Ideological Representation and Power in Social Relations

Economy and Society

Edited by
Economy and Society **editorial board**
Talal Asad   University of Hull
Beverley Brown   University of Edinburgh
Mike Gane   Loughborough University
Terry Johnson   University of Leicester
Gary Littlejohn   University of Bradford
Maxine Molyneux   University of Essex
Ali Rattansi   Open University
Grahame Thompson   Open University
Harold Wolpe   University of Essex
Jonathan Zeitlin   Birkbeck College, University of London
Sami Zubaida   Birkbeck College, University of London

Economy and Society paperbacks

This new series focuses on major issues which have been the subject of debate in the journal *Economy and Society*. Books in the series include:

Keynes, Beveridge and Beyond
Tony Cutler, Karel Williams, and John Williams

The Value Dimension
Marx versus Ricardo and Sraffa
Edited by Ben Fine

Towards a Critique of Foucault
Edited by Mike Gane

Ideology, Method, and Marx
Edited by Ali Rattansi

Soviet Industrialisation and Soviet Maturity
Edited by Keith Smith

Reading Weber
Edited by Keith Tribe

Ideological Representation and Power in Social Relations: Literary and Social Theory

Edited by Mike Gane

ROUTLEDGE
London and New York

First published 1989
by Routledge
11 New Fetter Lane, London EC4P 4EE
29 West 35th Street, New York, NY 10001

© 1989 Economy and Society

Typeset by Leaper and Gard, Bristol

Printed and bound in Great Britain by
Biddles Ltd, Guildford and King's Lynn

British Library Cataloguing in Publication Data

Ideological representation and power in social
    relations : literary and social theory.
    1. Society. Role of ideologies
    I. Title
    306.'42

Library of Congress Cataloging in Publication Data

Ideological representation and power in social relations : literary
    and social theory / edited by Mike Gane.
        p.   cm.
    Bibliography: p.
    Includes index.
    1. Literature, Modern—History and criticism—Theory, etc.
2. Criticism—France. 3. Ideology and literature. I. Gane, Mike.
PN441.I34   1989
801'.95'0944—dc 19

ISBN 0-415-02861-2

Contents

Notes on contributors

Graham Burchell lectured in Philosophy and Education at Westminster College, Oxford, before being made redundant in 1986. He was editor of *I&C*.

Pasi Falk studied Sociology at Helsinki University. He is currently research fellow in the Academy of Finland, where he has done research in theoretical and methodological issues.

John Frow is Professor of English at the University of Queensland in Brisbane, and is author of *Marxism and Literary History* (1986) and of numerous articles, including a recent group on legal discourse.

Mike Gane teaches Sociology at Loughborough University. He has edited *Towards a Critique of Michel Foucault* (1986) and is author of *On Durkheim's Rules of Sociological Method* (1988). He is a member of the editorial board of *Economy and Society*.

Ian Hunter took his first degree in English and History at LaTrobe University in 1971. Since 1976 he has lectured in the School of Humanities at Griffith University in Queensland, Australia. His research is focused on the theory and history of cultural insitutions, with a particular interest in literary criticism and pedagogy. He has published numerous articles in this area.

George Salemohamed is Lecturer in European Studies at the University of Loughborough. Educated at Keele and Paris Universities, his main interests are language and phenomenology.

Michael Shortland has taught History and Philosophy of Science at the Universities of Leeds, Lancaster, and Oxford. During 1989 he is a visiting professor in the History of Science at the Indian Institute of Technology (Madras), and then takes up teaching at the University of Sydney. He is author of *Medicine and Film* (1989) and co-editor of *Let Newton Be!* (1986) and *Teaching the History of Science* (1986).

Introduction

Mike Gane

It is hoped that the reader will find the present collection of essays, though written from a number of different perspectives, a stimulating introduction to some contemporary topics of literary analysis. In this brief presentation, I have no intention of trying to impose on them a false and unnecessarily formal sense of unity, but I do want to suggest that taken together they do reveal some important themes of modern social analysis, and illustrate the openness of the present situation.

Certainly one of the most significant themes is the fertile meeting of literary and social theory in the search for a better understanding of the functioning of ideologies. In the context of the general project of the journal *Economy and Society*, from which these essays have been gathered, the consideration of literary theory has been vital in the renewal of Marxist and Freudian theories of ideology and culture. Of course, for many Marxists, the choice once posed by the famous critic Georg Lukács – between either progressive realism (Thomas Mann) or depressive modernism (Franz Kafka) – is still valid. If the reader judges Lukács right to have set out the alternatives in this way, and to have settled the matter against modernism, this collection will be seen at best as irrelevant or nihilistic (Lukács 1962: 47–92). On the other hand, Michel Foucault remarked that modern literature was virtually a closed book for him while his principal intellectual nourishment was a diet of phenomenological and existential Marxism (1987: 174), implying that perhaps a realisation of the liberating power of modernist literature is itself dependent on certain ideological conditions. Lukácsian criticism, however, has been decisively displaced by the kind of writing and criticism represented here, and the crucial problems today concern not the struggle for or against modernism and postmodernism, but the struggle within it.

This collection well illustrates some principal current concerns, but without pretending that these discussions are exhaustive. Rather, these essays proceed by treating issues modestly; even the more prospective pieces are sketches and make no claim to be other than partial. The collection begins with highly critical assessments of aspects of work which has come to exercise a significant influence over recent literary theory: the work of Roland Barthes and Jacques Derrida, the first a leading exponent of literary structuralism, the second of post-structuralism (deconstruction theory). The first assessment, by Michael Shortland, concentrates on Barthes' attempt to develop a modern characterology, a theory of corporeal representation related specifically to the so-called inscrutability of the Japanese; although Barthes does not in this area put into play a fully blown structuralist analysis Shortland argues that some of the great weaknesses of Barthes' methods are starkly revealed. He compares Barthes' ideas with those in works written in the eighteenth century by Lavater and brings to light some striking similarities. The result is, for Michael Shortland,

> a dogmatic utopia. The coloniser of the body surface lays down the rules, formulates the law of reading, and sets into play a pretence autonomy of signifiers. Text and image put into circulation body, face, writing, but only the last possesses any freedom of development . . . (p. 45)

The second assessment considers Derrida's theory of the text, and particularly the concept of dissemination, by looking at what Derrida claims is produced or not produced on the surface by a deconstructive reading. On the one hand Derrida's writing appears as a major leap towards a theoretical approach which seems immediately to be more adequate to the complexity of texts than previous structuralist efforts. But I suggest that there appears to be a bizarre naturalism even in Derrida's idea of the text, and, corresponding to this odd anti-ontology, Derrida is unable or unwilling to specify a terrain of action of deconstruction. Elements of conversation taken from a short story by D.H. Lawrence are juxtaposed against Derrida's writing.

Following these two critical pieces are four textual analyses: of a Perrault tale ('Le Chat Botte' — known in English as 'Puss in Boots') and a Pascal short story by Louis Marin, of Tournier's *Friday, or the Other Island* by Gilles Deleuze, of Eco's *The Name of the Rose* by Pasi Falk, and my own investigation of Borges's short story 'Pierre Menard, Author of the Quixote'.

Marin's brilliant textual analysis of Perrault and Pascal '. . . testifies to the active, creative function of language as opposed to the reflective function to which representational theory consigns it.' (p. 84). But Marin uses Perrault and Pascal to go much further: language produces social power. Pascal tells the story of the shipwrecked mariner who, because he resembles a lost king, is welcomed by islanders as a king. Both, says Marin, are ensnared into this relation of power as an effect of narrative: '. . . the power trap is not set by anyone . . . both parties find it there.' (108).

In the next analysis a completely different outcome to shipwreck is imagined: Deleuze finds Tournier's modern Robinson Crusoe an exemplary text on the psychodynamics of the introduction of another (Friday) into a world without others. Deleuze's objective is therefore frankly didactic: where other writers have been content to

> do no more than invoke The Other a priori, [we] have attempted to show . . . how the Other conditions the whole of the conceptual field, the application to this field of the categories of the perceived object and of the dimensions of the perceived subject, and finally the distribution of other people in their particularity in every field. (133)

If Deleuze makes some acute observations on the differences between Defoe's and Tournier's novels, the next piece in this collection is my fictive pastiche of Borges's extraordinary story of Menard's twentieth-century 'rewriting' of *Don Quixote*. Menard specifically avoids the sort of enterprise undertaken by Tournier: he attempts to arrive at an exact word-for-word reproduction of the 'original' text, or so we are led to believe by the critic who tells the story in order to dispel other obviously mischievous interpretations. Itself in the fictional mode, the piece examines a number of readings of Borges's story: if each is possible, do these constructions exist in the story? Or, as Borges himself suggests, is reading always inevitably a mode of (re)writing? One of the most important issues raised in this story is the significance of the known author in reading: experiment, says Borges, with authorial attribution.

The final textual discussion, Pasi Falk on Eco's *The Name of The Rose*, itself a text profoundly influenced by Borgesian techniques, immediately poses the question of reading as provocatively raised, in 1979, by Eco himself: 'If there is a "jouissance du texte" (Barthes), it cannot be aroused and implemented except by a text producing all the paths of its "good" reading' (154). Falk concludes that Eco's subsequent development seems to have been towards a position similar to that of Derrida, which he describes as an 'unlimited semiosis' founded on 'endless abduction' (162). Perhaps Eco has indeed written at a number of levels and set in place pre-structured paths for readers, argues Falk. If this is true, what is required is an explication of the text layer by layer, which is what Falk undertakes to do. But here the expert modern theorist turned novelist seems to pose the ultimate puzzle, and to approach the position of Borges himself. If the principle of intertextuality is embraced, in the construction of the novel iteself, at one level at least, the number of paths of reading becomes, in principle, infinite. This crucial characteristic of the modern theory of ideology, as infinitely labyrinthine (curiously parallel, in its implication of passivity, to the traditional Marxist theme that ideology is not a decisively active element in the social whole), is the central paradox raised by modern theory for any social theory of ideology.

In the final section of the collection, problems of the wider theory of discourse and power are raised. The two contributions here cover rather different ground and appear to reach somewhat different conclusions. The basic directions of their discussion, however, seem surprisingly aligned. Hunter's discussion embraces a critical review of literary and linguistic theory to reach a conclusion which recommends an approach close to that of Wittgenstein or Foucault – something that Hunter calls a 'rhetoric of capacities', emphasising the need to break with concepts of the social totality. Frow, by contrast, provides a critique of theories of ideology, from Engels to Althusser, to arrive at a position which again seems close to Foucault's, but with the emphasis that the theory of power should not be divorced from conceptions of social struggle. The question remains as to whether these elaborations are as yet sufficient for an analysis of complex ideological and political struggle.

But let us ask a less complex question: What questions does imaginative fiction pose to social theory? Can it inform the processes of power and representation, or is it to be merely the object of a 'sociology of literature' or of a 'Marxist analysis' of a particular 'form of consciousness'? In one sense the question has a central fascination, even for modern writers of fiction. And today it should come as no surprise to learn that some writers of fiction are masters of theory, particularly the theory of their own art. At the present time, paradoxically perhaps, some of the most interesting and important social theory is to be found not in university departments of social sciences but in departments of languages and literature. This seems to be linked to the fact that whereas basic questions of language and ideology (from ethnomethodology to structuralism) were faced, and then in large measure marginalised or driven underground, in the social sciences, particularly in sociology, in the 1960s, in the cultural disciplines this encounter has only been effervescent in the last decade.

Given the – still current – domination of theory by questions concerning the nature of ideology and culture, this confrontation of theoretical fiction with theories of fiction remains a central configuration and it shows no sign of becoming infertile. Indeed, the tensions immediately evident in this very collection are indicative of the unresolved nature of the meeting between two or more modes of thought based on quite different assumptions and aims. For example, I have grouped the essays into three: the first group embraces direct assessment and criticism of two seminal French writers (Barthes and Derrida) and presents discussions of the two sides of the modern debate on the nature of representation; the second group considers fictional material by Perrault, Pascal, Tournier, Borges, and Eco, and the discussion concentrates on the critical explication, in various modes of writing, of fictional 'thought-experiments'. The final group includes two recent attempts to work towards a new and more adequate framework for analysis. The evident distance between the aspirations of this latter group and the achievements of the previous ones reveals the nature of the remaining tensions in the general project of cultural theory.

As a way into a discussion of this project, I here discuss a particular piece of fictional writing. If we start from the question 'what can fiction about fiction tell us?', perhaps we should commence with a story about writing and reading fiction: we can treat it as a contribution to the understanding of lived ideologies through an example of an analysis, itself fiction, of the secrets of writing and reading; we can also examine how other readers have approached it and, if it has given rise to different interpretations, ask what this might mean. One such possible piece is Henry James's exemplary story concerning the obsessional search by a literary critic for the fundamental 'figure' in the works of an author called Hugh Vereker.

To begin with, a brief synopsis of the story. The critic is introduced to the problem by a critic friend called George Corvick who, because he has to leave for Paris, passes over a work of fiction by Vereker for review. The critic, in writing the review, believes he has been able to 'unveil' the essence of Vereker's literary technique. But Vereker himself, when presented with it, is scornful: the critic has indeed missed the 'exquisite scheme' in his work and merely written the usual 'twaddle'. The author taunts the critic: there is something in my works, he says, which 'stretches . . . from book to book, and everything else, comparatively, plays over the surface of it. The order, form, the texture of my books will perhaps some day constitute for the initiated a complete representation of it.' (The question is whether or not James himself has some master scheme or concept of representation in the same sense, and is it at work in the current story?)

How could a literary critic not be tempted by such a juicy carrot? The existence – on the author's own word – of texts with a hidden secret, perhaps even the secret of life itself . . .? The critic announces the mystery to his friend Corvick, who, joined by Corvick's friend Gwendolen Erme, begins to search for the hidden scheme. Vereker himself goes abroad for an indefinite period, and Corvick leaves for a job in India. After a while a telegram arrives from India announcing that Corvick has found the secret ('Eureka. Immense.'). Corvick dashes off to Italy to meet Vereker, who confirms that this is indeed the case ('not a note wrong,' says Corvick). But Corvick announces, to the dismay of the narrator critic, that he will only tell Gwendolen, and then only after their marriage, which has hitherto been blocked by Gwendolen's mother. ('It's tantamount to saying . . . that I must marry him straight off,' she remarks). After their marriage (Gwendolen's mother dies before Corvick's return), Corvick is tragically killed on the honeymoon. The critic, desperate for the secret, cannot get it out of Gwendolen; perhaps, he muses, he will have to marry her as well, for she is likely to be the only one left in possession of the secret, as it becomes known that Vereker is struck down with malaria and his wife also dies. But Gwendolen marries again, to another critic, Drayton Deane, and the narrator reflects on what Deane will do with such a priceless 'nuptial gift'. Gwendolen herself dies in childbirth. The disconsolate critic eventually meets Deane and recounts the quest for the complex hidden figure in Vereker's fiction, but it is clear that the secret has not been entrusted to him:

> So abrupt an experience of her want of trust had now a disturbing effect on him; but I saw the immediate shock throb away little by little and then gather again into waves of wonder and curiosity . . . I may say that today as victims of unappeased desire there isn't a pin to choose between us . . . (1986: 400)

Let us examine some readings of this story by some recent theorists: Iser, Todorov, Kapeller, Macherey, and Rimmon. Iser's reading latches on to the differences between the critic's first reading (called 'twaddle' by Vereker) and the suggestion accepted by the author that the secret is a figure in a carpet, or the string on which the pearls are strung. Iser argues that the position of Vereker is a rejection of the idea that a work of fiction has a referential meaning which can be abstracted by criticism. Rather, he suggests, the work creates its own meaning and cannot be 'sucked dry'. Now this meaning, born at the same moment as the text, which so dramatically changes Corvick's life, can only be approached by the reader on condition that the reader abandons certain prejudices and ceases to search for an external conceptual meaning seen to be somehow represented in the text. For Iser, then the real meaning of Vereker's indications is that the thread in the story exists in a specific modality: it exists in the mode of imagery. The text represents a 'guide to the imagination', but the unfortunate critic 'remains blind to the difference between image and discourse'. Iser goes on to suggest that Corvick realises this but cannot convey it because he simply refuses the critic's mode of discourse: 'the meaning as effect is a perplexing phenomenon, and such perplexity cannot be removed by explanations – on the contrary it invalidates them' (Iser 1978: 10).

For Iser, then, the story is a moral tale – the story must be experienced as imagery, not reduced by explanatory concepts 'which dull the effect, for they relate the given text to a given frame of reference, thus flattening out the new reality brought into being by the fictional text' (1978: 10). Remarkably, Iser does not seem to be aware of the irony of his own explanatory and conceptual reading here. He finds it child's play to identify the secret treasure, and to castigate the naive realism of the critic. But Iser forces his interpretation against certain points in the story: Corvick has a project of revealing the secret in an article which remained unfinished, and Gwendolen reports that 'the opening pages were all that existed; they were striking, they were promising, but they didn't unveil the idol' (James 1986: 389); nowhere is it suggested that Corvick refuses the critic's mode. Clearly Iser has sought to appeal to James to lend authority to his own theoretical position.

Another reading is offered by Todorov, who again without much difficulty finds the secret treasure and reveals it immediately since he has 'no desire to make the reader impatient' (unlike James!). The secret, he announces, is that 'James's tales are based on the quest for an absolute and absent cause.' The cause can be an object or event – even the simple suspicion of its existence is sufficient – but its unveiling would bring the story to a dead end. The whole tension and dynamic of the story concern the pursuit of this object: every effort is made to reach it but James so manipulates it that it always remains out of reach. Complementing this is the use of the technique of indirect reference to the object so that various degrees of distanciation are developed. This atemporal spiral of distanciation is often doubled with historical distanciation. Thus Todorov reaches conclusions similar to those of Iser. It is a kind of complex writing, neither referential nor psychological.

Again, is it not true that Todorov has simply named the unnamable? As if struck down by remorse, he says with more than a tinge of bad conscience,

> The search for the secret and for truth is never anything but a search, a search without any content whatever . . . Are we not betraying James' fundamental precept . . . of the impossibility of describing truth by its name? But criticism too (including our own) has always obeyed the same law. It is the search for the truth . . . the quest for the treasure can only be absent.' (In Robey 1973: 101)

This rather astonishing expansion of the theme of the search is not only without any foundation in Todorov's own theory, it is in contradiction with Todorov's own explanation which suggests that James's technique (establishing the all-pervasive role of the absolute but absent cause) is deployed only during a limited period of James's work. It has also been hotly contested even for this period (Miller 1983: 302–13).

Another reading, by Susanne Kappeler (1980), examined linguistic and semiological theories in order to unravel James's own treatment of the same themes, and particularly the type of reader brought into existence in post-traditional society – a reader who will seek and find in a story 'more than its story' (1980: 75). The issue at the heart of this particular one, she suggests, is the illegitimate blurring of the lines between literature and criticism. The problem is actually set in train by the meeting of author and critic, and something approaching literary incest takes place when the author admits to the critic that there is something in his work other than that which the critic sees. The author has crossed the line of a division of labour which is structurally essential to the modern literary community. Kappeler goes on to note that this is also the problem in the case of Gwendolen, who is also a novelist. As the quality of her work seems to be dependent on the company she keeps, perhaps James wishes to imply that the writer should keep to his or her side of the divide.

Pierre Macherey has also considered this story, and finds in it an 'exemplary mystification' perhaps not even to be taken seriously, since the 'paradoxical ending naturally suggests that perhaps there was no secret'. However, Macherey ventures some observations: perhaps the story suggests that the author is already a kind of critic (a superior kind, no doubt) who expresses an already given and superior understanding, or alternatively, the critic is a kind of author (an inferior one). In any case, these two positions revolve round a rejection of the traditional realist view of the critic, as was suggested by Iser also, but only to bring to light the existence of a basic code in the text of the story which is available to both fictional and non-fictional modes, authorial and critical (as suggested by Todorov). In this 'structuralist' approach to the text, says Macherey, all questions posed to the text remain on the terrain of its own textual principles: 'the work is never related to the real conditions of its production, but its principle, its ideal possibility (which is its simulacrum).' This explains the constant problem of the contradiction between author and critic: both want to say the same, but both struggle for a superior way of saying it. But Macherey, who takes a different approach to the criticism of structuralism from someone like Derrida, here seems, perhaps against the tendency of his own position, to overemphasise the need to escape the terrain of the text itself, and although wanting to analyse literature as a practice, seems dangerously close to taking up a position which acknowledges only the elements which are purely external to the text. Unlike other critics Macherey specifically rejects what he identifies as James's position, which he quite clearly regards as the enunciation of a serious theoretical standpoint expressed in the form of a demonstration.

Finally, Sholmith Rimmon has examined the story from the point of view of its use of techniques whereby ambiguity is produced in the text. She examines the story in two different essays. The first, using notions taken from Barthes, concentrates on the way that James manages to frustrate the search for the secret. There are two quite separate 'motivations' for the suppression of information about the secret: unmediated forms, where there is a temporary or permanent absence of an informant, and mediated ones, where there are evasive tactics adopted by informants. She then analyses the main encounters in the story from this point of view. Her conclusion is that in the end there is no way that the reader can decide if the secret really exists or not, there are two 'equally consistent, coherent and tenable interpretations' (1973: 204). In the second essay, Rimmon analyses the way in which the suspicion that there is no secret is, or could be imagined to be, awakened (this unconvincing analysis rests largely on pointing to the changes of mind on the part of Vereker and Corvick), and then examines how the structure of the clues as to the nature of the secret (the differences between images used to refer to it, the radically incomplete and illusive descriptions of it, etc.) builds up an unrelenting and unrelieved tension of ambiguity (1977: ch. 4). It is perhaps surprising that Rimmon does not attempt to argue the far more plausible case that James's technique is not designed to induce ambiguity but is an exercise in the manipulation of desire – its induction, stimulation, appeasement and frustration – through the use of a register of obstacles and their maintenance or removal. This seems more fundamental than ambiguity and less problematic.

What is commonly accepted here is that James's story acts as the statement and illustration of a theoretical position and its technical accomplishment, and receives its force from the very fact that it demonstrates its understanding in a practice of imaginary realisation. Unfortunately, there is no general consensus as to what the position or the technique actually is, and no appeal to the author himself is possible in this case. But it would certainly be a mistake to think that, in general, authors understand perfectly their own technique, even their own plots (see Wilkins on Musil, 1967: 451 n. 1). Indeed, even where authors have attempted to explain their own methods, how are we to be sure that we are not being treated to yet more fiction (see Foucault 1987: 5)? It is also a mistake to think that the fictional mode is limited to imagery as opposed to concept, for there is perhaps no more powerful surrealist fiction than Borges's stories – often cast in the conceptual mode. Even the author's declared intention is not an infallible criterion. James's comments on the story suggest an intention to point up the irony of 'analytic appreciation', and the central problem of this story is whether the particular 'secret of perception' has been lost; but this does no more than repeat the terms of the story itself.

Certainly there is no reason in principle to refuse the challenge thrown down by James, and to search for the figure in the carpet. Both Iser and Todorov take up this challenge and conclude that the secret has not been lost. On the other hand some, including Macherey and Rimmon, have entertained doubts as to whether there was any secret at all, or at least have questioned whether there is sufficient evidence for it. James himself, in his comments on this story, leads the reader in a different direction from this suggestion, but what kind of reading would be produced from such assumptions: they are entertained by the narrator at one point or other in the story itself – it was perhaps a 'bad joke', he ruminates in a moment of irritation (1986: 370), a 'lie' in another (1986: 376)? In this reading the story is a sordid tale of power, suggestion, deception, manipulation, and gullibility. It thus tells of rivalries, jealousies, and petty acts of spite and vengeance (and it is not difficult to see that the story is indeed littered with them). The narrator could thus be seen as a poor unfortunate who is faced not only with the paradoxes of the secret itself, but also with the deceptions, and especially the 'discrepancies' between the various accounts, as well as the unjust accusations (as he imagines any) that he is superficial, and capable of insulting the memory of the dead.

Such a reading certainly diminishes the story; it is not necessary to adopt such a cynical position in order to place the interpersonal struggles within the orbit of analysis. Kappeler has rightly raised the question of the doubling of the textual/sexual themes (unveilings, penetrations, nuptial gifts, the fruits of such unions, etc.), for it is one the characteristics of the story that textual desires and obstacles to its fulfilment are reflected and interwoven with the theme of sexual desire and obstacles to its fulfilment. The search for the secret brings its joys, passions, and ecstasy; indeed for Corvick and Gwendolen 'they would scarce have got so wound up [about the secret] if they hadn't been in love . . . [and the search] gave them endless occasion to put and to keep their young heads together' (1986: 375). Now if the two sides are so deeply interwoven in this story, is it at all sufficient to think that there is one secret, one fundamental object of desire, or one absolute cause? In this story there seems to be at least another set of desires which revolve around Gwendolen herself and in which the narrator unwittingly, indirectly, ensnared. Indeed, Gwendolen is the motive cause for the commencement and conclusion of the story itself: Corvick's visit to Paris is comprehensible only from the point of view of his desire for her and the conclusion of the story can only mean that the narrator avenges himself against her by making Deane feel that she did not trust him. The central episodes of the story concern the relationship of the narrator to the secret via her: first as a rival (vis-à-vis Corvick), then as guardian of the secret (she is also a novelist and thus takes the place of Vereker), then as object of revenge. The narrator half suspects there was a secret but that it wasn't in the end very interesting or significant – he finds Corvick gullible (1986: 376), and Gwendolen's own novel, written in the light of it, 'overmastered' and only 'tolerably intricate' (1986: 392).

On analysis it becomes clear that the mysteries surrounding Gwendolen's character (the narrator seems able to develop only a highly stereotyped characterology) are, for the narrator, more impenetrable than those around the literary mystery: he admires her intelligence, passion, and her handsomeness; if she has no sense of humour yet she has faculties (for invention) which he cannot fathom; she stands on the authorial side of the literary division of labour and sticks to it. Yet, at the same time, the narrator cannot really take her very seriously: she could, he maintains, never create or discover the secret for herself; he is contemptuous of her novels; he distrusts her; and her unwillingness to pass on the secret he finds perverse. Yet in her presence he sometimes feels 'tepid' (1986:

380), he is sometimes corrected (1986: 381), or he intends to do one thing and does another (1986: 392). Out of her presence he is sure she will insult him behind his back, and so on. With Vereker, the narrator had really, as he admitted, 'taken to the man still more than . . . ever to the books' (1986: 378), and Corvick was his 'best friend' (1986: 389). What was Gwendolen to him but a complication, a mysterious centre of rival initiatives (behind Corvick's moves) and an effective barrier? It is also impossible to say that he is never seduced by her personal or authorial mysteries in themselves; these interest him only insofar as they reveal the charms of Vereker. The mysteries of Vereker are described as 'beautiful', the 'loveliest thing in the world'; Gwendolen is called 'interesting' and 'handsome', and though at one point, after the death of Corvick, the narrator notes that she presents herself as leading a life of 'singular dignity and beauty' (1986: 390), there is no hint of a possibility of adoration and veneration as there is towards Vereker and Corvick.

One of the key dramatic scenes in the short story is the meeting between the narrator and Gwendolen after Corvick's death. Clearly he realises that in order to get at the secret he has to find a way around Gwendolen's resistance. On this level, however, he is utterly unable to play any sort of game with her. He more than once considers the possibility of a personal relationship with her: the first time he dismisses the idea as an 'absurdity', the second time as 'madness'. At the crucial moment, all he can see is the 'torch she refused to pass on flame away in her chamber of memory – pour through her eyes a light that shone in her lonely house' (1986: 391). Thus the disappointment of the narrator is doubled: he is unable to discover the secret for himself, and is unable to find a way through Gwendolen's obstinate refusal. He does reflect on his own weaknesses in relation to trying to get the secret from Vereker: Gwendolen, he thinks scornfully, would not have been so scrupulous, so restrained by 'superior reflections' (1986: 394). She has come to possess the secret without effort of her own as part of the nuptial exchange. However much the narrator valued the knowledge of the secret, his own personal independence from Gwendolen was more highly prized, and thus in the end, although frustrated, he remains sane.

Todorov, as with other formal and structural analysts of Poe, has searched for a principle which determines the position of each character and event in relation to the story as a whole. But it is highly likely that such a 'last analysis' principle can only function if a number of other complex elements are also present, and any analysis which relegates these is likely to miss crucial tensions. In this particular story the counteracting principle enables James to play with textual (one sort of incest) and sexual (not only heterosexual) imagery, which implicates the story in the web of modern gender ideology as well as aesthetic theory. In this story, then, there is a struggle to uncover a secret, but there is also a struggle between beings of different gender to seize and retain possession of the secret.

There is a further dimension, however, which complicates the story: this is the apparent cross-over of gender attributes. Vereker's attractiveness and his secret are feminine – beautiful, lovely, warm, gay, etc. – while Gwendolen is interesting, intellectual, cold, handsome (not pretty) with white face and fixed eyes (nevertheless, when excited, her face could be 'luminous' or 'radiant' in the reflected light). The narrator's relation to Vereker is unashamedly sensual; his very presence is 'brilliant', his face is 'fine and clear, all bright with the desire to be tender to my youth' (1986: 364). Gwendolen, on the other hand, is reported to be, on first meeting, 'chilled' by the behaviour of the narrator; when she refuses to give up the secret it is denied with the 'largest finest coldest "Never!"' (1986: 392); and when she brings him news from Corvick he sees her with the note from an upstairs window and imagines her at the 'foot of the scaffold' (1986: 383). After Corvick's death the presence of Vereker's secret in her is a 'warm' compensation (1986: 391). Her reasons for not divulging the secret are deeply mysterious: there is only the hint of some promise in the report that she was 'tongue-tied by her perversity, by her piety', by her not being the 'right person' to break the silence (1986: 391). But the strong implication is that she was under no pledge to remain silent: 'I heard everything', she says, 'and I mean to keep it to myself' (1986: 390). Thus a reversal has taken place; the indicated secret is a form of gift from Vereker (revealed in a state of excitement in secret to a young critic in his bedroom – which no doubt a writer like Lacan would call the primal scene); the expression on Gwendolen's face when she withholds the secret from the narrator (in another sad moment of an attenuated character-ology), on the other hand, is read as one of 'remote disdainful pity'. A physical moment is also mirrored: Vereker at the opening of the story placed his hand on the young critic's shoulder 'feeling for a fracture' (1986: 362), yet about to deliver the gift; when the critic seeks the secret from Gwendolen, he this time lays his hand 'firmly on her arm', poses the inevitable question – and is denied.

The last scene of the story, that between the narrator and Drayton Deane, is a remarkable, but negative (utterly disproportionate, and therefore less than ironic) resolution; after a period in which the narrator has intimated his interest in Deane at a distance and has had his stares 'queerly' returned, he lays his hand on Deane's shoulder (1986: 399) as he reveals the existence of the secret and he himself notes the emerging 'throb' of 'wonder and curiosity' he is able to evoke; finally, he reflects afterwards that 'the poor man's state is almost my consolation, there are really moments when I feel it to be quite my revenge' (1986: 400).

If we now return to the question of what fiction can give to theory, it is evidently a lesson in subtlety. The story examines the dynamics of liter-ary and critical relations as interpenetrated with sexual and gender relations. And if it examines ideological and ritual attitudes towards creativity and authoriality, it also examines them in the context of critical engagements between men and women. In fact, the latter struggle envelopes the former. For the narrator the higher mysteries of literary structure are as incomprehensible as those of the modern woman: he is, as he says, impotent. The revenge he finds available for his frustrations and disappointments is taken not against Vereker but against her memory in Deane. This is an antagonism which is born in this text, and the text has been launched into social discourse itself riven with such antagonisms; the text is not simply a representation of such struggles, it is a positional statement inserted within them. Analysts have sought James's authority for dubious theories of the text, but few of them have noticed that he also concerns himself with a particular exploration of a bitter social struggle. If it can be held that in James 'the real woman stands in the way of the highbrow artist's consummation of his joy' (Kappeler, 1986: 178), in this story things are more complex. Maybe social and literary theory are on the point of grasping this as it concerns social struggle.

References

Foucault, M. (1987) *Death and the Labyrinth: The World of Raymond Roussel*, London, Athlone.

Iser, W. (1978) *The Act of Reading*, London, Routledge & Kegan Paul.

James, H. (1986) *The Figure in the Carpet*, Harmondsworth, Penguin.

Kappeler, S. (1980) *Writing and Reading in Henry James*, Basingstoke, Macmillan.

Kappeler, S. (1986) *The Pornography of Representation*, Cambridge, Polity Press.

Lukács, G. (1962) *The Meaning of Contemporary Realism*, London, Merlin.

Macherey, P. (1978) *A Theory of Literary Production*, London, Routledge & Kegan Paul.

Miller, J.E. (1983) 'Henry James and the language of literature and criticism',

Revue de Littérature Comparée, 3, 303–13.

Rimmon, S. (1973) 'Barthes' hermeneutic code and Henry James's literary detective: plot-composition in "The Figure in the Carpet"', *Hebrew University Studies in Literature*, 1, 183–207.

Rimmon, S. (1977) *The Concept of Ambiguity – The Example of James*, Chicago, Chicago University Press.

Robey, D. (1973) *Structuralism: an Introduction*, Oxford, Clarendon.

Wilkins, E. (1967) 'The Musil manuscripts and a project for a Musil Society', *The Modern Language Review*, 62, 451–8.

PART I

Language and Representation: Two Critiques

CHAPTER 1

Skin deep: Barthes, Lavater, and the legible body

Michael Shortland

Can the body be read as a text and, if so, how? Is it *lisible* or *scriptible*? What is entailed in an exploration of the outer appearance of the body in search of the human essence within? Can the look of the body be a reliable and accurate indicator of psychological life beneath the skin? If there remains a residue of mental life hidden from the outside gaze, what status is the physiognomist to assign to it? If on the other hand the body-as-text is simply what is inscribed upon it, should it be regarded as to all extents and purposes empty? Does the excavation of the body put character to death or bring it to life? What, in short, is the status of physiognomy; what are its possibilities and constraints, its foundations and implications, its theory and practice?

Such questions as these are suggested by Roland Barthes' *Empire of Signs*, a work which casts a great deal of light on the problematic status of character in narrative. How character is formed and what it *does* in a work of fiction are issues Barthes had already brought to the surface in *Writing Degree Zero* and inspected more carefully in the course of his entanglement with Balzac in *S/Z*. Here, at last, they are brought fully into the open – or, at least, it at first appears. The initial reading of *Empire of Signs* suggests its place in the Barthian oeuvre; it seems to set out from where *Mythologies* left off, with a quasi-technical (and equally unsatisfactory) discourse on signs, linguistics and symbolic systems. It seems also to contribute something to the answer Barthes gave in his first book *Writing Degree Zero* to the question 'what is writing?' Some critics have treated this book and that question as a continuing presence in all Barthes' work; Barthes' first text, on this reading, represents 'a veritable microcosm of his basic attitudes' (Lavers 1982: 47). This is, I think, unsatisfactory at least because it footnotes the *Empire of Signs* rather than acknowledging its profound originality of purpose. Put another way, if we adopt a view of Barthes' writings growing from the soil of his early work, *Empire of Signs* is bound to seem poor fruit. This, perhaps, accounts for the perfunctory and generally dismissive treatment the book has received from critics like Annette Lavers who have treated it as a minor contribution to a long-standing problem. A more careful reading of *Empire of Signs*, one which traverses Barthes' work and goes some way beyond it, allows one to refuse this rejection and to acknowledge the true value of the text. It is such a reading which this article intends, amongst other things, to provide.

Empire of Signs occupies a peculiar place in the body of Barthes' work since it fails to offer any developed, or even articulate, structuralist system. That perhaps is one of its attractions. Barthes here can be found in something of a hedonistic, playful, even anti-critical mood. Moving ground from the Occident to the Orient, Barthes leaves behind his '*rêve euphorique de la scientificité*' (Barthes 1975b: 20). The work derives from Barthes' sojourn in Japan; it resembles the collection of picture-postcards sent home, traveller's jottings which are fresh, lucid and occasionally contradictory. Further, the work possesses a dreamy quality which is difficult to reproduce but which seems to derive in part from Barthes' deliberate disjointing of image and text – his messages seem almost to have been scribbled on the backs of the wrong postcards. This, as we shall see, is no accident, for the role of the 'illustration' here becomes a dominant and coherent feature of Barthes' conception of the body, character and physiognomy.

Barthes ended *Writing Degree Zero* with the vision of a 'Utopia of language'. He opens *Empire of Signs* with the discovery of Japan, another utopia, but a fiction which becomes increasingly hideous and menacing as we are introduced to its landscape. To travel there affords Barthes a situation of writing, and the possibility of dealing directly with the relation of writing about bodies and writing on bodies, a relation treated in other texts of 1970 but addressed here far more directly. Barthes, indeed, has adopted the pose of the physiognomist and this, as we shall see, allows him the freedom of certain kinds of exploration and perception. But the Barthian physiognomy presses to its logical conclusion an obscured tenet of the widely-known physiognomy of Lavater, so much so that for bodies to be legible they must, to Barthes, be empty.

Signs and Surfaces

Many critics have remarked, quite properly, on the resemblance *Empire of Signs* has to the earlier 'travelogue' popular in the eighteenth century, the utopian portrait of another, more rational and perfect, society which served to put into question native life and manners. Barthes' dislike of the values of the Enlightenment is well known, but one cannot read his own text without being reminded of Montesquieu's *Lettres persanes* and the Eldorado episode of *Candide*, not to speak of de Stael's *De l'Alle-magne*. Barthes opens by declaring, 'If I want to imagine a fictive nation, I can give it an invented name, treat it declaratively as a novelistic object

. . . so as to compromise no real country by my fantasy' (Barthes, 1983: 3). But of course what is compromised is all that is not Oriental; at every juncture, historical, philosophical, cultural and political, 'fictive' Japan lives by its contrast to the Other: a less-than-fictive West. And always to the detriment of what is left unstated and assured, for there is nothing at all in Japan that Barthes finds not to his liking. The riots of the *Zengakuren*, symptom one might have thought of the tensions in post-Meiji restoration Japan, are dismissed as 'expressing nothing'. Indeed, those conflicts and contradictions endemic in a social formation which has grafted feudal familial forms on advanced capitalist structures, are never seen – they remain a massive 'region of darkness' (ibid.: 103).

What his eye focuses upon are what we might expect the casual Westerner to sample: the colours, the bows, the theatre, Zen rituals, *bunraku*, food. The food is a real revelation, and expresses by its texture, taste, design, presentation and consumption something of the essence of the Orient. It is fresh, natural and diversified, whereas the food of Europe is bland and overbearing, swollen with conceit and drowned in heavy, pretentious sauces. It is colourful, theatrical, ritualistic. It is the site of a *praxis*, of a process of decomposition and reorganization to the rhythms of eating. It is light, tiny, harmonious, aerial, fragile and almost absent. Our food, by contrast, is what is left on the plate before we set to: a solid and unitary presence. We eat according to rules, following the itinerary of the menu, clumsily wielding the knife and its predatory substitute, the fork. Moreover, we eat when and because we are hungry; our desire demands instant satisfaction, so we cut, pierce, rip, and mutilate our fare the more efficiently to eradicate it. In the East, fantasy replaces function and culture dispenses with natural drives. The vacancy of form supplants the Benthamism of the empty belly.

What is not replete with meaning is rejected by us as illusory and hypocritical. For example, we regard politeness with suspicion, as a form of play-acting. Having divided the person into an inner and outer, and labelled the first authentic and the second false, all that does not spring naturally from inside is put immediately on trial. The Japanese, of course, have their etiquette, but it subverts the metaphysics of the Occident. The quite empty gesture salutes no one, intends nothing, and refuses to institute that distance which our perverse punctilio maintains. Impossible to answer – and probably to ask – in Japan is the question 'who is saluting whom?'. In the west acting is suspect because the actor performs under a pretence that what is made manifest, feelings and conflicts for example, should have been a secret, and what is conceded is merely the artifice of that manifestation. Moreover, that artifice is, as it were, ashamed of declaring itself, and moves are always afoot to naturalize performance, to dispense with make-up, sets and spots, to eradicate theatrics. *Bunraku*, the Japanese theatre of dolls, each moved by a trio of quite impassive and quite visible men, presses relentlessly in the opposite

direction, towards total exhibitionism. It enforces the visibility of action
and gesture, putting on parade simultaneously the act and the labour. To
be sure, *bunraku* does not completely overturn the curious relation of
'theatre' to 'house' we hold so dear; it does not purport to be street
theatre or to occupy the fringe. But in its own way it is more provocative,
for it remains on the site of the stage whilst denying the possibility of the
true expression of inward character.[1]

The passages by Barthes on *bunraku* recall familiar themes in his other
works, particularly his championing of Brecht and his persistent challenge to the 'natural pose' in life, language and literature. Clearer echoes
may be found in Barthes' treatment of the wrestler, a figure which
perhaps transcends the space between East and West. It is easy to accept
that wrestlers openly proclaim that nothing they do is to be taken seriously, for it is this understanding that makes their spectacle possible.
Larvatus prodeo, 'As I walk forward, I point to my mask', is the image
which underpins Barthes' categorical description of language and theatre
as semiotic rather than mimetic both in *S/Z* and in *Sade, Fourier, Loyola*.
The grandiloquence of the wrestler is of the same order as that of the
ancient Roman actor. But there is a difference, which assumes increasing
importance as the *Empire of Signs* falls into place. By bearing the mask
(even though it is so obviously a pretence), the classical actor creates a
series of ambivalences and contradictions in his performance. Not so the
wrestler, for whom 'nothing exists except in the absolute', for whom there
is 'no symbol, no allusion [and] everything is presented exhaustively'
(Barthes 1973: 24–5). Whereas the stage allows – even demands – a
measure of subtlety and intrigue, the wrestling ring must offer instant
legibility of character and performance. A reading is made possible by the
fact that the wrestler bears his message on his body; his physique is a
basic sign of absolute clarity, a type which expresses the part assigned to
him. He lives the character of his body and, on demand, plays it out. His
physique is the key to the contest: from it one can predict what might
otherwise (if he were a boxer for example) be unpredictable.

If wrestlers are perfect physiognomical specimens, if they announce
themselves unproblematically by their corporal imagery, they do so in
collusion with their public. Wrestlers have no means of concealing that
which they have in any case no reason to hide; sport is not hidden behind
spectacle, it is dissolved into it. What the sumo or amateur wrestlers
embody are crude and clear signs and characters. In the case of Thauvin,
the famous French wrestler, to whom Barthes refers, a unitary essence of
baseness and bestiality is displayed in his animal ugliness. His actions
'perfectly correspond' to what is perceived to be his personage (ibid.: 17).

Other figures present something of a physiognomical problem. The
Abbé Pierre, made famous through a more detailed Barthian icono-
graphy, combines the marks of legend and modernity, to offer a doubling
of visual complexity. Or more exactly, a three times increase since his

image includes a benign expression, a Franciscan haircut, and an apostolic beard. The whole was intended to proclaim the intensity of the Abbé's devotion to the Christian ideal and his sublime indifference to the secular world. A more difficult figure than the wrestler to decipher, yet surely more difficult than even Barthes allows. Take the Abbé Pierre's beard, for instance. Barthes claims that it is part of a 'mythological routine' (ibid.: 48), but there is surely no routine to pogonological mythology. Indeed, the Abbé's beard, as such, signifies precisely nothing – that perhaps is its true function. To read it, or read through it, demands a more detailed perception and a broader cultural inventory. For instance, what *kind* of beard was it (if indeed we can, except for economy's sake, speak of kinds) – Uncle Sam, *fer à cheval*, Natal, Belgrave, St James, Masonic, *collier*? And what colour, texture, and luminosity? The 'long, flowing beard' of Abbé Pierre evokes a welter of signs, which excludes, one might hazard, the natural and the religious. Christ, it is true, is often represented bristling with facial fertility and the angels represented as smooth. But Adam has proved a more difficult subject, often smooth in his primal innocence and then, after the Fall, having as Byron wrote 'a beard entailed upon his chin.' St Francis was bearded but his immediate followers were not; St Jerome and St Cyprian objected to shaving, yet according to the *Catholic Encyclopedia* the earliest legislation declared that *Clericus net comam nutriat net barbam*. In isolation, cultural and corporal, the beard can and has been associated with divinity and devilness and anything betwixt, and taken as a sign of sexual conquest, a symbol of excess, an emblem of dignity, the mark of the beast, a natural protection. The first beards of Egypt, one should perhaps recall, were *false*, and tied to the chin for ceremonial occasions. They had a curious and problematic status between the natural and the artificial; they were equivocal emblems, part-truth, part-deceit. False beards have been adopted ever since and heavily taxed or forbidden by law for almost as long; and it is this association of the beard with the illicit which throws light on its curious history.

Associated in various discourses with the sexual, the religious and the political, beards occupy a space in the popular imagination through their links with the masquerade, with entertainments such as the *barbatoriae* and *barboires*. On stage they arm and protect the actor like a mask. *Larvatus prodeo*. 'What beard shall I best play it in?', Bottom asks before he takes the role of Pyramus. Used in this manner, they can be devastatingly effective in concealing character – 'your beards forbid me to interpret that you are so', laments Banquo, wholly deceived as to the power, sexuality and intentions of the witches. This is far more than a theatrical phenomenon, for beyond the stage, the implication of the cover-up has often been made quite explicit. In Dr Belcher's 'Hygienic Aspect of Pogonotrophy' (in his 1864 *Tractatus Medici*) the beard is praised because it can deflect the onlooker's gaze.

> It serves to conceal the thoughts . . . saving the man from those
> betrayals which would pull down his dignity and render him often as
> unequal combatant in the competitive struggle of everyday life.[2]

The beard-as-mask suggests to us, as it seems to have done to Barthes, the wider general problem impeding physiognomical readings of character from the make-up and appearance of the face and body. Hair lends itself to artificial reproduction in wigs, perukes, toupees and 'fronts' in part because of its peculiar status as insensible matter organically attached to the sensible body (matter which continues to grow after the body has died).[3] Indeed, it is quite explicitly intended to be a form of disguise and diversion, a device to entangle perception. As a result, the feigned naturalism and piety of the Abbé Pierre is not only misjudged, but rebounds to leave him open to the charge of hypocrisy. While he presents a more complex physiognomical subject than the all-in wrestler and the roman actor, his masks of fraternity, charity and piety as such fool nobody. The pretence that the hair he wears is part of his living body, that it emanates spontaneously from the essence of his character, may be punctured by the astute observer. But having demythologised the image, we are still no closer to the thoughts which, as Dr Belcher and many others have noticed, the beard conceals.

Hypocrisy: the noise and politics of the body

The hypocrite – $\dot{\nu}\pi o\kappa\rho\iota\tau\eta\zeta$, figure of the consummate actor – has often proved an insurmountable obstacle to the physiognomist, as to the artist attempting to portray character on canvas and to the moralist seeking to build a world on openness and truth. Even once hair and other faddish accoutrements are accounted for, the body itself can still adopt any number of disguises of expression. The hypocrite, wrote Hogarth, may 'so manage his muscles, by teaching them to contradict his heart, that Little of his mind can be gather'd from his countenance, so that the character of a hypocrite is entirely out of reach of the pencil, without some adjoining circumstance to discover him.' (Hogarth 1753: 126). What adjoins the body are its movements, and these Hogarth finds to be a surer indicator of life beneath the skin. While the countenance remains to all extents and purposes drowned in noise, 'deportment, words, and actions must speak the good, the wise, the humane, the generous, the merciful, and the brave.' (ibid.: 131; 30–38). Action, unlike appearance, forms a coherent language with its own grammar rules and provides the basis for pictorial communication. Hogarth's scenes are described by the artist as 'my stage and men and women my players, who by means of certain actions and gestures are to exhibit a dumb show.'[4]

Were the hypocrite to present merely a problem of representation,

Hogarth's solution to it would form little more than an episode in the history of art. But hypocrisy, labelled by Molière in *Don Juan* 'the familiar vice', was to Hogarth and many others a target not only to be confronted artistically but also to be dealt with on a political and moral level. In Hogarth's case, it may not be too far-fetched to trace his own scepticism about power (which notwithstanding some recent suggestions to the contrary remained clear and consistent throughout his life),[5] to the pervasiveness of acting in the socio-political world. His close associate Fielding makes the hypocrite even more explicitly 'the Bane of all virtue, Morality, and Goodness', and the recent experience of the cut-throat jostle of places after the fall of Walpole in 1742 added political urgency to Fielding's denunciations (Fielding 1972: 4). On the truth or falsity of physiognomical diagnoses seemed to rest the future of a general reformation of the moral and political character of man in and out of power. 'Those great Arts', Fielding wrote, 'which the Vulgar call Treachery, Dissembling, Promising, Lying, Falsehood, etc. are by GREAT MEN summed up in the Collective Name of Policy, or Politicks, or rather *Pollitricks*.'[6]

'It is', Fielding noted, 'a melancholy Instance of the Great Depravity of Human Nature, that whilst so many men have employed their utmost Abilities to invent Systems, by which the artful and cunning Part of Mankind may be enabled to impose on the rest of the World; few or none should have stood up the Champions of the innocent and undesigning, and have endeavoured to arm them against Imposition' (ibid.: 153). The problem here can be simply stated. Should the way people seem truly reflect what they are, or must they always be as artificial as the appearances they adopt for reasons of fashion, custom, influence, and conscious deceit? Contemporary comment suggests that this issue put into question some central tenets of Christian morality. The correspondent of the *Gentleman's Review* in 1756, for example, gave a remarkably candid answer to the question Fielding posed in both his essays and novels.

> The old maxim, that 'honesty is the best policy', has long ago been exploded; but I am firmly of the opinion, that the *appearance* of it might, if well put on, promote a man's interest, tho' the *reality* must destroy it. I would therefore recommend it to persons of all locations . . . to put on now and then the *appearance* of a little honesty . . . To deceive behind the mask of integrity, has been deemed the most effectual method.[7]

The honest clearly have little chance so long as hypocrisy has the upper hand and deceit can proffer advancement on the unscrupulous. Picking up as he so often did the *theatrum mundi* imagery in his satires, Fielding writes that 'the whole world (has become) a vast *Masquerade*, where the greatest Part appear *disguised under false Vizors and Habits*; a very few showing their own Faces, who become, by so doing, the Astonishment and Ridicule of the rest.'[8] The world described is one fissured by political identity and cultural and ideological values, one composed, as E.P. Thompson has described it, of 'the rulers and the ruled, the high and low people, people of substance and of independent estate and the loose and disorderly sort.'[9] Fielding's 'few' might have acted as a buffer, but at least until the 1760s, the professional and industrial middle classes along with the substantial yeomanry offered little deflection to the basic polarities, so powerful were the relations of clientage and dependency. The world was also one of patricians and plebs, of actors and spectators. *Theatrum mundi* served as a particularly effective metaphor because of the weakness of traditional organs of control – the church and state – and the absence of other forms such as the schools and the mass media. The oligarchic gentry therefore relied on symbolic forms of hegemony (as well as systems of influence and preferment, and the terror of the law).[10] The contest for symbolic authority was real enough to allow a wide variety of 'theatrical' modes, from those of affectation and hypocrisy to those of sedition, charivaris, effigy-burning and threats.[11]

Each of these brutal spectacles of power evolved its own appropriate repertoire of behaviours, but none stood out as more obviously symbolic of the age of affectation than the social embodiment of the beard, the eighteenth-century *barbatoria*, a form of masquerade. Addison in *The Spectator* had earlier set the tone for subsequent attacks with his fulminations against the midnight masque, declaring in 1711 that 'the whole Design of this libidinous Assembly seems to terminate in Assignations and Intrigues'.[12] In *The Masquerade* (1728), a theoretical articulation of Hogarth's 1724 *Masquerades and Operas,* Fielding noted that 'The misfortune of things is, that People draw themselves in what they have a mind to be, and not what they are fit for.' (Fielding 1728: 3). The masquerade imposed a distortion firstly on the body, and thence on the body politic; it was the first step along the road of wholesale moral and social degeneracy.[13]

Like the hypocrite who attends them, masquerades can only thrive because people fail to make adequate moral distinctions, to judge what are their best interests. Fielding's 'few' resort to the posture of the simpleton for there are no other means available to detect the actor-hypocrite. Parson Adams's imbecility is the only quality which 'when set on its Guard, is often a Match for Cunning.'[14] We may recall that having despaired of the powerful pretences of the hypocrite, Hogarth reckoned that only by actions and speech would that creature's true character be betrayed. Fielding appears to offer more hope for the physiognomist; speaking of the same figure he claims that 'however foreign to his Age, or Circumstance, yet if *closely attended to*, he very rarely escapes the *Discovery of an accurate Observer*; for Nature, which unwillingly submits to the Imposture, is ever endeavouring to peep forth and shew herself;

nor can the Cardinal, the Friar, or the Judge, long conceal the Sot, the Gamester, or the Rake . . . if we employ sufficient Diligence and Attention in the Scrutiny.'[15]

What is involved here is first of all the rejection of simple equations as between beauty and goodness, ugliness and evil. The notion that the body spoke in general terms about broad-ranging moral categories, that it was a 'letter of recommendation' was ancient and proverbial, and frequently reiterated during the eighteenth century.[16] Fielding, however, satirizes it throughout his novels and declares that to place any faith in such simplistic assumptions would be 'to throw our Arms open to receive the Poison, divest us of all kinds of Apprehension, and disarm us of all Caution.'[17] Secondly, Fielding, like Hogarth, is here renouncing common neo-classical aesthetic notions that beauty is only to be found in the general, and that minuter discriminations mark low forms of representation. Articulated early in the century by Jonathan Richardson, such views came to found the system elaborated in Reynolds's *Discourses*.[18] According to these criteria the artist needs to avoid details and portray 'the great and general ideas which are fixed and inherent in universal Nature.'[19] Not that in Reynolds's case such ideas are Platonic forms, as some have suggested, but rather visual distillations from the appearances of the world.[20] What is involved is an unfocused, reverse visual discrimination which aims to raise and to improve nature. As Reynolds states:

All the objects which are exhibited to our view by nature, upon close examination will be found to have their blemishes and defects. The most beautiful forms have something about them like weakness, minuteness or imperfections. But it is not every eye that perceives these blemishes. It must be any eye long used to the contemplation and comparison of these forms; and which, by a long habit of observing what any set of objects of the same kind have in common, has acquired the power of discerning what each wants in particular.[21]

The general, or uniform – what Burke terms the '*compleat, common form*'[22] – results from a rational, rule-governed and trained cognition (rather than, say, 'inspiration'). But a cognition the reverse of that involved in Fielding's 'accurate observation'. When Fielding suggests that the mask of the hypocrite can be penetrated by the 'discerning Eye' (Fielding 1972: 161), his aim is precisely to *see through* the common forms – the beautiful and the ugly for example – to particular aspects of the countenance. Yet having set out a perceptual programme for doing so, that is, a means to 'extirpate all Fallacy out of the World' (ibid.: 175, 19–29), Fielding has reluctantly to admit that this has little chance of success. Such was the extent of deception, posing and hypocrisy in the world that to Fielding the bulk of mankind was doomed to 'mistake the Affectation for the Reality' (ibid.: 161–62). Put another way, the power of neo-classical modes of perception was so entrenched that a revolution in aesthetics, criticism, morality and politics was required before physiognomy could lay claims to be able to see through villainy.

In an intriguing passage which was not included in the published version of his *Analysis of Beauty* (1753), Hogarth prophesied large-scale advances in visual power, such that one would be able to make words 'speak to the eye'.

> What further Improvements, the Eye is capable of, is hard to say, but this particular is known to many, with regard to hearing, that some deaf people can hold a conference, and understand almost every word that is said, by the motions of the mouth, without so much as hearing the least sound of the voice, which is an almost inconceivable, and extraordinary, improvement of the sight, and more so, than that of a Musicians ear with reguard to sounds (*sic*).[23]

In the printed text however, Hogarth explains his reliance on actions and speech as indicators of character by arguing that the '*art of seeing*' necessary to find truth in the writing on the body has yet to be perfected. In like fashion, Fielding resorts to the 'Actions of Men' as the justest Interpreters of their Thoughts, and the truest Standards by which we may judge them.[24] That bodily appearances do not serve him as physiognomical clues may be seen from Fielding's method of character portrayal in his novels. Tom Jones and Joseph Andrews are both introduced not with descriptions of their countenances but by biographies: Tom is given a whole book, and Joseph a couple of chapters, which set out their past actions and reactions to certain events, incidents and people. The biographies draw on the art of life-writing, not on face-painting: of Tom we are told merely that he is handsome, over six feet tall, and that he is a member of a group of men possessing an 'open countenance'. Partridge, another central character in the same work, is described still more perfunctorily – he is slightly less than six feet tall. Of Squire Allworthy, Thwackum, Square and Squire Western in *Tom Jones* (1749), we know nothing whatsoever respecting their appearance. Parson Adams, a central figure in *Joseph Andrews* (1742), is bearded like the Abbé Pierre, but we only gather this by accident, after blood flows down it following a punch-up.[25]

A science of physiognomical perception

That the body becomes legible in the nineteenth century, and that this legibility redirects character description in the novel, character depiction in art, and character definition in the sciences, owes more to Johann Caspar Lavater (1741–1801) than to any other figure.[26] Lavater's work, by breaking with the aesthetics and constraints of earlier treatises on physiognomy, set the perspectives for all subsequent approaches, including that of Barthes, as we shall see. Though he continues to occupy an obscure place in the intellectual landscape of Europe as a result of the outreach of his interests, his shifting religious and political affiliations, and his diverse network of admirers and collaborators, Lavater continues to be remembered primarily as the author of *Physiognomische Fragmente* (1775–78). Translated into English shortly after its original publication, the impact of Lavater's claims was immediate and considerable. But physiognomy defined as a mode of distinguishing character by outward appearance was not founded by Lavater. When Homer describes the vicious Thersites as having a game foot, bandy legs and a repulsive expression and has us assume that Achilles is handsome, he is in a primitive sense relying on physiognomical assumptions. Likewise Pythagoras, who is said to have used bodily appearance as an admission criterion to his school. So too Socrates, who according to Plato foresaw the promotion of Alcibiades from the pleasing configuration of his features.[27] To describe such ventures as physiognomical, however, is to systematize practices which are little more than crude manifestations of the 'letter of recommendation' – something Plato himself acknowledged in warning that appearances are liable to be deceptive (Plato 1978: *Protagoras* 309a, 356d).

The earliest extant treatise on physiognomy is the *Physiognomonica* attributed to Aristotle, in which human and mental characteristics are related to those of animals and differentiated as between the sexes and different races.[28] Based squarely on analogy (though occasionally resorting to the theory of the humours), the body here is split into areas of physiognomical significance and insignificance. A 'complete list' is given of the important legible signs: 'movements, gestures of the body, colour, characteristic facial expressions, the growth of hair, the smoothness of the skin, the voice, condition of the flesh, the parts of the body, and the build of the body as a whole' (Aristotle 1913: *Physiognomonica* 806a, 27–33). Less important than the list itself was the method of classification into types, for this rudimentary framework provided a starting point which was later extended and amended as new species and peoples were discovered, and then overlain by further correspondences established in nature, in the cosmos and through time. This mode of analysis imposed severe limitations on the range of physical and psychical characteristics available for inspection; only those shared by men and women, or man and beast, or the primitive and the civilised, formed part of the discourse of physiognomy. Against this background Lavater's *Essays on Physiognomy* (my edition is the 17th, issued around 1870 in one volume translated by Holcroft) appears not only as an important restatement of the truth and viability of physiognomy but also as a genuinely novel attempt to extend the doctrine and to found it on systematic grounds.

The innovation wrought by Lavater may best be seen if we consider his project as the establishment of a *science* of *physiognomical perception*. These three terms are initially defined in the written text of the *Essays* in a manner which is designed to mark the discourse off from previous physiognomies, which Lavater holds in contempt. Having staked out his terrain in broadly theoretical terms, Lavater then proceeds to defend it and create its practice through images and commentaries on these images with rules, examples and what he terms 'physiognomical exercises'.

If physiognomy, science and perception define the project, each concept is contrasted to another: *pathognomy, philosophy* and *sensation* respectively. Physiognomy deals with man's character and stable features rather than with his passions and expressions, the latter being the province of pathognomy (the two were, as in the *Physiognomonica*, often collapsed). Next, scientific physiognomy has the object of arranging, specifying and defining those stable features while philosophical physiognomy is what we would today term the physiology of expression – the domain investigated by Descartes, Le Brun, James Parsons, Cureau de la Chambre and John Bulwer before Lavater, and following him by Charles Bell and Darwin.[29] And lastly, having defined his perceptual object as those stable parts of the body observable from the exterior, Lavater distinguishes the physiognomical sensation, which is a universal attribute of all creatures, a vague understanding that form speaks of content which underpins the majority of description, from physiognomical perception which man alone can develop and which allows him to *think* rather than feel physiognomically. The scientific physiognomist assumes that the body speaks, yet recognizes that before its language can be deciphered a number of obstacles need to be overcome. As Lavater makes plain, the body will always tend to babble, to revert to a state of apparent disorder, and this anarchy needs to be dissolved not by the adoption of easy general aesthetic categories but by visual penetration.

The practice of scientific physiognomy proceeds from and through a peculiar, trained, visual perception corresponding in many ways with the 'new art of seeing' Hogarth, Fielding, and others had deemed to be necessary before the relations of outward appearance and inner constitution could be established systematically. At the risk of banalization, one might say that the physiognomist perceives things *differently*. For one thing, analogies based on sexual and racial difference, like those comparisons of man and beast so much a feature of previous physiognomies, are firmly rejected. *De humana physiognomonia* (1586) by Giambattista della Porta (Giovanni Battista Porta) was amongst the most renowned attempts to establish physiognomical relations between man and beasts, and it did so by reducing each animal species to a fixed bodily type corresponding to its governing passions and then seeking expressions of this type in humankind. Socrates, who figures half a dozen times in the work, is the physical and psychological embodiness of the deer (see Figure 1).

Figure 1 Socrates as Deer (from Giambattista della Porta, *Della Fisionomia dell'huomo ... Libri sei*, Venice, 1644)

Here as elsewhere in Porta's text what are being compared are general types; no characteristic differentiations are posited within species. The first important statement of the existence of such distinctions was probably delivered in a 1671 lecture during which Charles Le Brun queried Porta's approach. The text of Le Brun's discourse has been lost, but the images which accompanied it show remarkably subtle variations on the theme of the 'humanised' beast and the 'brutalised' man (see Figure 2). J. Blanquet, who made the images available in a folio collection of lithographs, announced quite correctly that

> This skilful man was far from coinciding in opinion with those who admit a certain instinct to a certain species of brutes in general, and without regard to the particular propensity, suppose at first sight, an analogous affection with men whose physiognomy bears some affinity to these animals. It was doubtless, to remove this opinion that he drew a group of heads of oxen, whose variety of character at first sight, causes one to attribute a different instinct to each. (Blanquet 1827: 3)

This image (see Figure 3), as Blanquet emphasizes, requires careful scrutiny if its message is to be understood, particularly since it is not accompanied by any caption or verbal explanation. Are the eyes of the oxen human or bovine? And what of the leontine figure in the bottom left: part-Zeus, part-Leonardo; a caricature like one of Cruikshank's *Zoological Sketches* (1834), or a genuine attempt to explore the range of human and animal character?

Figure 2 Le Brun's Zoomorphism (from L.J.M. Morel d'Arleux,
Dissertation sur un traité de Charles le Brun, Paris, 1806)

From orthodoxy to optic power

Le Brun was not known for these sketches (which were, it appears, locked
away in the *Cabinet du roi* until well after Lavater's *Physiognomische
Fragmente* had been published).[30] His authority derived from his role as
the chief impulse behind the grandiose decorative schemes at Versailles,
as the *Premier peintre du roi* from 1662, and as director of the *Académie*
and the reorganized Gobelins factory. From the mid 1660s he was widely
recognized as the 'dictator of arts in France'.[31] From this post he
dispensed patronage and gave authority to the view that every aspect of
artistic creation could be reduced to rule and precept. One of the
concerns of Le Brun was the representation of human passions in art, a
concern which Poussin had first articulated in a schematic manner as he
assigned each of his subject-actors a recognizable and discrete expression. Le Brun studied under Poussin's guidance in Rome, following the
master there in 1642; then in October 1667 he lectured on *Les Israélites
recueillant la manne* and from this important discourse probably derived
the main lines of the treatise which was published posthumously in Paris
in 1698 as the *Conférence de M. Le Brun sur l'expression générale et
particulière* (translated into English in 1701 and again in 1734 as *A
Method to Learn to Design the Passions*).[32]

Accepting the ancient distinction of the two appetites of the soul
(irascible and concupiscible), Le Brun argues that whenever the soul
experiences attraction towards something outside itself, the brain is
stimulated and the eyebrows begin to ascend; conversely, they fall when
the soul experiences repulsion from something as they lose contact with

Figure 3 The Range of Animal Instincts (from J.I. Blanquet,
Lithographic Drawings . . . from the Designs of Le Brun, London, 1827)

the brain (or perhaps the pineal gland), whose power declines under negative emotion (Le Brun 1734: 21–22). Compound passions, so named, are monitored in similar fashion: hope, for instance, which results from the soul wishing for something yet fearing the results of the wish unfulfilled raises the eyebrows close to the nose and lowers them at the far ends (Figures 4 and 5).

Each of these representations is accompanied by a short description which bears a direct one-to-one correspondence with the image. There is a fluid interchange and translatability between the verbal and the visual, and because the latter is so limited, the former is set down with the barest outline. The French art historian Roger De Piles had claimed that 'the expressions are the touchstone of the Painter's understanding', but had failed to provide any theoretical guidance which could inform that understanding (De Piles 1780: 29). Artists like Raphael, Dürer, Holbein and Titian had all been concerned with the human countenance as the reflection of the motions of the mind, but their guidance had been merely by example.[33] As such, what had been portrayed was a wide variety of types of expression conveyed in a multiplicity of genres; in Le Brun's treatise, the range is severely limited, most obviously by his focus on the face and the eyebrows. Even the recently-published drawings which Le Brun used to illustrate his lecture on the depiction of human passions offer only minor diversification and do not provide any means to adjust

Figure 4 Laughter (from Charles Le Brun, *A Method to Learn to Design the Passions*, London, 1734)

Figure 5 Hope (from Charles Le Brun, *Method to Learn to Design the Passions*)

expression for age, sex, temperament and complex character (Figure 6).[34] Some, like Félibien, sought to undercut Le Brun's dogmatism by extending the range of physical expression to other regions of the body, but this in itself did not provide any latitude for individual variation (Félibien 1685: I, 291–316; II, 16–58, 595–600). Constrained by the poverty of language, of description, and of range in the face of the apparently endless variability of human expression, Le Brun fell into dogmatic formalism. Each of his figures seemed to be cast in the same mould, as De Piles noted:

> [Le Brun's] expressions, in all his representations, are beautiful. He studied the passions with extraordinary application, as appears by the curious treatise he composed on them, which he adorned with demonstrative figures; nevertheless, even in this he seems to have *but one idea*, and to be *always the same* . . . What I have said of the passions may serve for his designs, both of figures and the airs of his heads, for they are *almost always the same.* (De Piles 1780: 341)

Though Le Brun intends to provide the resources for the depiction of compound passions, the blandness and homogeneity of the expressions in his text prevents him from so doing, just as the single-minded focus on the eyebrows vitiates the translation of emotional conflict and contra-

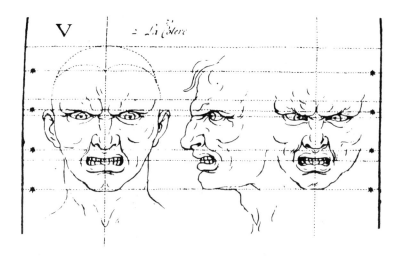

Figure 6 Fright (an illustration accompanying Le Brun's *Conférence sur l'expression générale et particulière*, probably delivered in 1668, from the Cabinet des dessins, Louvre, Paris)

diction on to canvas. His drawings are, as Hogarth noted, 'but imperfect copies', too general and unpenetrating, too fixed to capture 'that infinite variety of human forms which always distinguishes the touch of nature from the limited and insufficient one of art.' (Hogarth 1753: 127–129). This is why Le Brun resorted to the use of other markers and emblems to convey the passions, why, as Bryson (1981) shows, his zoomorphic images are means to conceive of mental states outside the control of the will and reason.

The dogmatism and restrictedness of Le Brun's *Conférence* is completely overhauled by Lavater, who reiterates *ad nauseam* that his project is intended explicitly as a series of *fragments*, as consciously shapeless and unmethodical.[35] To be sure, the claim is a welcoming invitation to readers, beckoning them to come closer to 'the touch of nature'. And when Lavater repeats 'I neither can nor will state anything but what is known', his intention is to disengage himself from the centuries of scandal, stigma, and secrecy which had cast physiognomy as one of the divinatory black arts (Lavater 1870: 400, 47). The ritual obeisance is to common sense, to the empirical tradition, and this intrudes into the text of the *Essays on Physiognomy* so as to unkennel the rehabilitated science to the broadest ranks of readership and discipleship. Physiognomical facts are intended not only to 'silence all doubts', but to claim a privilege over the physiognomical treatises deriving from the *Physiognomonica*, which Lavater contends to have simply repeated and extended analogies 'like beads on a rosary' (Lavater 1795: II, 59).

It is impossible to miss the tension in the *Essays* between a naive empiricism and an unshakable dogmatism, between the decisiveness of 'facts' and the pressing need to formulate a new science which will submit to rules. Further strains are strongly present in Lavater's treatment of free-will and determinism, heredity and environment; and the generosity of his editors and translators in manipulating the text must be put down to their impulses to systematise the fragments, and of course to point erstwhile Lavaterians in the right moral and political direction. A more unitary perspective does, however, arise spontaneously from the work once we view it as articulating a science of physiognomical perception. This should not imply that physiognomical perception is in any sense innocent or objective, as we shall see: simply, many problems which appeared in previous physiognomical treatises and were debated during the eighteenth century are now posed, and to some degree resolved, on the perceptual plane. To illustrate the point, one may consider briefly an example from Lavater's work.

The example concerns a figure who attracted both opprobrium and respect: the first for his body, the second for his mind. The figure appears in almost every physiognomical and anti-physiognomical treatise, at least by name – Socrates (See figure 7).[36] The problem of Socrates is in a word his fractured presence: his proverbial ugliness and his equally proverbial wisdom. According to traditional accounts, the ancient physiognomist Zopyrus judged from the philosopher's countenance that its owner was inwardly dull, brutish, sensual and addicted to the vice of drunkenness.[37] This assessment was put to Socrates by one of his less than respectful pupils, who received the reply that though all the Egyptian had presumed was correct, Socrates had yet managed to elevate himself by the persistent pursuit of learning.

The example is in many ways a variant on the age-old problem of dissimulation, and Lavater's treatment of it forms part of his general approach to what he terms 'altered physiognomies'. Substantially, his response is to argue that only pathognomy can be misled by the deceptions of the conscious hypocrite and the reformed character; that changes of the body can only manifest themselves on the most superficial level of expressions. But it remains that the Socrates case is 'pregnant with physiognomical discussion', and that this discussion revolves about the possibility and the practice of delving beneath the surface to the organs and structures which more accurately signal stable character (Lavater 1870: 113).

One response to Socrates – undoubtedly the easiest and the commonest – was to picture him as a natural freak, as the exception to the rule that goodness resides in beautiful vessels and evil announces itself in ugliness. But Lavater moves instead in the opposite direction so as to make that rule the exception and the exception the rule. His claim is not that the 'good' is the 'ugly', but rather that such terms are inappropriate to physiognomical discourse – as useless, he says, as those of 'good' and

Figure 7 Rubens' Socrates (from John Caspar Lavater, *Essays on Physiognomy*, London c. 1870)

'poor' health would be to the physician making diagnoses. The letter of recommendation, in other words, is rewritten. Appearances and essences, body and mind, are complex terms made up in difference – and that is the rule. The outer surface of the body, like that which it covers, is inconsistent and contradictory even though man's exterior stands in a harmonious relationship to his interior. And this, Lavater contends, is something of which the Greeks, like the theoreticians of Ideal Beauty, were unable to conceive. Socrates was living proof that humans could not be slotted into preconceived categories, whether these were founded in aesthetics or in racial and sexual types.

An important corollary of Lavater's position is the call to expand vastly the vocabulary of visual and verbal description, distending and contracting language as suits the demands of the new perception. To those still gripped by the discourse of conventional aesthetics, freedom lies in developing 'A register, the most perfect that can be obtained, of all characteristic countenances [as] a very necessary aid for the student, which he must compile from the writings of those who have known men best, and from his own observation' (ibid.: 150–1). Such a register of epithets should include invented and portmanteau expressions designed to disengage perceptual difference from the uniformitarianism of the first glance, the basis of mere physiognomical sensation.

That vision and knowledge, knowledge and power, are coupled is a fundamental assumption of Lavater's discourse, one more evident perhaps in the French edition of his work where great play is made with the terms *voir*, *savoir* and *pouvoir*. But this assumption is unfortunately never clearly developed. Lavater is insistent that observing is not seeing and experimenting not equivalent to experiencing. The seeing, experiencing, 'sensing' person lacks focus, or rather trains the eye on the horizon or on what is in immediate contact with the body. His or her object is, as it were, given physiologically according to the laws of perspective, the immediacy of the corporal, and the construction of the eye. Moreover, the sensation is clouded by subjective feelings, and these, rather than perceptual discrimination, inform the miscognition of immediate appearances.

Lavater's world is bifurcated into the observed and the observers; the equivalent, one might say, of the world-as-stage distinction of humankind into actors and spectators. But with one difference: not all people can become actors, but 'all men who have eyes ... have talents to become physiognomists'. Yet, Lavater adds immediately, 'not one in ten thousand can become an excellent physiognomist' (ibid.: 62–63). The chosen few are the scientific practitioners, those who have so refined their visual perceptions that they are able to observe 'more than ten thousand of the observant, produce more than ten thousand of the productive' (ibid.: 452). Nothing can appear more easy than to observe, yet nothing is more uncommon. So at the heart of the new physiognomy is a peculiar mode of cognition which one commentator in *The Reflector* in 1810–11 aptly termed 'optic power'. Accepting that the body is legible, that it is possible to 'read the mind's construction in the face' this critic wrote, it remains that:

> in every species of *reading*, so much depends upon the eyes of the reader; if they are blear, or apt to dazzle, or inattentive, or strained with too much attention, the optic power will infallibly bring home false reports of what it reads.[38]

This 'optic power' strains for a verbal account in Lavater's text, and one is impelled to view the many descriptions of it as substituting for what is at heart a theoretical solution to the problem. From cover to cover, the *Essays on Physiognomy* bathe in a sea of visual metaphor as we are presented with a startling array of perceptual terms: the gaze, the stare, the gape, the careful scrutiny, the complete survey, the idle contem-

plation, the close inspection, the viewpoint, standpoint, outlook – here for
once, the language of the land of empiricism is richer than its rationalist
continental counterpart. But the prolixity of expression serves a definite
purpose as each kind of look can fathom different regions of the body,
penetrating to hidden layers of meaning, and prising off deceits and
postures. From the crude sensation, students (and it should be remembered that Lavater's is a manual to reading true character) are instructed
how to increase their optic powers by continual practice. From A to B
then, the physiognomist is helped to 'turn calmly, but determinedly, from
indiscreet curiosity' to the scientific summit of 'the singleness of eye'
(ibid.: 167, 399).

Underlying the *how* of perception lies of course a *what*; the method is
only developed to claim its object: those significant parts of the body
which Lavater sets out in his 'hundred physiognomical rules'. This object
though is always tantalisingly out of reach, for even once the nose, lips,
forehead, eyes and chin are marked out as semiotically important,
concrete problems – those we have sketched above – will intrude to
muddy the perceptual waters. For this reason, Lavater accepts that vision
unaided may prove insufficient to unmask the hypocrite, that a 'third
eye' – the magnifying lens or 'solar microscope' – may be required (ibid.:
43, 190).

Physiognomy, while it succeeded in shaking off attachments to
fortune-telling, was viewed in many quarters as a powerful perceptual
probe. Numerous artists and critics took up the new physiognomy both as
a doctrine of character and as a discourse heralded as having, in Herder's
phrase, revived 'the noble spirit of observation'.[39] Others on the receiving
end held it in fear and contempt. Such, Lavater maintained, ran
frightened 'because they dread the light of physiognomy', trembling 'lest
others should read the truth in themselves' (ibid.: 21–22). 'The truth is',
wrote Chateaubriand, 'that most men reject physiognomy because they
would appear very badly in its light' (Chateaubriand 1978: 95). Already
in 1786, the *English Review* forecast that physiognomists would soon
become a national pest, that they would renounce 'the excellent rule of
their master, "*jujez peu*"' and obtrude into polite society.[40] And so they
did. In a striking reversion to the rhetoric of the eighteenth century
theatrum mundi, an entry in the *Encyclopaedia Britannica* for 1853–60
first noted how Lavater's work had everywhere caused a 'profound
sensation' and then went on:

Admiration, contempt, resentment and fear were cherished towards
the author. The discovery was everywhere flattered or pilloried; and
in many places, where the study of human character from the face
became an *epidemic*, the people went *masked through the streets*.
(quoted in Graham 1960: 108)

Mask or no mask, no one was safe from the scrutinizing, all-seeing gaze of the physiognomist. Even Emperors fell into focus.[41] There were those, it is true, whose lives were whittled away in secrecy, the self-abusers who seemed at one stage to be rocking the country into apoplexy – the onanists (Shortland 1982). R.H. Allnatt, writing on 'excessive masturbation' in the 1840s, described a patient of his who 'entered the room with a timid and suspicious air, and appears to quail like an irresolute maniac *when the eye was fixed resolutely upon him*' (quoted in Skultans 1979: 73). All the more reason for the physiognomist to seek him – or her – out, and to meet this demand, a special, powerful, 'onanistic physiognomy' was pioneered.[42] Physiognomy had launched the struggle against dissimulation, secrecy, and hypocrisy, and in favour of truth, clarity and openness.

Barthes, physiognomy, and the emptiness of the body

To link the names of Lavater and Barthes must seem fantastic, however attractive the techniques in the physiognomical tool-kit might be. For though the term 'physiognomy' makes more than one appearance in his works, Barthes nowhere mentions or discusses the theories and methods of Lavater. Without seeking refuge in the notion of an invisible physiognomical presence in French cultural discourse, one might hazard that Barthes may have been exposed to many features of Lavaterian characterology through his deep and lengthy contact with the Balzacian corpus. There is no doubt that a great portion of the psychology and fictional techniques of the *Comédie humaine* derive from the physiognomist. Balzac himself purchased a copy of the '*superb Lavater*' in 1822.[43] Before he had done so, there had already appeared at least eight other versions of the text; afterwards, at least twenty more were published during the nineteenth century (Graham 1961, 1979). The Lavaterian 'interrogation of the eye' was still running rampant through France in the 1850s, according to contemporary witness (Scoutetten 1862: 21–2). Accepting the documented importance of physiognomical perception in Balzac's work, one might expect Barthes' study of *Sarrasine* to account for this.[44]

The very format of Balzac's short story itself imposes severe constraints on any author's techniques of characterization, and lengthy physiognomical portraits only appear in Balzac's novels; moreover, *Sarrasine* is by almost any criterion an eccentric work, marginal to his great historical cycle. Nonetheless, Lavaterian themes and attitudes do make frequent, if brief, appearances in Balzac's story (first published in *La Revue de Paris* in 1830). As should be clear from our discussion of Lavater's work, his physiognomy does not consist solely in pictorialism, in accompanying the description of character with that of appearance. That description itself is the *labour* of physiognomy, for even assuming the legibility of the body (or rather of its parts), what is required is to undertake a process of visual scrutinizing, to excavate, to probe, to visit and to explore the body, as Barthes notes (Barthes 1975a: 168). This is the means to penetrate the surface and so reveal the stable structures lying beneath. Different modes of perception reveal different aspects of the observed – and the observer. In a work based on the interplay of appearance and truth, form and content, misjudged sex and character, Balzac deploys just this form of discourse in his development of narrative. To see truth necessitates that eyes be 'trained', and this Sarrasine gradually understands; 'only the most avid onlookers', Balzac remarks at one crucial juncture, were 'able to perceive the uneasiness of the heads of the house, who could conceal their feelings with unusual skill' (ibid.: 226). The tragedy of the artist Sarrasine, as Barthes shows, is that he has mistaken general appearances (which are embodied in culture and are therefore liable to deceive) with the essence he has tried to capture in his work.

This is an important recognition, in tune with Barthes' acknowledgement that the body is 'a duplicate of the Book', that La Zambinella's beauty is superficial, and that passions and their expression lie at the heart of *Sarrasine* (ibid.: 50). 'Femaleness' is judged to be a composition of essentially arbitrary signs; yet having, as he phrased it elsewhere, 'attacked and destroyed the notion that signs are natural', Barthes may locate the site and process of that composition in the writing itself, in the subtle dialectic of the stated and the signalled, the tale and its telling (Thody 1977: 137). The text is open and provides no final signifiers which can be read off as indicators of signifieds; no meaning is to be explicated in criticism. Applied to the body, this notion has quite fatal implications, for physical superficiality is a screen floating on emptiness producing a noisy babble. There exists, in other words, no fixed character since the body itself is quite empty – transparent enough to be penetrated 'like the ray of sunlight going through ice.'

We know already from his *Michelet par lui-même* that Barthes' readings often dwell on the physical, and from *Roland Barthes par Roland Barthes* that the autobiographer writes to the dictation of his body, so it is perhaps no particular surprise to find him captivated by the physical superficies of the body in Japan. The outer surface of the humans he sees does not connote the blank or the bland, but rather the smooth, glazed and unctuous. The unctuous, indeed, is as powerful an attraction here as it was to Sartre in his famous chapter on the body in *L'Etre et le néant*.[45] But for Barthes, unlike Sartre, the body may be an empty vessel; or, at least, its exterior packaging does not possess any necessary relationship to any 'thing' that is being revealed or concealed. In this respect, in East and West, packaging itself may follow similar patterns – the visual quality of oriental cuisine, for example, is almost identical to that recommended by the magazine *Elle* (Barthes 1973: 78–80). The character of each, such as it is, results from outline, colour, shadow and surface. Inside there is nothing. Food is a text, and like the text presents itself as a problem of language, of possible readings. The equivalence of the verbal and the visual necessitates that what is seen can be read and that what is read must be pictorial.

Nevertheless, language in Barthes' hands is a hindrance as much as a revelation, for what he sees cannot, he confesses, be captured by a vocabulary, even one strained to breaking-point with neologisms from French and English and buttressed by the incomprehensible Japanese. To break free is to settle in a state of *a-lang'uage*, a state which precludes verbal communication (Barthes 1983: 75). Once the poverty *and* the power of the verbal are accepted, it is the visual that comes to occupy front rank in the *Empire of Signs*. The implication might seem to be that the illustrations deployed somehow add to or substitute for the word, that they can claim a privileged access to the real. But Barthes opens with the statement that 'The text does not "gloss" the images which do not "illustrate" the text.' A useful caution, yet it leaves us with an ambiguous understanding of the role the photographs in the book are intended to serve. To combat the purported realism of the photograph Barthes instructs us throughout to *read* the image: food is written, the brush writes, the city is to be read, femininity is not to be seen, the face is not painted but written. But images, precisely because they do not illustrate the text, cannot be reduced to the level of the text; moreover, the fact is that we can only read Barthes' writing *about* the image, and it is this activity of writing which is problematic. Unless the image is decisively wrenched from the script or we are provided theoretical access to it, writing will also revert to a position of envelopment about an illustration. The only escape is to claim that the image is not generated, and this is the fail-safe of mimesis which assumes that it does no more than reproduce the real. This surprisingly seems to be Barthes' solution, since he purports not to have created images or even to have translated them into print. 'Japan', Barthes writes, adopting the depersonalising journalistic tone, 'has starred him with any number of "flashes"; or better still, Japan has afforded him a situation of writing' (ibid.: 4).

This gesture imposes limits on what Barthes can write – he meets no one and records no conversations, for example. It further allows him the pretence of reproducing lines of seemingly infallible description based only on the collection and setting down of the visual. 'Where does the writing begin?', he asks, 'Where does the painting begin?' (ibid.: 21). The answer in this kind of naive photo-journalism, which employs the empty camera as an extension of the eye, is impossible to give: the work is intended as a consummation of refined visual perception and verbal outpouring.

The naturalism of the photograph commands ready acceptance, since in the absence of any visible generation of meaning from within the text, sense is felt to intrude from a world outside. This is a deceit, and it remains so long as the photograph effaces the traces of its own manu-facture and conceals the independent material existence of the signifier. To suggest that a textual accompaniment is necessary in order to make it explicit is to admit that the intrinsic sense of the photograph is buried by the complications of production and needs to be pulled free. In other words, the suggestion carries force in as much as the relation of photo-graph to caption mimics that of reality to the text.

In the *Empire of Signs* there appears a photograph with the caption: 'This Western, lecturer, as soon as he is "cited" by the *Kobe Shinbun*, finds himself "Japanned", eyes elongated, pupils blackened by Nipponese typography'. This conjunction implies that the image has a privileged status. Once informed of the process which moves from the real through the representation to the explanation, we look to the caption for guidance in retracing those same steps in reverse. The image (that is, the representation) is severely undertheorised, for the message derives in large measure from its situation in a text by Barthes, with a caption by Barthes, and with Japanese script alongside. The real is Barthes himself and the caption permits us to look for techniques of distortion at work. A comparison of the 'Japanned' image with the 'true' representation (conveniently given on the rear dust-jacket of the volume) puts the identity of the *Kobe Shinbun* portrait beyond doubt, even though the 'true' image is not captioned. The photograph goes one length further than merely illustrating a statement; it provides its foun-dation. The accompanying text does not merely explain the image, it assigns it the rank of the real, even though this real has been tampered with. To say that a real portrait has been distorted supposes that it might have been true.

If images do not stand in an easy relationship to reality and to the text, it follows that they may serve a variety of critical ends; they may, as they do in the *Essays on Physiognomy*, function to demonstrate the manner in which conventional aesthetic and perceptual systems impose themselves on purportedly mimetic representations. The portrait of Socrates in Lavater's work (Figure 7) derives from Rubens, widely celebrated as a local, concrete, particular artist committed to the laborious reproduction of minute detail. Recognisably similar images of Socrates have percolated through western art, so much so that the testimony of Zopyrus we have referred to would seem unreliable were it not for the sage's acceptance of it. What is recognisable in the Rubens is the 'other' Socrates; what has been depicted is the essence of wisdom and virtue. Moreover, the process of beautification finds legitimation in Socrates' claim that his inner self had improved. Assuming that this improvement would have been manifest on his countenance, what Rubens has reproduced is a real image of his subject. But Lavaterian physiognomy does not strive straight-forwardly for fidelity to nature, particularly since 'altered physiognomies' reveal little of use to the scrutineer. Rubens may well have revealed

Socrates as he really appeared, beard and all, but not the way he really was. The portrait suggests what he may have looked like, not how the scientific physiognomist would perceive him.

That Socrates was dead when Rubens depicted him was a drawback to faithful portraiture, but not for physiognomical diagnosis and representation. For one thing, even the living presence does not offer an unambiguous source of reference; for another, as eighteenth-century critics relentlessly pointed out, the living actor-hypocrite actually *impedes* the observer's search for true character. If mobile subjects are to be properly scrutinized, Lavater argues, they ought to be mounted like a statue on a pedestal which can be rotated in a way which allows the body to be considered 'from head to foot, before, behind, in profile, half profile, quarter profile.' Alternatively, the physiognomist can resort to the silhouette or freeze the subject in a sculpture (Lavater 1870: 251, 163, 187, 95).[46] Better still, particularly for the physiognomist who has yet to reach the pinnacle of scientific perception, is a visit to the asylum or the prison, where extreme forms of human development will be on show and where, moreover, subjects either will not or cannot adopt 'masks and vizors'. Best of all are the dead, frozen with the basic character they possessed when the spirit of life abandoned them. 'Their settled features are much more prominent than in the living, and the sleeping. What life makes fugitive, death arrests; what was indefinable is defined. All is reduced to its proper level; each trait is in its true proportion.' How good it would be, Lavater muses dangerously, for the physiognomist to be faced with a world populated only with the significant traces of the departed (ibid.: 149, 370–71).

What those traces would resemble may be gathered from four images (of eight) depicting Socrates in Lavater's work (Figure 8). The realistic portrait has been used as the datum on which the physiognomist sets perceptually to work, casting off the masks, the flexible armature, the semiotically unimportant. The result is 'unnatural' since it fails to mirror what the immediate impression conveys: shade, texture, 'feel'. Even so, such images still convey little, for they are physiognomical exercises, like the skeleton in the anatomist's cupboard or the map on the geographer's wall. They are Weberian types perhaps, or more probably intended to fulfil a function analogous to Hogarth's painting *The Bench: on the different meaning of the Words Character, Caracatura, and Outré in Painting and Drawing* (1759), that is, to articulate theoretical problems through the category of the visual by putting the status of each into question.

To sift the face on non-physiognomical matter does not render it into a meaningless space, any more than does its representation by the barest half-outlines (Figure 9). Our natural tendency will be to compensate by filling the expanse and completing the boundary, but we would do so at the cost of pathognomical confusion. The physiognomical portrait is

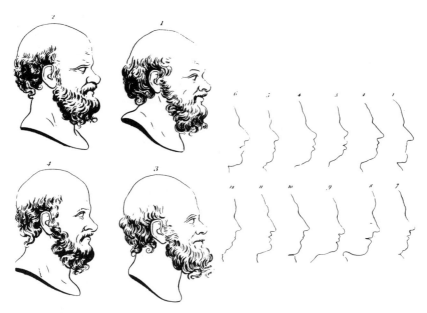

Figure 8 Lavater's Socrates
(from John Caspar Lavater,
Essays on Physiognomy)

Figure 9 The Physiognomical
Face – realised or dissolved? (from
John Caspar Lavater, *Essays on
Physiognomy*)

delicately balanced between caricature and 'character', offering, as it
were, plain legibility rather than, on the one hand, noise, and on the
other, silence. It speaks coherently only to the trained scientific perceiver.
The act of physiognomical perception, as should be clear, strives relentlessly to decipher uniqueness in diversity and significance in the uniform.
So whilst Barthes can speak of the 'Japanese face' as a coherent sign, the
physiognomist would meet and then fracture the racial type so as to
analyse and probe its underlying constituents. Lavater clearly and
characteristically admitted that the 'Oriental form' was a misnomer
which only existed because of its rarity in European thought; to claim, as
one critic has done, that he contributed to racism is to completely
misunderstand the anticlassificatory tenor of Lavater's thinking.[47]

Barthes' reading of the Japanese character is more problematic, not as
the result of any vicious racism, but because we are invited once again to
contemplate 'it' as enigmatic and inscrutable. The emptiness of the
bodies he meets with in the Orient is a match, an explanation even, for
the blankness of the face. Both make it impossible to decipher the
Japanese physiognomically. The Japanese face, writes Barthes, 'cannot be
read "in depth"' by an eye subject to the 'mythology' of the soul which
radiates towards the exterior (Barthes 1983: 102). Like their cities, their

food, their poetry and their packages, the Japanese themselves are empty centres with desolate but inscribable exteriors. They present a blank page without content or character, and this permits Barthes to write about them *on* them; their superficiality has, as he puts it, afforded him the situation of writing. In the west we are to struggle against the imposition of meaning; the east, however, is a 'matter of indifference' and simultaneously the 'possibility of a difference' (ibid.: 3).

The reference here turns again towards language, to the terms within the text itself; for notwithstanding the associations of the *Empire of Signs* with the travelogue, the sentences, like the image, are not intended to mirror something outside the work's own boundaries. The utopia of language offers the possibility of an endless series of substitutions by which a thing is not named directly but by way of contiguous features. The replacement of words is justified and legitimated only by the implied ontological link in reality. Phrased another way, the formation of the text suggests that some connections of similarity and causality actually exist in the world between the thing and something adjacent to it in space and time. Another reality is posited, or at least made possible, by the devices of metonymy and synecdoche, yet this other world is subverted by the intransigent journalistic objectivity of the reporter's stance. In an earlier essay, Barthes called attention to the role of the 'irrelevant detail' as a device for establishing the authenticity of what is depicted and for conveying the '*effet du réel*' (Barthes 1968). Certainly, the congestion of local description has the result of arresting reality, but having done so one requires to know what is relevant and what irrelevant in the stilled image.

A central aim of the *Essays on Physiognomy* is to come to grips with this issue in theoretical terms and by the deployment of images and language, and it deserves to be read for this reason. The decision as to which features of appearance are significant and which insignificant founds scientific physiognomy and casts it in its complex and ambivalent relation to the 'real' of realism. There is never any suggestion that the insignificance of pathognomy relegates that layer of appearance to the status of unreality – on the contrary, it is all too pervasively and powerfully 'real'. The distinction of the relevant and irrelevant is made theoretically and perceptually – one might say cognitively if that term could be unburdened of its empiricist implications. In a utopia such as the *Empire of Signs*, which falls neither into the camp of fact or fiction (Japan is not 'real', and Barthes has never visited 'it'), such distinctions are correspondingly more difficult to draw. Barthes in fact makes no efforts to do so, still less to tackle the issue, and the luxuriance of detail provided serves to deflect the criticism that his is in a pejorative sense a fantasy, and at the same time to anticipate the comment that there might be another way to tell the tale. Like those eighteenth-century travelogues which *Empire of Signs* seems at so many points to mirror, Barthes' work is a dogmatic utopia. The colonizer of the body surface lays down the rules, formulates the law of reading, and sets into play a pretence autonomy of signifiers. Text and image put into circulation body, face, writing, but only the last possesses any freedom of development; the *Empire of Signs* turns around an empty, nonetheless powerful, centre. The yellow hole.

The Body in question

Lavater and Barthes both posit the body as visible, legible and meaningful. Both recognize the immense theoretical labour and perceptual acuity required to decipher the writing of the body, yet each adopts different procedures for doing so. The image of the body when reproduced in a printed text may, like any other image, purport to serve as a privileged space in which the real is transmitted literally. But this claim cannot be upheld. The literal, the 'naive', and the 'pure' message is always constituted in relation to a convention of 'literalness', 'naivety' and 'purity'. After all, was it not Barthes who told us how the 'third meaning' remains present even after the connotative and denotative messages of an image have been evicted? The image of the body may of course be read narratively, but for Lavater its function derives precisely from the manner in which it can go beyond the dead end of the verbal; it can sustain, extend, and enrich language. Hogarth set down a prophesy concerning the potential developments in optic power; Lavater suggests that the physiognomist might at one point be able to set down in print a complete description of what has been seen, and then from that description reproduce the visual image without loss; he is, one might say, straining to match Hogarth in the realm of verbal power.

The claim that Lavater's physiognomy succeeded in developing a perceptual language which conjoins the verbal and the visual would seem to be undercut by the apparent conventionality of the relation of illustration and text in the *Essay on Physiognomy*. But that relation is far from ordinary. There is a powerful and at times incredible interplay between word and image – so far-fetched did this seem to Lavater's contemporaries that he was often denounced either as a charlatan who had failed to understand what he had written, or as a genius flashed with truth who could not set down in language what he had seen. Though word and image in the *Essays* lie under the same covers, they do not share the same bed. Lavater strives continuously to put into question the familial union of the pictorial and textual traditions as he seeks, with the assistance of the word, to place, return and retain physiognomy in the space of the perceptual.

Relationships between text and image have always been subject to complex transpositions and disruptions, not least because the former is restricted by line, space and form in a way the image of itself is not. Of course, this freedom is to some degree illusory and certainly compromised once the image takes its place in the text, particularly as it becomes inter-twined with verbal description and elaborate systems of cross-reference are developed. Of itself the image is polysemous, implying, as Barthes has termed it, a 'floating chain' of signifieds underlying the signifiers. The caption, the text, criticism and interpretation are all intended to fix this chain. If designed and produced to be set in a text, the image may become swamped, and the liberty of its signifiers repressed. Thus banalized, the image will no longer be worth 'more than a thousand words'. It may indeed require bailing out by the thousand-word elucid-ation; Le Brun's zoomorphic images fail to be self-supporting not because they have come down to us with a caption but because they were designed to have a caption which no longer exists. In this case, the image is under-informed and does not bear the surplus of meaning we might expect to see overflowing from it. That said, the image in a book will need in most circumstances to be treated not only as a possible extension of a verbal statement but as a statement in itself, one with its own conventions, traditions and grammar rules.

When we turn to Lavater's work we find a *development* in visual discourse which does not match that in the written text. What is striking is that by creating a perceptual space for the imagination Lavater is disclosing the site of a praxis. This imagial site is under constant pressure from the text itself, yet against it the text seems impossibly restricted, flat and poverty-stricken. The designation of the text as a series of fragments is particularly appropriate since on their own the theoretical positions staked out do seem disjointed, piecemeal and contradictory. However, the images in the work go some way to solder the fragments together; they provide a unity-in-development. As I have said above, coherence arises from the whole work as the reader adopts a participatory role in physiognomical reading, as that reading is invested with interests. The images do not mimic reality by giving the stamp of authority to what might, if the verbal description was not embellished, seem a mere fiction. They profoundly alter the nature of the writing, and hence of the reading of the complete text – most decisively by breaking down the work's isolation (as a piece of 'writing'; as 'authored'; as 'inspired'; as 'literary') and casting it within a network of correspondences which involve reader, text, interests, power, knowledge. The *Essays on Physiognomy* does not present a pell-mell confusion of still images steadied by captions, but something closer to a filmic (at times even evolutionary) sequence. A single image is not sutured to another single snippet of text by cross-reference; it is the struggle of appropriation by the reader of the literal and the figurative which establishes the possibility and the practice of physiognomical science.

Lavater's images are of course not photographic, and we must not think that later developments in photography would have assisted his work – the photograph was of some use in pathognomy, but even in this realm its cluttered detail was often baffling.[48] Unlike the drawing, the photograph represents the significant and the insignificant without distinction; except in the case of a *trompe-l'oeil* or a retouched image like the 'Japanned' Barthes, it reproduces everything without the purity of line or content of the physiognomical depiction. But as Barthes argued in 1970, the year which saw the publication of *S/Z* and *Empire des signes*, the photograph also possesses a 'third meaning'.[49] This constitutes a level of the message, along with the symbolic and the informational, which is at once evident and yet obstinately resistant to description.

Barthes' essay on the third meaning forms a body with his other contemporaneous works since it is on the plane of the superficial that this message is displayed. It is the expression of bodies which is obtuse – or rather the residue of that expression left after the historians, sociologists and psychoanalysts have taken their share. Lavaterian physiognomy, were Barthes to deal with it directly, would find a space between that which is obtuse and that which is obvious in the physicality of the body surface. But as we have seen, Barthes' reading of corporal signs is obviated by the series of reductions he makes and by his refusal to grant interiority to the body. The interest of Barthes' reading of some Eisenstein stills is that what serves as the major interference to the understanding and transposition of the third meaning is the *disguise*. This is symbolized not by the masquerade but by the *barbatoria*; the dance of the beard from the raised chin of Ivan the Terrible. The beard is far more problematic than it was in the case of the Abbé Pierre, partly because Barthes has by this stage recognized the dimensions and purport of physiognomy through his reading of Balzac, and partly because in Ivan's case the beard declares its artifice without abandoning the good faith of its referent, the figure of the Tsar. The Abbé had to be demythologized and exposed as the consummate actor; here Ivan is disguised twice over, once as the actor in the anecdote, once as actor in the film. Barthes' essay allows us to see clearly that what is being described in *Empire of Signs* is a series of objects ranged at the level of the third meaning. These objects are the bodily equivalent of the Japanese *haiku*. They are anaphoric bodies without content. Their emptiness is precisely what makes them inarticulable. To the utopia of language then, Barthes in 1970 could offer only the dystopia of the death of character.

Notes

1. The puppets of *bunraku* theatre are treated in Barthes' 'Lesson in Writing', in Barthes, 1977.
2. Quoted in Reynolds 1976: 277. On the beard as a symbol of masculine sexuality see remarks in Ellis 1939: II, 1, 173–5; Darwin 1901: 877, 885, 912; Lurie

1981: 170–6; and Walker 1977: 31–2.

3. See Woodforde 1971 and, for more general treatments, Polhemus 1978: 132–46, Berg 1951, Chesterton 1960: 489–95 and Banner 1983: 63, 124 and *passim.*

4. Hogarth quoted in Antal 1962: 104–5; see also Wright's description of Hogarth's representations as 'a series of *speaking* pictures' (Wright, 1968: 122, 133) and Hogarth's own comments in his autobiographical notes in Hogarth 1955: 209, 215.

5. I here follow Jarrett 1976: 159 rather than Paulson's purely aesthetic reading in Paulson 1971: II, 204.

6. Fielding 1973: II, 5 (as customary, my references to Fielding's novels are by book and chapter). See also Irwin 1941: 48–49, which treats Fielding's use of the theme of the trickster/hypocrite/politician. On Fielding's early political views, see Goldbar 1976 and for later ones, Cockshut 1980: 103–4 provides a concise summary. The issue is further discussed in Shortland 1988.

7. *Gentleman's Magazine*, XXVI, 1756: 335; see also *Gentleman's Magazine*, XXI, 1751: 79–80 (future references to this publication will be abbreviated to *GM*).

8. The problem of falsehood in physiognomical diagnoses is discussed in many issues of the *GM*, e.g. XVII, 1747: 229–31; X, 1740: 117–18; VII, 1737: 549–51, 553–55. Sennett (1976) provides an insightful sixth chapter on man-as-actor.

9. See Thompson 1974: 395; Thompson 1978: 143.

10. On the growing upper-class distrust of the clergy, scriptures and moral theology, see Stone 1977: part V.

11. On this see Thompson 1971: 135–6, Thompson 1972: 285–312, Brewer 1976: 163–200, Holton 1978.

12. Addison 1967: I, 26–7 (9 March 1711); Steele in ibid., 43–6 (16 March 1711).

13. On this see Paulson 1971: I, 116f. and Atherton 1974: 219–23.

14. Fielding 1974: VII, 6. See also Fielding's essay on human nature in *The Champion* of 11 December 1739, in Miller 1961: 62 and his remarks in Fielding 1972: 119–52, especially 126–7.

15. Fielding 1972: 155. In his poem 'To John Hayes, Esq.', Fielding writes:

> Men what they are not struggle to appear,
> And Nature strives to show them as they are;
> While Art, repugnant thus to Nature, fights,
> The Various Man appears in different Lights. (ibid.: 53)

16. For classical expressions, see Diogenes Laertius 1925: I, 461–3 and Ovid 1915: II, viii, 54. Steele provides the early eighteenth-century account in *The Spectator* of 15 August 1711 (Addison, Steele and others 1967: I, 434–7).

17. Fielding 1972: 158 and 30–5. For accounts in the novels, see Fielding 1962: IX, 5 and Fielding 1974: VII, 10.

18. Richardson 1715: 162 and 1762: 23, 73, 95. For another interesting example: Lairesse 1738: 102. Hazlitt neatly sums up Reynolds's view in 'two words': '*That the great style in Painting consists in Avoiding the details, and peculiarities of particular objects*' (*The Champion*, 25 December 1814 in Reynolds 1981: 326); see also Hazlitt 1944: 619 and Trawick 1965.

19. Reynolds, 'To the Idler', 20 October 1759 in Reynolds 1852: II, 128. Two important studies of the topic are Elledge 1943 and Hipple 1952–3. More discursive but equally interesting is E.H. Gombrich's essay 'Meditations on a Hobby Horse' in Whyte 1952.

20. Strong Platonic elements in Reynolds' work have been isolated by Bredvold 1934 and Gombrich 1948; more convincing, however, are the filiations to Aristotle and Locke. These are traced by Blanchard 1949: chapter 2 and Trowbridge 1939, respectively. Discourse III and Discourse XIII seem especially empiri-

cal in their orientation, but Discourse IX much less so.

21. Reynolds 1981: 44; see also 65–73 and Reynolds 1852: II, 312.

22. *A Philosophical Inquiry into the Origins of our Ideas of the Sublime and the Beautiful* in Burke 1906: I, 84. Reynolds' principles of taste derive substantially from Burke, especially from the *Essay on Taste* prefixed to the second edition of the *Inquiry* in 1759. On this, see Thompson 1917: 357–60 especially; Bryant 1939: 53–4; the memoir in Reynolds 1852: I, 185, 258–71; and the editor's remarks in Reynolds 1981: 132n.

23. Hogarth 1753: 123. The term 'art of seeing' derives from Richardson (on this see Antal 1962: 142–3).

24. Fielding 1972: 162. As Miller shows, this follows the approach Fielding adopted in his earlier work (Miller 1961: 193). See also the *GM*, XL, 1770: 445 where this aspect of Fielding's method is discussed and, for a more general treatment, *GM* III, 1733: 6.

25. On the role of literary pictorialism in biography, see Wendorf 1983; the classic discussion of *ut pictura poesis* is Hagstrum 1958.

26. Two studies of Lavater stand out: Guinaudeau 1924 and Tytler's brilliantly researched but analytically disappointing study of 1980. Tytler has an extensive bibliography to which should be added: Heisch 1842, Brooks and Johnson 1980, MacAlister 1911 and Ysabeau 1862. I have treated certain aspects of Lavater's work in Shortland 1986.

27. On classical modes of character description according to bodily appearance, see Evans 1969; Cooper 1790; Duprat 1905; and Armstrong 1958.

28. On its authenticity see Rose 1854; Forster 1889. Ross judges it to be a 'combination of two treatises, both perhaps Peripatetic' (Ross 1923: 12).

29. Descartes 1649; Parsons 1947; La Chambre 1640–62; Bulwer 1649; Bell 1806; Darwin 1872.

30. See Lavater 1806–7: IX, 85–90; and Morel d'Arleux 1806 (where the sketches were first made public).

31. See Blunt 1953: 226–30, 242–5 (quote from 22), Blunt 1944, Jouin 1889, Marcel 1909, and Montagu 1964.

32. Le Brun's text had earlier appeared in Henri Testelin's *Sentiments des plus habiles peintres sur la pratique de la peinture et sculpture* (Paris, 1680). For details, see Marcel 1909: 124 and Paulson 1971: I, 536n10. On Le Brun, important studies include Fontaine 1909: chapter III, Smart 1965, Rogerson 1953, McKenzie 1978, Baltrušaitis 1957: 8–46, and Ross 1984.

33. See Pope-Hennessy 1966, Piper 1957, and Gombrich 1962: chapter IX.

34. See the *Nouvelle revue de psychanalyse*, 21, 1980: 110–21.

35. For example, see Lavater 1870: 11. In *The Monthly Review* (LXVI, 1782: 481) one critic noted how in the French edition of Lavater, the chapters were clearly marked as 'fragments': 'Those who think they have composed a complete and regular system of any science, divide it usually into *books* and *chapters*; but our author, however adventurous in point of genius, is modest enough to look upon the science of physiognomy as far from being completed . . . and therefore he calls his chapters Fragments.'

36. For eighteenth-century examples, see *GM*, LXIX, 1799: 948; *The Monthly Review*, LXVI, 1782: 495; Clubbe 1763: 5; and Parsons 1947: 41.

37. The typical statement of this confrontation appears in Cicero's *De Fato* (see Cooper 1790: 414–15).

38. *The Reflector*, I, 2, 1810–11: 424 (an article on 'The Danger of confounding Moral with Personal Deformity').

39. Quoted in Tytler 1980: 81. The impact of physiognomy and phrenology on art and art criticism in mid-century forms the subject of Cowling 1982.

40. *English Review*, VII, 1786: 388.

41. Some nobility, it is true, did submit to the diagnoses willingly, and Lavater received visits from, amongst others, Mary Empress of Russia and Prince Edward of England; see Maier 1909: 143f. and Lavater 1870: cviii. Joseph II was perhaps more typical and held Lavater in distrust: 'Ah!' he said on being introduced to the prophet from Zurich, 'You are a dangerous man, and I know not whether I may venture to show myself before you . . . one must be on one's guard on approaching you!' (quoted in Heisch 1842: 95).

42. See Mantegazza 1880: 269–70 and Giovanni 1837: 331, 368.

43. Balzac to Surville, 20 August 1822 in Balzac 1960, I: 204; see also Bonard 1969: 40.

44. See Fess 1924, Baldensperger 1927: 81–97, Baldensperger 1910, Thiele 1927, and Abraham 1931.

45. See Barthes 1954: 33, 35, 74, 75, Barthes 1964: 33, 114.

46. Newhall (1964: 11–12) has judged that the European interest in profiles was largely generated by physiognomy. Ysabeau (1862: 119–24, 147–56) claims that portraits and statues are invariably better sources for the physiognomist, particularly when the subject is a nervous female or a male hypocrite.

47. See Mosse, 1978: Chapter one. In the heyday of physiognomy, its anti-classificatory bias was widely recognized even by its opponents: see, for example, Hazlitt's comments in Hazlitt 1944: 54–70, 55 especially.

48. Darwin, for one, was frequently unable to 'see' the expressions and signs which were described by the photographers who sent him materials for his *Expression of the Emotions*.

49. See Barthes 1977: 52–68. I should emphasize that this paper does not deal with Barthes' later work on photography, particularly that represented in Barthes 1981.

References

Abraham, P. (1931) *Créatures chez Balzac*, Paris, Gallimard.

Addison, Joseph, Steele, Richard and others (1967) *The Spectator*, 4 vols, London, Everyman's Library.

Antal, F. (1962) *Hogarth and his Place in European Art*, London, Routledge & Kegan Paul.

Armstrong, B.A. (1958) 'The methods of the Greek physiognomists', *Greece and Rome*, V, 52–6.

Atherton, Herbert M. (1974) *Political Prints in the Age of Hogarth*, Oxford, Clarendon.

Baldensperger, F. (1910) 'Les théories de Lavater dans la littérature française', *Etudes d'histoire littéraire*, 2nd series, Paris, 51–91.

Baldensperger, F. (1927) *Orientations étrangères chez Honoré de Balzac*, Paris: Bibliothèque de la revue de la littérature comparée, number 31.

Baltrušaitis, J. (1957) *Aberrations*, Paris, O. Perrin.

Balzac, Honoré de (1960–5)

Correspondance de Honoré de Balzac, 5 vols, edited by Roger Pierrot, Paris, Garnier.

Banner, Lois (1983) *American Beauty*, New York, W.W. Norton.

Barthes, Roland (1954) *Michelet par lui-même*, Paris, Seuil.

Barthes, Roland (1964) *Essais critiques*, Paris, Seuil.

Barthes, Roland (1968) 'L'Effet du réel', *Communications*, XI, 84–89.

Barthes, Roland (1973) *Mythologies*, translated by Annette Lavers, London, Paladin.

Barthes, Roland (1975a), *Le Magazine Littéraire*, 97.

Barthes, Roland (1975b) *S/Z*, translated by Richard Miller, London, Cape.

Barthes, Roland (1977) *Image-Music-Text*, translated and edited by Stephen Heath, London, Fontana.

Barthes, Roland (1981) *Camera Lucida*, translated by Richard Howard, New York, Wang & Hill.

Barthes, Roland (1983) *Empire of Signs,* translated by Richard Howard, London, Jonathan Cape.

Bell, Charles (1806) *Essays on the Anatomy of Expression in Painting,* London, Longman & Co.

Berg, Charles (1951) *The Unconscious Significance of Hair,* London, George Allen & Unwin.

Blanchard, Frances (1949) *Retreat from Likeness in the Theory of Painting,* London.

Blanquet, J.P. (1827) *A Series of Lithographic Drawings illustrative of the Relation between Human Physiognomy and that of the Brute Creation from Designs by Charles Le Brun, with Remarks on the System,* London.

Blunt, Anthony (1944) 'The early work of Charles Le Brun', *Burlington Magazine,* LXXXV, 165–73, 186–94.

Blunt, Anthony (1953) *Art and Architecture in France 1500 to 1700,* Harmondsworth, Penguin.

Bonard, O. (1969) *La Peinture dans la création Balzacienne,* Geneva.

Bredvold, L.I. (1934) 'The tendency towards Platonism in neo-classical esthetics', *English Literary History,* I, 91–119.

Brewer, John (1976) *Party Ideology and Popular Politics at the Accession of George III,* Cambridge, Cambridge University Press.

Brooks, G.P. and **Johnson, R.W.** (1980) 'Johann Caspar Lavater's *Essays on Physiognomy*', *Psychological Reports,* 46.

Bryant, Donald Cross (1939) *Edmund Burke and his Literary Friends,* St Louis: Washington University Studies in Language and Literature, number 9.

Bryson, Norman (1981) *Word and Image: French Painting of the Ancien Régime,* Cambridge, Cambridge University Press.

Bulwer, John (1649) *Pathomyotomia; or, a Dissection of the Significative Muscles of the Affections of the Minde,* London, Humphrey Moseley.

Burke, Edmund (1906) *The Works of the Right Honourable Edmund Burke,* 6 vols, London, Henry Frowde.

Chateaubriand, Vicomte de (1978) *Essai sur les révolutions,* Paris, Garnier-Flammarion.

Chesterton, G.K. (1960) 'On keeping your hair on' in Raymond T. Bond (ed) *The Man who was Chesterton,* New York, Image Books.

Clubbe, John (1763) *Physiognomy; being a Sketch only of a Larger Book upon the Same Plan,* London: R. and J. Dodsley.

Cockshut, A.O.J. (1980) *The Novel to 1900,* London, Macmillan.

Cooper, Thomas (1790) 'Observations respecting the history of physiognomy', *Memoirs of the Literary and Philosophical Society of Manchester,* III (partly reprinted in *The European Magazine,* XIX, 1791, 122–6, 204–8).

Cowling, Mary Christine (1982) *The Conception and Interpretation of Character in Victorian Modern Life Art,* Leeds University PhD.

Darwin, Charles (1901) *The Descent of Man and Selection in Relation to Sex,* London, John Murray.

Darwin, Charles (1872) *The Expression of the Emotions in Man and Animals,* London, John Murray.

De Piles, Roger (1780) *The Art of Painting, with the Lives and Characters of about 300 of the most Eminent Painters,* London, J. Osborn.

Descartes, René (1649) *Les Passions de l'âme,* Paris, Chez Henri le Gras.

Diogenes Laertius (1925) *Lives of Eminent Philosophers,* 2 vols, translated by R.D. Hicks, London, Heinemann.

Duprat, G.L. (1905) 'La psychophysiologie des passions dans la philosophie ancienne', *Archiv für die Geschichte der Philosophie,* XVIII.

Elledge, Scott (1943) 'The background and development in English criticism of the theories of generality and particularity', *PMLA,* LXII, 147–82.

Ellis, Havelock (1939) *Studies in the Psychology of Sex,* 4 vols, New York, Random House.

Evans, E.C. (1969) 'Physiognomics in the Ancient World', *Transactions of the American Philosophical Society,* 59, 5.

Félibien, André (1685) *Entretiens sur les vies et les ouvrages des plus excellents peintres anciens et modernes,* 2 vols, Paris, S. Mabre-Gramoisy.

Fess, G.M. (1924) *The Correspondence of Physical and Material Factors with Character in Balzac,* Philadelphia: Publications of the University of Pennsylvania, Series in Romance Languages and Literature, Number 10.

Fielding, Henry (1728) *The Masquerade,* London, J. Roberts and A. Dodd.

Fielding, Henry (1962) *Amelia,* edited by A.R. Humphreys, London, Oxford University Press.

Fielding, Henry (1972) *Miscellanies by Henry Fielding, Esq*; *Volume One*, edited by Henry Knight Miller, Oxford, Clarendon.

Fielding, Henry (1973) *The Life of Mr Jonathan Wild the Great*, edited by Claude Rawson, London, Oxford University Press.

Fielding, Henry (1974) *The History of Tom Jones, A Foundling*, 2 vols, edited by Fredson Bowers and Martin C. Battesin, Oxford, Clarendon.

Fontaine, André (1909) *Les Doctrines d'art en France*, Paris, H. Laurens.

Forster, Richard (1889) 'Handschriften und Ausgabe des pseudoaristotelischen *Secretum Secretorum*', *Centralblatt für Bibliothekwesen*, VI, 1–22, 57–76.

Giovanni, P. (1837) *Saggio di Fisiognomonia e Patognomonia*, Milan.

Goldbar, B.L. (1976) *Walpole and the Wits*, London, Methuen.

Gombrich, E.H. (1948) 'Icones Symbolicae: the visual image in neo-Platonic thought', *Journal of the Warburg and Courtauld Institute*, 11, 163–92.

Gombrich, E.H. (1962) *Art and Illusion: A Study of the Psychology of Pictorial Representation*, London, Phaidon.

Graham, John (1960) *The Development of the Use of Physiognomy in the Novel*, Johns Hopkins University PhD.

Graham, John (1961) 'Lavater's *Physiognomy*: a checklist', *Papers of the Bibliographical Society of America*, 55, 297–308.

Graham, John (1979) *Lavater's Essays on Physiognomy*, Bern.

Guinaudeau, Oliver (1924) *Jean-Gaspard Lavater*, Paris, F. Alcan.

Hagstrum, Jean H. (1958) *The Sister Arts: The Tradition of Literary Pictorialism in English Poetry from Dryden to Gray*, Chicago: Chicago University Press.

Hazlitt, William (1944) *Selected Essays of William Hazlitt 1778–1830*, edited by Geoffrey Keynes, London, The Nonesuch Press.

Heisch, P.I. (1842) *Memoirs of John Caspar Lavater*, London, S. Bagster & Sons.

Hipple, Walter J. (1952–3) 'Generality and particularity in the *Discourses* of Sir Joshua Reynolds', *The Journal of Aesthetics and Art Criticism*, XI, 231–47.

Hogarth, William (1753) *The Analysis of Beauty*, London, J. Reeves.

Hogarth, William (1955) *The Analysis of Beauty*, edited by Joseph Burke, Oxford, Clarendon.

Holton, Robert J. (1978) 'The crowd in history: some problems of theory and method', *Social History*, 3, 219–33.

Irwin, W.R. (1941) *The Making of Jonathan Wild*, New York, Columbia University Press.

Jarrett, Derek (1976) *The Ingenious Mr Hogarth*, London, Michael Joseph.

Jouin, H. (1889) *Charles le Brun et les arts sous Louis XIV*, Paris, Imprimerie Nationale.

La Chambre, Marin Cureau de (1640) *Les Charactères des passions*, Paris, P. Blaise.

Lairesse, Gerard de (1738) *The Art of Painting in all its Branches*, London, printed for the Author.

Lavater, J.C. (1795) *Secret Journal of a Self-Observer*, 2 vols, London, T. Cadell.

Lavater, J.C. (1806–7) *L'Art de connaitre les hommes par la physiognomie*, 10 vols, edited by L.J. Moreau de la Sarthe, Paris, L. Prudhomme.

Lavater, J.C. (1870) *Essays on Physiognomy*, 17th edition, London, W. Tegg.

Lavers, Annette (1982) *Roland Barthes: Structuralism and After*, London, Methuen.

Le Brun, Charles (1734) *A Method to Learn to Design the Passions*, London, printed for the Author.

Lurie, Alison (1981) *The Language of Clothes*, London, Heinemann.

MacAlister, A. (1911) 'Physiognomy', *Encyclopaedia Britannica*, 11th edition, XXI.

McKenzie, Alan T. (1978) 'The countenance you show me: reading the passions in the eighteenth century'. *The Georgia Review*, XXXII, 3, 758–73.

Maier, Heinrich (1909) *An der Grenze der Philosophie*, Tübingen, J.C.B. Moke.

Mantegazza, P. (1880) *Physiognomy and Expression*, London, Walter Scott.

Marcel, P. (1909) *Charles Le Brun*, Paris, Plon-Nourrit.

Miller, Henry Knight (1961) *Essays on Fielding's Miscellanies*, Princeton, Princeton University Press.

Montagu, J. (1964) 'Le Brun Animalier', *Art de France*, IV, 310–14.

Morel d'Arleux, L.J.M. (1806) *Dissertation sur un traité de Charles Le Brun concernant les rapports de la physiognomie humaine avec celles des animaux*, Paris.

Mosse, George L. (1978) *Towards the*

Final Solution: A History of European Racism, London, J.M. Dent and Sons.

Newhall, Beaumont (1964) *History of Photography*, New York, Doubleday.

Ovid (1915) *Tristium Libri Quinque ... Fragmente*, edited by S.G. Owen, Oxford, Clarendon.

Parsons, James (1947) *Human Physiognomy Explain'd: in the Crounian Lectures on Muscular Motion* (supplement to the *Philosophical Transactions*, XLIV, 1746).

Paulson, Ronald (1971) *Hogarth, his Life, Art and Times*, 2 vols, New Haven, Yale University Press.

Piper, David (1957) *The English Face*, London, Thames & Hudson.

Plato (1978) *The Collected Dialogues*, edited by Edith Hamilton and Huntingdon Cairns, Princeton, Princeton University Press.

Polhemus, Ted (ed) (1978) *Social Aspects of the Human Body*, Harmondsworth, Penguin.

Pope-Hennessy, John (1966) *The Portrait in the Renaissance*, London, Phaidon.

Reynolds, Joshua (1852) *The Literary Works of Sir Joshua Reynolds*, 2 vols, edited by Henry William Beechey, London, George Bell and Sons.

Reynolds, Joshua (1981) *Discourses on Art*, edited by Robert R. Wark, London, Collier-Macmillan.

Reynolds, Reginald (1976) *Beards*, New York, Harcourt Brace Jovanovich.

Richardson, Jonathan (1715) *An Essay on the Theory of Painting*, London, J. Churchill.

Richardson, Jonathan (1762) *The Works of Jonathan Richardson*, London, Strawberry Hill.

Rogerson, Brewster (1953) 'The art of painting the passions', *Journal of the History of Ideas*, XIV, 68–94.

Rose, Valentin (1854) *De Aristotelis Librorum Ordine et Auctoritate Comentatio*, Berlin, G. Reimer.

Ross, Stephanie (1984) 'Painting the passions: Charles Le Brun's *Conférence sur l'Expression*', *Journal of the History of Ideas*, XLV, 1, 25–47.

Ross, W.D. (1923) *Aristotle*, London, Methuen.

Scoutetten, H. (1862) *Eléments de philosophie phrénologique*, Metz, F. Blanc.

Sennett, Richard (1976) *The Fall of Public Man*, Cambridge, Cambridge University Press.

Shortland, Michael (1982) Secret sins and unnatural follies', *Literary Review*, July 1982, 31–3.

Shortland, Michael (1986) 'The power of a thousand eyes: Johann Caspar Lavater's science of physiognomic perception', *Criticism* 28: 379–408.

Shortland, Michael (1988) 'Setting murderous Machiavel to school: hypocrisy and politics in the novel', *Journal of European Studies* 18: 93–119.

Skultans, Vieda (1979) *English Madness: Ideas on Insanity, 1580–1890*, London, Routledge & Kegan Paul.

Smart, Alastair (1965) 'Dramatic gesture and expression in the age of Hogarth and Reynolds', *Apollo*, LXXXII, 90–7.

Stone, Lawrence (1977) *The Family, Sex and Marriage in England, 1500–1800*, London, Weidenfeld.

Thiele, F. (1927) *Balzac als Physiognomiker*, Berlin.

Thody, Philip (1977) *Roland Barthes: A Conservative Estimate*, London, Macmillan.

Thompson, Elbert N.S. (1917) 'The discourse of Sir Joshua Reynolds', *PMLA*, XXXII, 339–66.

Thompson, E.P. (1971) 'The moral music": Le charivari anglais', *Annales*, 27, 285–312.

Thompson, E.P. (1974) 'Plebian society, plebian culture', *Journal of Social History*, 7, 382–405.

Thompson, E.P. (1978) 'Eighteenth-century English society: class struggle without class?', *Social History*, 3, 133–65.

Thompson, E.P. (1971) 'The moral economy of the English crowd in the eighteenth century', *Past and Present*, 50, 76–136.

Trawick, I.M. (1965) 'Hazlitt, Reynolds, and the Ideal', *Studies in Romanticism*, IV, 240–47.

Trowbridge, Hoyt (1939) 'Platonism and Sir Joshua Reynolds', *English Studies*, XXI, 1–7.

Tytler, Graeme (1980) *Physiognomy in the European Novel*, Princeton, Princeton University Press.

Walker, Benjamin (1977) *Body Magic*, London, Granada.

Wendorf, Richard (ed) (1983) *Articulate Images: the Sister Arts from Hogarth to Tennyson*, New Haven, Yale University Press.

Whyte, Lancelot Law (ed) (1952)

Aspects of Form: A Symposium on Form and Nature in Art, London, Lund Humphries.

Woodforde, John (1971) *The Strange Story of False Hair,* London, Routledge & Kegan Paul.

Wright, Andrew (1968) *Henry Fielding:*

Mask and Feast, London, Chatto & Windus.

Ysabeau, V.F.A. (1862) *Lavater et Gall: physiognomie et phrénologie rendues intelligibles pour tout le monde,* Paris, Garnier frères.

1985

CHAPTER 2

Textual theory: Derrida

Mike Gane

Texts reviewed:

J. Derrida, *Writing and Difference*, trans. Alan Bass, Routledge & Kegan Paul, 1978. This collection contains eleven essays ranging from '"Genesis and structure" and phenomenology' (of 1959) to 'From restricted to general economy: a Hegelianism without reserve' (of 1967).

J. Derrida, *Positions*, trans. Alan Bass, Athlone Press, 1981a. This collection contains three interviews: 'Implications' (of 1967), 'Semiology and grammatology' (of 1968) and 'Positions' (of 1971).

J. Derrida, *Speech and Phenomena*, trans. David Allison, Northwestern University Press, Evanston, 1973. This contains the essay 'Speech and phenomena' (1967) and two other essays: 'Form and meaning' (1967) and 'Difference' (1968).

J. Derrida, *Of Grammatology*, trans. Gayatri Spivak, Johns Hopkins University Press, 1976.

J. Derrida, *Dissemination*, trans. Barbara Johnson, Athlone Press, 1981b. This contains 'Plato's pharmacy' (of 1968) and 'The double session' (of 1970) and 'Dissemination' (of 1969), all prefaced by 'Outwork' (1972).

> *'for those who are willing to read*
> *the most general title of the problem*
> *would be castration and mimesis'* (1981a: 84)

A

'The staging of a title, a first sentence, an epigraph, a pretext, a preface, a single germ, will never make a beginning. It *was* indefinitely dispersed' (1981b: 43).

B

In a sense the 'review' of Derrida's works is strictly impossible. But we have to be careful here, on many scores, and especially perhaps of the oblation, or the singular *reading* of Derrida.[1] If texts are doubly written and infinitely dispersed then this text is already divided (this is evident) in the most 'natural' manner of the horizontal interruption: the excerpts quoted are linked by the linear text of the review.[2] In order, however, to mark the development of dispersion it is essential to note the vertical division, which Derrida points up as both the marginalia, footnotes, etc., but also the insertion of the *other* text into this.[3] For this reason Derrida, and he is not the first, is tempted to practise the most explicit divided writing. To read Derrida therefore it is appropriate to stage what is going on in this review itself (outside itself within itself).[4]

C[5]

The texts of *Dissemination*, for ease of reference marked D, are articulated around the break with the metaphysics of the text and the essay called Outwork and discusses what Derrida calls the extratext of which this review is no doubt a 'double'.

'I'm afraid you waited for me.'

Outwork polarizes the logocentric extratext against the disseminated one: 'From the point of view of the fore-word which recreates an intention-to-say after the fact, the text exists as something written – a past – which, under the false appearance of the present, a hidden omnipotent author . . . is presenting to the reader as his future, you will have anticipated everything that follows . . .' (D:9).

'No. We're very little later than usual . . .'

'Isabel tells me that you have not suffered unbearably from the loss of sight . . . are there any compensations?'

And this kind of (logocentric) extratext exists as a kind of superfluity: 'fore-words, introductions . . . have always been written, it seems, in view of their own self-effacement . . .' (D:9).

'Yes, you cease to bother about certain things.'

On the other hand:

'. . . Dissemination endlessly opens up a *snag* in writing that can no longer be mended, a spot where neither meaning, however plural . . . can pin/pen down (*agrapher*) the trace . . .' (D:26).

Therefore to write an a-Hegelian preface is: '. . . to lose one's head, no longer know where one's head is . . . the signifying precipitation introduces an excess facing . . . the gap between the empty 'form', and the fullness of 'meaning' is structurally irremediable, and any formalism, as well as any thematicism, will be impotent . . .' (D: 20–1).

So the extratext of the disseminated type cannot be contained in the triadic dialectic of the Hegelian kind: '. . .The written preface . . . the outwork, then becomes a fourth text. Simulating the post-face . . . it is another text entirely, but at the same time . . . it is the 'double' of what it goes beyond . . .' (D: 27–8).

This brings into question the relation of the inside to the outside, since the fourth term seems to lie outside of the dialectic altogether. '. . . to allege that there is no outside of the text is not to postulate some ideal immanence, the incessant reconstitution of writing's relation to itself. What is in question is no longer an idealist . . . operation which, in a Hegelian manner, would suspend and sublate what is outside discourse, Logos, concept, or the idea. The text *affirms* the outside . . . If there

'And that is a relief. But what is there in place of bothering? What replaces the activity?'

'Oh, I don't know. There's a good deal when you're not active.'

'Is there? What exactly? It always seems to me that when there is no thought and no action, there is nothing.'

'There is something . . . I couldn't tell you what it is.'

'You came to look for me?'

'Isabel was a little uneasy.'

'I don't know . . . sometimes I feel it isn't fair that she's saddled with me . . . is my face much disfigured?'

was nothing outside the text, this implies with the transformation of the concept of the text in general, that the text is no longer the snug airtight inside of an interiority . . . but rather a different placement of the effects of opening and closing . . .' (D: 35–6)

Derrida's affirmation of the text's generativity is not then a symbolism: '. . . dissemination . . . explains itself . . . as the heterogeneity and absolute exteriority . . . seminal difference does constitute itself into a programme, but it is a programme that cannot be formalized. . . . It is attached, so to speak, to the incessant falling of a *supplement to the code.* Formalism no longer fails before an empirical richness but before a queue or tail . . .' (D: 52)

Again the polarity is established for '. . . the simulacrum can also be play-acted: while pretending to turn around and look backward, one is also in fact starting over again, adding an extratext, complicating the scene, opening up within the labyrinth a supplementary digression, which is also a false mirror that pushes the labyrinth's infinity back forever in mimed – that is, endless – speculation . . .' (D: 27)

But: '. . . dissemination . . . displaces a whole onto-speleology, another name for mimetology: not mimesis, an enigma of redoubtable power, but an interpretation of mimesis that misapprehends and distorts the logic of the double . . .' (D: 40)

'There is the scar. Yes it is a disfigurement. But more pitiable than shocking.'

'A pretty bad scar though?'

'Oh, Yes.'

'Do you mind if I touch you?' The lawyer shrank back instinctively. And yet, out of very philanthropy, he said, in a small voice: 'Not at all.' But he suffered as the blind man stretched out a strong naked hand to him. 'I thought you were taller', he said . . .

'You seem young', he said quietly, at last. The lawyer stood almost annihilated, unable to answer.

. . . 'Touch my eyes, will you? – touch my scar.' . . . He lifted his hand, and laid the fingers on the scar, on the scarred eyes, covered them with his own hand, pressed the fingers of the other man upon

And: 'Dissemination question: . . .
what's the story with this auto-
graphy of pure loss and without a
signature?' (D: 41)

'The opening of the square, the
supplementary four . . . the more
or less which disjoins dissemination
from polysemy, are regularly and
explicitly associated with castration
. . . but with a certain *outside* of
castration . . . because of its
'affirmative' character (and) also
because . . . the concept . . . has
been metaphysically interpreted
and arrested.' (D: 25–6)

his disfigured eye-sockets. . . .
. . . (Isabel) was watching. . . . She
knew that he had one desire – to
escape from this intimacy, this
friendship, which had been thrust
upon him. He could not bear it
that he had been touched by the
blind man. . . . He was like a
mollusc whose shell is broken.

(Lawrence 1980: 55–75)[6]

D

This 'review' thus joins what has become virtually an established tradition for translators of Derrida who have put their own function directly
into question. And where there are 'prefaces' these too have become
problematized. These are indices of an effective transference of the
fundamental questioning Derrida himself undertakes in the works translated. The pressure to throw into question the nature of the review article, and this very clause in an index of it, is part of the same lure. For
Derrida the article form is itself held in place, in part, by the philosophical forces of *idealist* metaphysics. The struggle against these forces leads,
with Derrida, to a mode of writing that appears experimental, writing
that challenges certain well-ingrained assumptions, even though modern
literature in many of its branches has questioned these assumptions
throughout the current century, as have music, visual arts etc.

The reader of Derrida, then, has to be prepared for both highly
theoretical and practical-experimental modes of writing, but which all
have one fundamental enemy, one which might be called, initially,
communication *conceived as an absolute monologue*. The mode of
construction of this review itself can be scrutinized under this idea: for
example, what is being written now is a 'final' draft, written on the basis
of a 'first' draft which contained certain textual experiments which have
been displaced by others. Clearly, then, *from the point of view of a purely
empirical inquiry*, this review has no beginning or existence that can be
ascribed to a single uninterrupted thought: what does surface has a
fictional beginning and end (whether it is idealist or not); the problem
cannot be resolved at the level of a realism or nominalism of the beginning (1981b: 36).

If the text is not a monologue, it is heterogeneous. Not single, but multiple. Beginning is a repression. Derrida resorts, like Joyce, to the text as interruption: breaks become open, featured, rather than repressed manoeuvres. The edifice which rests on this repression is now brought into question as *a mode of rationality intimately collusive with idealism.* The 'article' in this conventional mode, is articulated as a system of hierarchized elements: monolithic, linear, corporeal (it has a head, body and tail). The text irrupts with a capital letter, a title, and may even have its own 'abstract' tucked in under its own head.[7]

Derrida's alternative textual practices have a playful character. If the text has a head and a body, Derrida is, at least formally, willing to consider the case for decapitation.[8] And if the text has a surfacing it does not need also to have a *First Word of All.* The facility of the connection of the first word and the theological haunts Derrida's work. Textual religiosity is for Derrida a monumental seriousness (an insecurity). The tendency of Derrida's work is towards a play that is not just experimental but subversive, a play which affirms the seriousness within play, the reverence which is inside the irreverent. In order to overturn this particular idealism of monolithic textual religiosity it is essential to practise textual division: textual multiplicity is a mode of realizing the return of the repressed, the essential nature of textual heterogeneity as intertextuality, as inter-irrupted textuality. This way a part of the main body of this text is vertically multiple: the reading of D.H. Lawrence in Derrida and vice versa. If the enemy is at all hurt by this, then this sacrilege will be felt as such.

Another possibility would have been to have inserted the works of a sociologist such as Erving Goffman into Derrida's. For Derrida appears, at least to this reader, to have a distinct Goffmanesque side to his writing; or, rather, Goffman has a distinctly Derridean side to his. The translation of the preface to *Dissemination* as Outwork (*Hors livre, hors d'oeuvre*) recalls Goffman's concept of Facework. The mode of conceptualization of the two writers appears very much to be a question of *ad hoc*ing. Both are interested in games and fun, and both are in their different ways interested in Freud: it is Goffman who, for example, notes the production of seriousness by the overdetermination of the game. But above all, both writers appear to play on the shift from the apparently secure to the insecure. For Goffman this shift is indicated towards the 'communication out of character', to 'the insanity of place' to the 'out of frame'.[9] For Derrida the whole of the strategy of his work is the destabilizing of the matrix which holds in position the most secure of all places: the metaphysics of presence, the security of the immediacy of presence to itself.

Not all games or modes of play are the same, of course. Some are less a mode of experimentation than a kind of indebtedness. For these latter modes, effectiveness depends entirely on pre-established values and

products, which, being highly charged, have a potential for being irrever-
ently discharged. A strong current of the modernist movement in the arts
exists as a quasi-parasitism: their humour or frivolity is only possible
because they are able to discharge an over-seriousness, or over-valuation,
of the traditional products. These forms of play leave the enemy
completely entrenched. Derrida's experimentation is without doubt
aimed at overturning the enemy. The question remains, for example (as
Lacan and Foucault have indicated), whether a blatant experiment such
as the insertion of the word *différance* into philosophical discourse, with
its resonances of the effectivity of the written, since it cannot be heard,
over the spoken, with its doubling of the verbs 'defer' and 'differ' in the
form of a simultaneous condensation-displacement, as a genre of diacritical novelty, is of the order not of the music of the so-called second
Viennese school (say Webern), but of the order of strictly parasitic
'music', as of the notorious 'piece' which is entirely silent, with the
performer instructed to take a position of anticipation (by Cage).[10] It is
clear that Derrida is aware that pure parasitism only heightens the ability
of the enemy to defend itself, and impedes the process of de-constructing it.

E

The works of Derrida are now being assimilated into English under the
category, predominantly, of 'post-structuralism'. It is true, of course, that
Derrida himself says: 'In the last analysis, *dissemination* means nothing'
(1981a: 44). But does this mean that the phenomenon of '*post*-structural-
ism' is some ghostly ectoplasm which emerges from the opening of his
texts? Or, because, in another image, according to Derrida, dissemination
'explodes' (*crève*) 'the semantic horizon' (1981a: 45), should one simply
not light the fuse and stand well back, to wait . . .? But there is, though, a
difference between the 'nothing' in Derrida's definition ('nothing . . .
cannot be reassembled into a definition') and the nullification of an
(structuralism's) alleged posteriority. Derrida's work puts into play a
rigorous scrutiny of absences, gaps, intervals, etc., and so it is deeply
ironic that Derrida's works are being fostered in English under a label
which designates an absence. What is more significant, the labelling is not
of Derrida's making. It is clear that 'post-structuralism' as a category is
an evasion and has no heart. It is strictly solidary with terms found in
profusion in history, sociology and aesthetics – post-industrialism, postmodernism, etc., which form part of naive and empiricist discourses of
those disciplines. It is precisely *against* those currents that Derrida's interventions are sustained. . . .

But 'post-structuralism' has become popular for more than one
reason. One of these is undoubtedly the image of apparent forward
movement visible in French philosophy, in, for instance, the linearity

'from Sartre through Althusser and Lévi-Strauss to Derrida'. That is to say the evolution of philosophy from existentialism through structuralism to *post*-structuralism. It was, in fact, from France that English philosophy heard of the 'end' of structuralism: the announcement came from J.-M Benoist amongst others. An article entitled 'The End of Structuralism' portentously introduced the work of Derrida in that perspective in 1970.[11] Benoist referred to Derrida's 'new, most rewarding approach . . . which overrides the artificial opposition between phenomenology and structuralism, yet links them together under the common accusation of being still caught up in the matrix of Western metaphysics . . . he scrutinizes, and in the process, *de-constructs* the foundations of culture.' From then on Derrida's name had been linked to the new nothing of this supersession.

Yet Benoist *had not in fact argued* that the end of structuralism had arrived, despite the title of his article. Derrida's work, he said in conclusion, was a development of structuralism, of new ends and objectives, and his work held out the promise of 'a new frontier for structuralism' – that is, a new mathematics and a new science of the written sign. It is enough to stress at the moment that the idea and phrase 'the end of structuralism' was a phrase which found a home, and appealed, and still does, to a certain current of Anglo-Saxon historicism. It is an idea which also has the great merit of indicating a fact of 'profound' progress in philosophy that is both linked yet sufficiently distantiated from Marxism (it might be said to shift *from Marxism to Marxisantism*), and is polarized towards the literary as against the scientific (for Benoist's claim that Derrida moves towards the scientific is flatly denied in Derrida's texts).

And, while the Nietzschean element is well to the fore, the expression 'post-structuralism' has been presented so earnestly that there cannot be the slightest doubt that the Nietzschean image of 'the beyond . . .' has been reduced to the anteriority of irony. An irony, that is, that is not intended. It is the assumption of an already achieved confusion. The evident embarrassment of the commentators here is interesting: from Culler's 'Derrida is one of a group . . . who can be loosely labelled "structuralist and post-structuralist" . . .' (Sturrock 1979: 155) to Harari's 'A definition of post-structuralism . . . will finally come . . . only from the results afforded us by post-structuralist theoretical practices . . .' (1979: 31). Hegelianism here is rendered naively in terms produced to define and depart from it (e.g. theoretical practice). It should be noted that Derrida himself is explicitly full square behind the critique of Hegelian empiricism: 'In order to define writing, the gram, *différance*, the text, etc., I have always insisted on the value of *practice*. Consequently, everywhere, from this point of view, that a general theoretical-practice of the "signifying practices" is elaborated, I have always subscribed to the task thus defined' (1981a: 90).

The interviews (1981a) indicate Derrida's complex relations with that development of Marxism which is a break with Hegelian empiricism. Derrida could be read, if the indications of these interviews are pushed to the limit, as a kind of ultra, if onesided, Althusserian.[12] Disguised, distanced, Derrida nevertheless appears to adhere to the programme of a materialist critique of idealism, which for Derrida is shifted into a critique of the matrix of idealism from the point of view of *absolute materialism.* And it is clear that Althusser's change of definition of philosophy (from 1967 on) moves in the direction already to some extent indicated in the writing of Derrida. ('I do not believe in decisive ruptures, in an unequivocal "epistemological break" ... breaks are always, and fatally, reinscribed in an old cloth that must continually, interminably be undone. This interminability is not an accident or contingency: it is essential, systematic, and theoretical ...' (1981a: 24). Whereas Derrida identifies the enemy as 'logocentrism', Althusser preferred to talk of the 'complicity between Logos and Being' (1970: 17 and 1976: 134–141). (An alternative classification has seen Derrida as a mode of 'left-Heideggerianism' but Derrida has insisted on precisely 'liberating' Nietzsche from Heidegger, and maintains that 'the Heideggerian problematic is the most "profound" and "powerful" defence of what I attempt to put into question under the rubric of the *thought of presence*' (1981a: 55).)

F

What is it that is produced in a Derridean reading or deconstruction? An ambiguity here was noted early on and was reflected in the difficulties recognized by Benoist: Derrida's 'main strength ... lies in the fact that he does not destroy anything – or even refute – but simply offers a diagnosis.' De-construction, which is said to be non-refuting and non-destructive, nevertheless appears to do something profound to the 'foundations of culture' (Benoist's phrase). One writer interprets this 'profundity' as simply an 'absolute licence': 'Derrida's argument that standards of judgment should be freed from Western standards of rationality conjures up the picture of absolute and probably uninteresting relativistic licence.'[13] This reading is said to be traced through another: that of Culler (1975) whose relevant chapter is carefully entitled '"Beyond" Structuralism' (no question mark, and the inverted commas are simply ambiguous), which cites Derrida as follows: 'the absence of an ultimate meaning opens an unbounded space for the play of signification.' For Culler, this means, immediately, 'the anguish of infinite regress' is replaced by 'the pleasure of infinite creation'. This composite perspective on Derrida leads to the astonishing view that Derrida is proposing the *absolute end of barriers* in discourse.[14] The couple seems to reinforce itself: absolute licence and absolute ineffectiveness (nothing destroyed or refuted).

But the issue of what Derrida does is complicated by the other side of the equation outlined by Benoist, that Derrida proposes new sciences. The argument on both sides is complicated by the fact that Derrida himself argues that his works are neither philosophical, scientific, nor literary (1981a: 71): the problem of the philosophy, or theoretical practice without an object. The more that Derrida's texts are studied now that they are in English the more they will be measured against the already fertile reception given to Althusser's. For, in English, the linearity 'first Althusser and then Derrida' does reflect the chronological appearance of works in translation, an obvious difference with the situation in France. In France the publications of Althusser and Derrida were almost exactly coeval (e.g., *For Marx* and *Writing and Difference* both cover the period 1960–5) but in translation the works are separated by a decade. It seems, therefore, that for Derrida to have become an appendage is a specifically Anglo-Saxon reaction to a determinate delay. The nothing (nullity) of *post*-structuralsim is a product of this interval. The positive and negative impact of Althusserian Marxism in English has been immense, and the intriguing question is not whether Derrida's works are to be seen as a kind of pale supplement of these developments, but *whether they are to be continued to be appropriated as a supplement.* '. . . Because it easily becomes a method of interpretation, deconstruction has succeeded in America in a way that Marxism and structuralism have not' (Culler 1981: 16) is a statement that is indicative perhaps of the quality, theoretically and philosophically, of the appropriation that dominates current Derridean discourse, and it must be said that with such an appropriation the potentiality of the deconstructive critique of metaphysics is lost. In order for it to find its target in the Anglo-Saxon climate, it is essential that the links between Derrida and materialist analysis be re-made.[15]

G

There are obstacles to this project, and these cannot simply be avoided. The Derridean project itself contains profound internal difficulties and problems which greatly reduce the impact of the critique of metaphysics. Although Derrida is able to identify clearly the limiting effect of the formalism-empiricism couple in Hegelian philosophy (see especially the pages on Hegel in 'Outwork', for example) it is not altogether clear that Derrida has been able to escape it himself. It is possible in this perspective to see Derrida's as a Marxism which has undergone, at specific points, a shift towards empiricism and at others towards formalism. The nature of Derrida's empiricism, although not unique, is certainly unusual (the nature of his formalism here is provisionally identified in so far as Derrida's project may in the end re-work it). Briefly stated, Derrida's project is an effort to work an overturning and a transcendence of the dominant modes of idealism in so far as they intervene in the disciplines which are articulated around the analysis of language and knowledge (especially philosophy, Marxism, psychoanalysis, literature, anthropology, etc). The first risk which Derrida takes is that his rigorous introduction of new concepts and the re-definition of traditional concepts may become a possible scholastic pedagogy, while his aim is to provide an exposure of the extent of metaphysical assumptions. Derrida's dissatisfaction with the concept of 'materialism' itself is an example: for him the opposition idealism/materialism is far too undefined to allow it to escape entanglement in the hierarchical opposition structures of traditional metaphysics. For idealism gets inserted within many forms of naive materialism (1981a: 64), and it is totally ineffectual, he argues, simply to hold on to one of the terms and to attempt a mere reversal. The possibility of linking Derrida's conception of deconstruction directly to the Marxist concept of dissolution is, as Derrida rightly points out himself, a 'theoretical naivety' (1978: 82); not only is it inaccurate, it neutralizes the specificity of the concepts. Derrida's method is to intervene in two quite separate operations: first, the reversal of the order of dominance (thus the word 'materialism' is retained) second, the action of inserting the structurally ambiguous, 'undecidable', new term which breaks the mould of the old matrix. The matrix which holds the idealism/materialism couple is logocentrism. The first problem is to work an overturning of the traditional couple in favour of materialism, and then to de-substantialize and pull the concept of matter towards the new idea of 'matter as absolute exteriority'. The deconstruction is an effort of intervention which aims to produce a new configuration which is dependent on a continual re-working of undecidables that are consolidated with others inserted at other sites. In this way it is possible to see that 'idealism' is not so much refuted or destroyed, because it is indestructible and irrefutable, as taken to pieces and replaced in a way that departs from the Hegelian sublation.

The proximity of Derrida's dialectic with that of Marx is evident, but so is Derrida's refusal to become identified with Marxism. Derrida explicitly adheres to the Althusserian project of the critique of the essentialist (empiricist and formalist) conception of history, yet refuses again to be identified with it and to use its terminology consistently.[16] The result is that Derrida's adherence is nominal, and in contrast to the elaboration of an analysis of philosophy as marked by breaks and irruptions (see Althusser 1970: 102), Derrida's conception of 'western metaphysics' becomes frankly undifferentiated, an homogenized issue of logocentrism. Derrida even begins to extend this: 'Western metaphysics constitutes a powerful systematization of this illusion, but I believe it would be an imprudent over-statement to assert that Western metaphysics alone does so' (1981a: 33). The sources of such homogenization are not analysed; it is the nature of the illusion and not its systematicity that is analysed. Curiously, at certain points the reader is conscious that Derrida is aware of the Althusserian critique of Mao (1969: 94). It is identical with the Marxist critique of Hegel mentioned by Derrida in 'Outwork': without the Marxist topography the dialectic becomes a delirious formalism inhabiting a ghostly medium created by itself. In 'Outwork' the new topography of the text is promised but does not arrive. And in the development of his analysis of 'instances of analysis' the tendency of his thought is to say that overdetermination, which can only work through a differentiated, stratified articulation of instances, is itself dependent on logocentrism: his reading of Freud's *Beyond the Pleasure Principle* moves decisively away from Marx and the early Freud, towards a mode of analysis without instances.[17] The theoretical tensions of this movement are as yet without definite outcome.

The tendency to formalism thus outlined in Derrida seems to be linked intimately with the problematic nature of the object of deconstruction, in other words the status of the 'beyond' which Derrida seeks to evoke and affirm. As Derrida defines his objective in terms of the overturning of the metaphysics of presence, it is inevitable that he seeks to avoid at all costs the production of yet another version of the same thing. This explains why we find so often in his works statements of the following kind:

There are only, everywhere, differences and traces of traces. (1981a: 26)

The gram as *différance*, then, is a structure and a movement no longer conceivable on the basis of the opposition presence/absence. *Différance* is the systematic play of differences . . . of the spacing by means of which elements are related to each other. . . . It is also the becoming-space of the spoken chain . . . (1981a: 27)

. . . the motif of *différance* . . . in effect plays neither the role of a 'concept' nor simply a 'word' . . . it blocks every relationship to theology. (1981a: 40)

. . . it has been necessary to analyse, to set to work, *within* the text . . . certain marks . . . that by analogy [I italicize J.D.] I have called undecidables . . . that can no longer be included within philosophical (binary) opposition, resisting and disorganizing it *without ever* constituting a third term. (1981a: 43)

. . . if dissemination, *seminal* difference, cannot be summarized into an exact conceptual tenor (*teneur*) it is because the force of its disruption explodes (*crèvent*) the semantic horizon. (1981a: 36)

. . . grammatology is less another science, a new discipline charged with a new content or new domain, than the vigilant practice of . . . textual division. (1981a: 36)

It is possible here to catch a glimpse of a determinate shift. Derrida plays with the process whereby the avoidance of the definition of the object is made in the form of an empiricism of the object, which, *being the becoming-nothing of substance cannot have its concept.*[18] The attraction of the Freudian concept of the unconscious in this context is therefore quite understandable, for as Derrida says '. . . the undecidable' . . . situates in a rigorously Freudian sense the *unconscious* of philosophical contradiction, the unconscious which ignores contradiction to the extent that contradiction belongs to the logic of speech, discourse, consciousness, presence, truth, etc. (1981a: 101). This complication of the concept of deconstruction (now become a quasi-psychoanalysis of philosophy) poses more problems: initially the 'undecidable' was inserted into a 'violent' hierarchy of contradictions, but under the pressure of the deconstruction of matter and rationality, the empiricism of the object (nothing) is associated with the production of an empiricist surrealism (the terrain of grammatology).

But these two elements, the becoming-nothing of substance, and the undecidable as the unconscious of philosophical contradiction, have a unity. The avoidance of the production of science (the negative side of deconstruction) and the insertion, and articulation of, undecidables, (the positive side), are both articulated around Derrida's conception of matter, defined as the radical or absolute exterior which, because it cannot be thought as a content, cannot operate as a concept in the scientific sense (1981a: 64). What appears to be the obstacle or barrier to the formulation of the concept is not its strategic role but a series of attributes of the exterior itself. A twilight zone of the text is evoked, a zone of indetermination, of ungraspable multiplicity which passes from the given to the unthinkable. Once Derrida has made this characteriz-ation, and has *answered it in advance* the question of the nature of the barrier to scientificity, it is clear that an unsurpassable epistemological-ontological obstacle, in the shape of a ghostly empiricism or, even better perhaps, an empirical ghost of the absolute exterior (matter), blocks off development. The concept of the ghost cannot exist because the ghost does not exist. The refusal is doubled under pressure from Derrida's politics: this nothing us unable to play the role of a master-concept, and thus for Derrida it blocks off the road to science and to theology. Derrida's 'beyond' is indicated in the apparent absence of the hierarchy of oppositions. . . .[19]

Thus a formidable barrier is erected: epistemological, ontological, and political, diverting the process of deconstruction from both theology and science into the twilight, for, this new deconstruction-grammatology is crepuscular, as is indicated in 'Outwork', suspended between the night of theology and the light of science.[20] The 'undecidable' is launched into this framework, as part of a project which has no master (and no master-concept), the levelling here produced by no work of overdetermination. Breaching logocentrism is made possible by the equalization of realism and surrealism, thus even the 'ambiguity' of the 'undecidable' is itself questioned as it too is tainted by the matrix of logocentrism. Determination is surrealized in this near nympolepsy.

H

The project of deconstruction can be followed clearly in Derrida's attempt to deconstruct Saussurian linguistics. Derrida's specific objective is to isolate the precise points at which metaphysics occupies Saussure's text, and to find in the heterogeneity of the text already existing moments of quasi-constituted opposition to such metaphysics. Having done this Derrida would seek to insert a lever of intervention into the text in the form of an 'undecidable' which is aimed to de-sediment the field and to begin the haul of displacement in the direction of an absolute exteriority (materialism). The text *Of Grammatology* (Part One) follows this procedure. Derrida's argument is that Saussure's specific logocentrism is a phonocentrism: for Saussure holds that speech is prior to and primary in relation to writing. Derrida claims that Saussurian linguistics is dominated at certain points, strategically important, by a metaphysical closure in the form of a complicity between logos and voice which is used to exclude writing from the terrain of semiology. But, at the same time, Saussure also argues that 'in language there are only differences *without positive terms.*' And there are other decisive formulations in the concept of the sign, of linguistic value, the environment of the sign, etc., which make it possible to begin to construct the text's heterogeneity internally. Derrida accepts none of these on Saussure's terms completely, but the paradox that Saussure is able to both define writing as a mode dominated by the law of difference and yet to disqualify it from semiology, is quickly seized and made the focus of the work of deconstruction: the overturning of the specific order of hierarchic oppositions and the insertion of the 'undecidable'. Derrida has thus shown, it must be said purely logically, that the Saussurian project for an all-embracing semiology has a metaphysical blockage, and the form of the Derridean intervention is conceived as an effort of liberation – but *not in the form of an already given philosophy which is simply applied.*[21] The Derridean dialectic is implacable in relation to the Saussurian attempt to privilege speech. A part of the classical philosophical tradition is quite opposed to the primacy of speech, and this current of natural theology Derrida is quite prepared to use as a weapon of reversal. It is clear, he argues of writers from Spinoza to Rousseau, that speech is regarded as derivative on the writing of God: 'natural law . . . is . . . engraved in the heart of man' (Rousseau, cited by Derrida 1976: 17). Derrida adds 'Natural writing is immediately united to the voice and to breath . . . Arche-speech is writing because it is a law.' This resource is, however, external to the text and is only an auxiliary to the main resource, which is internal, for Saussure has already seen that writing is determined by the action of difference (and, in this respect, is no different from speech). The lever which is necessary to level writing and speech is thus in part provided by Saussure: the absence of positive terms and the action of difference. But Derrida proceeds to lever writing above and beyond speech: 'we must think that writing is at the same time more exterior to speech, not being its "image" . . . and more interior to speech, which is already itself a writing' (1976: 46). The arche-trace, conceived on the basis of what is common to writing and speech, is at work at all levels in all systems, but the figure of writing takes precedence in this invertion-overturning, and is exemplified in the 'undecidable' *différance*, as written intervention. At this point Derrida can be quoted to show that his position is not developed without hesitation:

> . . .The 'unmotivatedness' of the sign requires a synthesis in which the completely other (*le tout autre*) is announced as such – without any simplicity, any identity, any resemblance or continuity – within what it is not. *It is announced as such*: there we have all *history*, from what metaphysics had defined as 'non-living' up to 'consciousness'. . . . The trace, where the relationship with the other is marked, articulates its possibility in the entire field of the entity (*étant*), which metaphysics has defined as the being-present starting from the occulted movement of the trace. The trace must be thought before (*avant*) the entity. But the movement of the trace is necessarily occulted, it produces itself as self-occultation. When the other announces itself as such, it presents itself in the dissimulation of itself. This formulation is not theological, as one might believe somewhat hastily. The 'theological' is a determined moment in the total movement of the trace. The field of the entity, before (*avant*) being determined as the field of presence, is structured according to the diverse possibilities – genetic and structural – of the trace. The presentation of the other as such, that is to say the dissimulation of it 'as such', has always already begun and no structure of entity escapes it. (1976: 47)

The trace is thus situated in a total movement which contains several moments. The apparent Spinozism of this passage is striking, as is its propinquity to the Althusserian *Darstellung*. The trace is prior (*avant*) occulted, dissimulated; and, further, the trace is active, determining doubly the structure of the field of presence, as precisely its own self-occultation.[22]

The structure of the relations of trace and presence begins to be displaced by movement. There is neither symbol nor sign but a 'becoming-sign of the symbol' (1976: 47). The introduction of the idea of passage, of 'becoming', develops the difficulties surrounding the barrier to the concept, already immense. 'The immotivation of the trace ought now to be understood as . . . an activity movement, a demotivation, not as a given structure' (1976: 51). This conception developed by Derrida liberates what Derrida claims as 'grammatology' from the dominance of the linguistic model dominated by phonocentrism. However:

> . . . it is because arche-writing, movement of difference, irreducible arche-synthesis, opening in one and the same possibility, temporalization as well as relationship with the other and language, cannot, as the condition of all linguistic systems, form a part of the linguistic system itself and cannot be situated as an object in its field. (Which does not mean that it has a real field *elsewhere, another* assignable site.) Its concept could in no way enrich the scientific, positive, and 'immanent' (in the Hjemslevian sense) description of the system itself . . . (1976: 60)

As the pages of *Of Grammatology* circle around this issue the argument seems to intensify as Derrida over-insists. Not only can grammatology not be a science, it cannot enrich it. A surrealist logic[23] emerges as the crepuscularity begins in earnest, or as we might interject, Derrida, in *so surre*alizing Saussure, is not *so sure.* Derrida appeals to the light: '. . . the deconstruction of presence accomplishes itself through the irreducible notion of the trace (*Spur*) as it appears in both Nietzschean and Freudian discourse. And finally, in all scientific fields, notably in biology,[24] this notion seems currently to be dominant and irreducible' (1976: 70). Thus it is possible to see that Derrida insists on the *principle* of the pure difference as an exteriority that cannot be thought, and on the *fact* that this exteriority cannot be experienced (though it is experienced as a nothing) and therefore has no conceptual content. It is for these conjoint reasons that grammatology, overdetermined politically and theoretically, must be thought as a practice without an object.

The change of definition of philosophy by Althusser (referred to already) towards the idea that it cannot be regarded as having an object in the scientific sense was greeted in England as a departure from the issue of epistemology altogether by one group of Althusserians, now ex-Althusserians (Hirst and Hindess), and this tendency also inserted itself into the translation of Althusser's *Elements of Self-Criticism* (compare, for example, the pages dealing with epistemology[25] to note how Althusser's attack on a theory of science in the singular is translated as an attack on science in general: Althusser plays on the difference between Epistemology and epistemology – his argument being that a de-limited epistemol-

ogy contained within the Marxist topographical structure was necessary
in order to prevent philosophy (Epistemology) appearing to create its own
substance). Althusser's redefinition moved explicitly to a recognition of
the political in theory, while Derrida's position appears to move to a more
negative conception: the interventions become a kind of torment of metaphysics producing an issue which is unacceptable, tending towards the
unthinkable, an impossible practice, of perpetual, if evanescent, prolepsis.

It is now possible to see why Benoist and others have such difficulties
in trying to state what it is that Derrida produces in his texts. It is also by
trying to evade this problem that literary criticism can appear so 'easily'
to assimilate deconstruction to the literary register. The temptation of the
literary resolution is a possibility which is made possible by Derrida's
evasion of scientificity. On this subject some of Derrida's assertions are
astonishing: although the 'practice of science has constantly challenged
[the] imperialism of the logos . . . [grammatology] . . . even if . . . it did
overcome all technical and epistemological impediments . . . runs the risk
of never . . . being able to define the unity of its project or its object . . .'
(1976: 3–4). Derrida continues: the future of grammatology '. . . can
only be anticipated in the form of an absolute danger. It is that which
breaks absolutely with constituted normality and can only be proclaimed,
presented as a sort of monstrosity' (1976: 4). The absolute has been noted
already: the absolute break, the absolute exterior (see 1981a: 64). It is
surely symptomatic that Derrida should so strongly insist on the barrier
as an absolute; for elsewhere he is equally insistent on the *inadequacy* of
the conception of the absolute nature of the epistemological break. If the
breaks (of sciences with metaphysics) are always interminable why is it
that grammatology is privileged in this respect? Why dangerous and not
useless? (Nietzsche's 'even if the existence of such a world were never so
well proved, it would be certain that knowledge of it would be the most
useless of all forms of knowledge . . .' (*Human, All too Human*, 9) is
hovering close.)

There is yet another more powerful representation of the barrier and
the forces behind it in Derrida, and it lies in the corpus of sexual images
and concepts taken over and reworked from Freud. Jameson has noted
this usage as a reversion to 'the oldest forms of . . . phallic symbolism'
(1972: 178). This seems altogether too narrow for what is at stake here,
for although Derrida is interested in imagery he is far more concerned
with the deconstruction of the received notion of symbolism of this order.
His position seems also on the other hand to be different from that of
Barthes, who writes as if the text is *directly* sexual. In relation to Rousseau's network of oppositions articulated around nature/culture, the
questions of incest and masturbation lead Derrida to propose the
'undecidable' 'supplement' as a lever of intervention: '. . . masturbation
re-assures . . . only through that culpability traditionally attached to the
practice, obliging children to assume the fault and to interiorize the

threat of castration . . . pleasure is thus lived as the irremediable loss . . . exposure to madness and death . . .' (1976: 150–1). Derrida continues:

> sexual auto-affection, that is auto-affection in general, neither begins nor ends with what one thinks can be circumscribed by the name masturbation. The supplement has not only the power of *procuring* an absent presence through its image; procuring it for us through the proxy (*procuration*) of the sign, it holds it at a distance and masters it. For this presence is at the same time desired and feared. The supplement transgresses and at the same time respects the interdict. This is what also permits writing as the supplement of speech; but already, also the spoken word as writing in general. Thus, the supplement is dangerous . . . in that it threatens us with death. (1976: 154–5)

This passage gives us a number of elements crucial to the understanding of the barrier. For it is surely not accidental that the idea that the supplement is 'dangerous' is linked to two threats: death and castration, 'pleasure lived as the irremediable loss'.

It is, though, the term 'dissemination'[26] which poses the problem of castration[27] most directly. It is developed against the hermeneutics of J.-P. Richard and Ricoeur in a deconstruction of texts by Mallarmé. Again it is necessary to quote Derrida here:

> is dissemination the *loss* of that kind of truth, the *negative* prohibition of all access to such a signified? Far from pre-supposing that a virgin substance thus precedes or oversees it, dispersing or withholding itself in a negative second movement, *dissemination* affirms that always already divided generation of meaning [Derrida inserts a footnote here]. Dissemination – 'spills it in advance.' The footnote is important. '. . . dissemination – which entails, entrains, "inscribes", and relaunches castration – can never become an orginary, central, or ultimate signified, the place proper to truth. . . . Castration is that non-secret of seminal division that breaks into substitution.' (1981b: 268)

The connections become more complex: the term 'division' is precisely that used to describe the practice of grammatology. And now it is apparent that deconstruction is conceived as being produced under the imposition of the barrier that is the absolute threat of castration. Derrida makes an explicit reference to Freud: '. . . more than ever attentive to undecidable ambivalence . . . to the process of interminable substitution – can, without contradicting this play, have recourse to castration anxiety, behind which no deeper secret would lie hidden, and to the substitutive relation itself, for example between the eye and the male member.' The emphasis is plain: castration is a nonsecret, an ultimate or absolute 'behind which no deeper secret would lie hidden'. The evasion here is surprising, the political overdetermination is announced (castration can never become an ultimate signified) so that its very denial seems less a form of castration threat than what it is: a form of prophylactic.

I

The danger in fact that faces, or seems to face, Derrida in the absence of topography (for the castration threat or even the prophylactic are inadequate for this purpose) is precisely the delirium of the Hegelian type, however much it is apparently faced and overcome in 'Outwork'. To express this provocatively in the Derridean context it might be evoked not so much as the problem of the labyrinth, of speleology, but rather of the space between west and east: the problem of Byzantinism, of the mosaic, for in the end without the Marxist or Freudian topography, Derrida seems destined to become the governor of a distant Byzantine province: an *exarch*. So another reading would have Derrida become, for Anthony Giddens has attempted what must be the most incredible of all efforts at appropriating Derrida. Giddens sees Derrida as a lost soul of phenomenology, and his reading is not so much a mis-recognition as a calling in the Byzantine wilderness (though it is no wilderness). Curiously enough Giddens actually tries to read Derrida against Wittgenstein (Giddens 1979: 28–45), but the interpenetrations are so formal and abstract that both are neutralized. Giddens proceeds to an immediate reduction: *différance* is simply an already given moment *within* Wittgenstein's 'meaning is created and sustained by the play of difference "in use" . . .' (1979: 33). Having thus 'seen' his quarry, Giddens appropriates the term *différance* as the basis of a theory of social structuration: threefold – in its rules, in its time, and in its physical basis (1979: 46). This squarely situates Derrida within the Giddensian project of rescuing the acting subject from the nightmare of structuralism, for it is clear, says Giddens, that it is the acting subject who constitutes social life through 'his reflexive monitoring of conduct' (1979: 39).

Four basic objections are made against this exarch in exile, or rather propositions that are designed to tempt him to come home. But they are really only aspects of one basic objection: that Derrida really adheres to Saussure's basic project. First Derrida does not connect what can be said with what can be done; second, Derrida places the referent outside of language; third, Derrida ignores the fact that identity within codes derives from the referent; and fourth, the consolidation of the signifier is only brought about by the fact that the referent or object is made into an impossible object. Giddens offers the simple remedy that the outside be thought, as with Wittgenstein, as 'forms of life' where the *cogito* is even more thoroughly expunged than in structuralism: but through, astonishingly, the reconnection of 'being and action'. The framework for this is political, for the attack on the subject, on the individual, threatens a form of totalitarianism.

Thus the critique of Derrida is not actually enjoined at all. Giddens, like Searle,[28] simply proffers an oblation to 'being and action'. Derrida's attack on the complicity of being and voice, of logocentrism, is made a part, quite directly, of logocentrism ... curiously presented as 'a recovery of the subject without lapsing into subjectivism' (1979: 44). Giddens's treatment of Derrida is interesting: the exarch is regarded as inflicting damage on himself. In relation to the debate between Derrida and Searle, which echoes so much of the debate between Chomsky and Skinner, and where Derrida seems not so much to deconstruct Searle's position as to explode it, Giddens says that the exchange was 'somewhat comic ... Derrida goes through absolute contortions in order to defend himself ... without having to employ the terminology, 'What I meant was ...' (1979: 266). The exarch has a disfigurement that is 'more pitiable than shocking'.

J

But if Giddens simply juxtaposes, and this is a form of reading and writing giving rise to the illusion of the mosaic, of the Byzantine, it is suggested by Derrida's *Glas* and Joyce's *Finnegans Wake*. It is the tactile *and* the visual *and* the oral, etc. In so far as the text becomes simply multiple the result is a textual mosaic. Derrida, however, suggests that the deconstructive mode of writing and reading is interventional: 'By means of this double and precisely stratified, dislodged and dislodging (*décalée* and *décalante*) writing we must also mark the interval between inversion ... and the irruptive emergence of a new "concept" ... This biface or biphase can only be inscribed in a bifurcated writing ... (1981a: 42, the English translation here omits a clause). The intervention makes an incision, which can, for example, 'erase' a word: 'the sign is that ill named ~~thing~~ ...' (Derrida 1976: 19). The text is scarred. 'Isabel watched him enter. He looked so strong-blooded and healthy, and at the same time, cancelled. Cancelled – that was the word that flew across her mind. Perhaps it was his scars suggested it' (Lawrence 1980: 66). But if Giddens can be assimilated to Bertram Reid and Derrida to Maurice Pervin (the blind man) this is simply a movement from juxtaposition to superimposition. The queston for deconstruction is the articulation of lines of force logocentrism/dissemination in Lawrence (and Derrida), and it is not for Derrida a question of rule and exception here ('. . . every mark, including those which are oral, [is] a grapheme in general: which is to say, . . . the non-present *remainder* (*restance*) of a differential mark cut off from its putative "production" or origin. And I shall even extend this law to all "experience" in general if it is conceded that there is no experience consisting of *pure* presence but only chains of differential marks' (*Glyph*, 1, 183)), but of law. There can be no purely logocentric text: every text is, in principle, not simply juxtaposed or superimposed as an external spacing, but *internally juxtaposed* in the sense that these divisions exist (see Althusser 1972: 132–3 and Culler 1981: 14–16) and are reproduced as logocentric doubles *or* disseminated by the work of reading. To say then that Derrida's reading (deconstruction) of Lawrence's story already exists in *Speech and Phenomena: Introduction to the Problem of Signs in Husserl's Phenomenology* is not the case.

Notes

1. '. . . protocols of reading. Why not say it bluntly: I have not yet found any that satisfy me' (Derrida 1981a: 63).
2. The horizontal gaps are filled artificially by the alphabetic series, about which Derrida has a lot to say. In practice he starts mid-way through.
3. In Derrida's case he inserts his own texts into themselves (1981a: 4) and, say, Hegel's into Genet's (see *Glas*).
4. Derrida often seems to want to treat writing as theatre: see A.
5. These texts can neither be spoken 'for' nor speak 'for' themselves. The appropriate outwork here would, perhaps, raise the question of the tactile that is inside the specular.
6. Lawrence's short story was suggested to me by my late friend G.R. Farren. See also J. Kristeva, 'Gesture: practice or communication?', in T. Polhemus (ed.) 1978: 264–84.
7. Derrida appears to practise the 'fiction' of absolute materialist textualism: the dispersion of the monologue and onto-polysemia (and its complement onto-speleology).
8. Derrida's political and theoretical ultra-leftism is made more explicit in his support and activity in the *Tel Quel* group.
9. F. Jameson has broached some of these issues in his 'On Goffman's frame analysis' in *Theory and Society*, 3, 1.
10. 'John Cage's school of performance rip-offs'. Goffman: *Forms of Talk* 1981: 162.
11. J.-M. Benoist, 'The end of Structuralism' in *Twentieth Century Studies*, 3, 1970, 31–54.
12. Dominique Lecourt's 'Epistemology and poetics' (in *Marxism and Epistemology*, NLB, 1975, 142–161) is interesting against the background of Derrida's presentation in the ENS as well to the left theoretically and politically of the Althusserian group (communication of 1972 to author).
13. J. Hall, *The Sociology of Literature*, Longman, 1979, 84–5.
14. This misleading view is perhaps the most tempting of all misreadings of Derrida. Its correction is highly instructive, for it draws attention to the barriers, first those articulated in deconstruction: the rigour appropriate to reading and misreading (see the debate between Derrida and Searle in *Glyph* 1 and 2), and the rigour necessary for the deconstructive incision which '*can be made only* according to the lines of force and forces of rupture that are localizable in the discourse to be deconstructed' (my emphasis, MG) (1981a: 82). In so far as Derrida is able to

develop a topography, it is precisely around the concept of these textual forces. Second, the political and epistemological barriers, which are crucial in this respect, are discussed in sections G and H.

15. This would first of all seek to establish the strategic unity of Derrida's absolute materialist deconstruction with the Marxist theory and critique of ideology. Developments in this direction have begun but not got very far. See for instance: F. Jameson (1972), R. Coward and J. Ellis, *Language and Materialism*, RKP (1977), C. Sumner, *Reading Ideologies*, Academic Press, 1979.

16. For example as developed by Althusser (1969), in 'On the materialist dialective: On the unevenness of origins' (orig: 1963).

17. See Derrida 'Speculations – on Freud', in *The Oxford Literary Review*, 3, 2, 1978, 87–97.

18. This empiricism can also be located in Lacan, where it is bound up with the conceptualization of the subject and the unconscious.

19. Cf. this utopia and the 'Utopia of a tired man', Borges, in *The Book of Sand*, Penguin, 1979, 64–70.

20. Cf. Lacan's 'The best image to sum up to unconscious is Baltimore in the early morning', in *The Structuralist Controversy*, ed. R. Macksey and E. Donato, Johns Hopkins University Press, 1972, p. 189.

21. Derrida's proposition to the materialist dialectic is to say that the critique of idealism can only be achieved by the constructive work of the lever of intervention *within the lines of rupture* of idealism itself. All else, as Derrida stresses, simply evades or neutralizes the effectiveness of the strategy.

22. For a savage critique of this kind of Spinozism see the unsigned article 'Introduction to Glucksmann' in *New Left Review*, 72, 1972: 61–7. Further discussion, only apparently remote, N. Rose, 'Fetishism and ideology' in *Ideology and Consciousness*, 2, 1977: 27–56.

23. Noted also by E.W. Said in *Beginnings*, Basic Books, 1975: 339–43.

24. Investigated by A. Wilden in *System and Structure*, Tavistock, 1972: 395–400.

25. *Éléments d'Autocritique*, Hachette 1972: 51; *Essays in Self-Criticism*, New Left Books, 1976: 124.

26. 'Dissemination generalises the theory of the graft without the body proper, the skew without a straight line . . .' (Derrida 1981b: 11); 'error without truth, deviation without a norm . . .' (Althusser, 'Lysenko: unfinished history' in *Marxism Today*, February 1977, 54).

27. 'Castration', a fundamental term in Derrida's work, can only be grasped through the Lacanian reworking of Freud's concept. The clearest introduction to this issue is J. Mitchell's *Psycho-analysis and Feminism*, Allen Lane, 1974. For Derrida's discussion the most direct text is 'The Purveyor of Truth', in *Yale French Studies*, 52, 1975.

28. Derrida 'Signature, Event, Context' (pp. 172–187) and J. Searle 'Reiterating the differences: a reply to Derrida' both in *Glyph* 1, Johns Hopkins University Press 1977; and Derrida 'Limited Inc.' in *Glyph* 2 (162–254), 1977.

References

Althusser, L. (1969) *For Marx*, London, Allen Lane.

Althusser, L. (1970) *Reading Capital*, London, New Left Books.

Althusser, L. (1972) *Politics and History*, London, New Left Books.

Althusser, L. (1976) *Essays in Self-Criticism*, London, New Left Books.

Bloom, H. *et al.* (1979) *Deconstruction and Criticism*, London, Routledge & Kegan Paul.

Culler, J. (1975) *Structuralist Poetics*,

London, Routledge & Kegan Paul.

Culler, J. (1981) *The Pursuit of Signs*, London, Routledge & Kegan Paul.

Derrida, J. (1974) *Glas*, Paris, Galilee.

Derrida, J. (1976) *Eperons*, Venice, Corbo and Fiore.

Derrida, J. *et al.* (1981) *Les Fins de l'Homme*, Paris, Galilee.

Descombes, V. (1980) *Modern French Philosophy*, Cambridge, Cambridge University Press.

Eagleton, T. (1978) *Criticism and Ideology*, London, New Left Review Editions.

Giddens, A. (1979) *Central Problems in Social Theory*, London, Macmillan.

Goffman, E. (1981) *Forms of Talk*, Oxford, Blackwell.

Harari, J.V. (ed.) (1979) *Textual Strategies*, Ithaca, NY: Cornell University Press.

Jameson, F. (1972) *The Prison House of Language*, Princeton, Princeton University Press.

Lawrence, D.H. (1980) *England, My England*, Harmondsworth, Penguin.

Macherey, P. (1978) *A Theory of Literary Production*, London, Routledge & Kegan Paul.

Polhemus, T. (ed.) (1978) *Social Aspects of the Human Body*, Harmondsworth, Penguin.

Saussure, F. de (1974) *Course in General Linguistics*, London, Fontana/Collins.

Sturrock, J. (ed.) (1979) *Structuralism and Since*, Oxford, Oxford University Press.

1982

PART II

Fictions:
Textual Explication and
Criticism

Marin: a Pascalian diversion

George Salemohamed

The text translated here, bearing the title of the book in which it features as the concluding as well as the most interesting chapter, has two earlier versions, one in Italian and the other translated into English and published by Diacritics (Marin 1977: 54–63). The present text differs from both in length. This is due to a more detailed treatment of the Puss-in-Boots tale, but also to the inclusion of the 'lost king' episode culled from Pascal. The famous French philosopher and mathematician is an important influence on Marin's works, which are almost exclusively concerned with seventeenth-century France – its philosophy, historiography, linguistics, literature and folk-tales. It is an influence that marks both Marin's philosophy and his approach to criticism. The philosophy, if it can be called that, is a variant of postmodernism, inspired in its opposition to all types of referents by Pascal's doctrine of 'infinitism'. For Pascal, all referents, including the subject and object, rather than being fixed entities, intelligible by themselves, are perspectival results and are thus capable of an infinite number of variations when the perspective is altered (Pascal 1966: 48). Pascal's argument is with Cartesian rationalism and its fixed perspective of a reason given as the source of all knowledge and with everything that such a conception entails: the possibility of a unified body of knowledge demonstrable *more geometrico* and the possibility of access to first principles. All these are denied in the name of a pluralism that also extends to the question of method in scientific procedure. Marin is Pascal's disciple in all this, even to the point of rejecting all methodological *a prioris* in his main preoccupation, which, again as with Pascal, is with Cartesian rationalism, but from the point of view of the representational theory that buttresses it. Marin's most serious statement and most sustained attack on representational theory is the *Critique du Discours* (1975), hailed by Lyotard (1976) as a classic. Since Marin himself describes the *Critique* as the precursor to Puss-in-Boots, it is as well to start with it, not just to show what the latter owes to the former, but also to highlight two different strategies to the same problem.

The *Critique du Discours*

The *Critique* is a work of deconstruction, aimed at dismantling the representational schema at the heart of the Port Royal Logic – an applied Cartesianism, as Marin so aptly describes it. The Port Royal Logic (Arnauld and Nicole 1662) is an attempt by the logicians of the Port Royal to render logic more intelligible and simple and, at the same time, to take into account the ideas of Bacon and Descartes. It is an endeavour to bring out the common sense nature of the rules of syllogism by, among other things, linking logic to grammatical considerations relevant to its use. The *Critique* uses Pascal in order to dismantle this but, in true constructive fashion, it does not seek to erect Pascal as a counter-model. The effect of this, Marin argues, would be to reproduce the very model that it is the intention to undermine (Marin 1975: 20). Model and representation, he states, entail each other. Both assume the existence of a fixed point – whether that of a subject thinking through the model or of the object the model is about. The *Critique*, therefore, uses Pascal as an internal critic, a possibility offered by the Port Royal text itself, which quotes Pascal for support at some decisive moments of its exposition on language. Marin's technique consists of displacing the Pascalian quotations in direct contradistinction to the intention of the Port Royal project.

Briefly, what the Port Royal logic attempts to do is to ground thought and discourse in logic. As this is an endeavour that requires a theory of representation which subsumes language under logic rather than rhetoric, the Pascalian displacement is shown to have the effect of shifting the focus from the former to the latter. Marin's thesis is that the quotations, three in all, concerning the origin of language with primitive terms, the existence of determinate logico-grammatical boundaries and the transcendental subject (the 'I think' of Cartesian rationalism), are pressed into the service of logicism, whereas abandoned to the influence of Pascal's 'thought of the infinitive', they yield directly opposite results. There are no primitive terms because there are no first principles. Definitions are therefore always nominal; there is no rational scientific language because every system, no matter how superficially coherent, rests ultimately on undemonstrable principles (axioms); and the 'I think' is a void to be filled up in a propositional statement and not a substance as Cartesianism implies. Each displacement demonstrates the arbitrary nature of language in contradistinction to the logical viewpoint's assumption that at least in some respects, and in relation to certain forms of knowledge, language has a necessary link with the thought it expresses.

The three Pascalian displacements constitute the first stage of the Port Royal theory of representation. The point about nominal definitions is of special significance. The denial of the existence of primitive terms raises the possibility of a constitutive role for language at the origin of society. It signals the absurdity of the logical conception that language merely reflects, a theme which the second stage of the deconstruction goes on to argue against. The aim is to show that the representational theory of language deconstructs as it constructs itself. The classical notion of representation constructs itself on the assumption of the primacy of things over thought (ideas) and the primacy of the latter over language.

Language is thus relegated to the status of a second order sign representing a first order sign (thought) in relation to reality. Marin's argument is that this notion is incoherent in its own terms and therefore deconstructs itself. The drift of his argument is something like the following. If a successful act of representation is assumed to have taken place, this must mean, on the evidence of the theory expounded, not only that the two signs (language + thought) have come together, but also that they have united with reality. However, if this is the case, no hierarchy such as that upheld as obtaining between signs and reality can any longer be held as valid, since, via the success of the representational act, reality becomes a sign – it is absorbed into the sign – which in turn becomes reality since it successfully acts as its substitute.

For Marin, representational theory and its ultimate requirement of a fusion of sense and reference is profoundly theological. Not the least interesting of all the deconstructive aspects of his analysis is that which identifies this linguistic theologism with the Eucharist formula of the Catholic ceremony of transubstantiation. For here in the statement – 'this is my body' – as sanctioned by religious belief, is what representational theory dreams of: the complete coincidence of an utterance – 'this is my body' – with its reference, the very presence of the body of Christ in the host. Marin shows how the Eucharist formula arises as a problem for the Port Royal authors. It surfaces in their debates with the Protestant reformers of the time. The latter sought to place a rhetorical interpretation on the formula in contrast to the Port Royal inclination to treat it as a special case of their logical theory of language, that is, as a marginal instance. Marin does not take up the reformers' case but argues that the Eucharistic formula is the occulted centre of the Port Royal theory of representation, as well as its distant 'periphery'. The reason is that where representational theory succeeds the most, it also succeeds the least because it dislocates the 'coextensiveness of language and thought' (Marin 1975: 41). Representational theory thus throws up a model of its own success, but a model it cannot really accommodate. At the periphery, however, the same model demonstrates an alternative to representation: that of a speech act which creates or transforms representations (or reality) in contradistinction to representational theory which only conceives of speech (language or sign) as means of reflecting and communicating an existing reality. Thus, the Eucharist formula both confirms and refutes representational theory – it refutes it because as a practical religious act it produces its own communicative system and its own meaning objects.

Marin has repeatedly emphasized the paradigmatic value of the Eucharist formula: how, occurring from within a non-rational field (religion), it nevertheless 'shows us the basic truth of the philosophy of representation' (Marin 1975: 56) – the way it seeks to ground the claim that representational systems and things are equivalent. Such a putative claim, he argues, proceeds from an operation by which a subject places himself at the centre of his representational systems and 'transforms himself by transforming things through them' (Marin 1977: 56). Marin describes this as a process of appropriation by which a subject gives himself the right 'to possess things legitimately' because he has replaced them with signs that are meant to represent them in their fullness (Marin 1977: 56). Thus in the Catholic ceremony Jesus is made to utter a formula whereby he transforms an external thing (the host) which is not signified but pointed to by 'this', into a signified element of the signifying system of representation: the word 'body' related to him by the possessive 'my'. As a result, he becomes a product, a 'word-thing' . . . to be exchanged in a communicative process, through a practical ritual of consumption in the religious community that thinks of itself as a universal one (Marin 1975: 56). He becomes, in other words, the centre-piece of an ideological system, with all its social and political implications.

As with the Eucharist ceremony, discourse as representation is the locus of an ideological process whereby a subject universalizes himself through an assumed transparency of what he utters in relation to a reality that is supposed to be under his intellectual control. This is a possible summary of the *Critique du Discours* which, on Marin's own showing, is concerned with representational discourse as ideology. Masking the language dimension from the ideological process of representational theory is an essential feature of the illusory objectivity with which rationalism deludes itself, he argues. Thus Port Royal never raises language as a specific problem of the analysis of thinking (except, significantly, in relation to theology). Yet, as Marin observes, the Port Royal text is concerned with nothing else but language (Marin 1975: 37). In *Le Récit est un Piège* (Marin 1978) he returns to this theme, but for a different purpose. The idea is to show both how discourse in the form of the narrative, especially of the historical narrative, exercises an entrapping effect leading to the illusion of a truth being described, and how this discourse of truth can be circumvented. The latter is what 'Puss-in-Boots' is largely about. In both cases the use of language tricks testifies to the active, creative function of language as oppposed to the reflective function to which representational theory consigns it.

Le Récit est un Piège

Le Récit est un Piège with the Puss-in-Boots story subtracted from it is largely an attempt to lay bare the ensnaring mechanism of the historical narrative. This is viewed as dependent on the ideology of representation. Although it is concerned with a variety of authors, Retz, La Fontaine, and Racine, showing how the judicious use of rhetorical tactics can lead to political point-scoring and even political victory, its main thrust is an analysis of Racine as history writer. Marin shows that history, as the truth of the events it purports to describe, in fact creates events which it then offers 'framed up' as if the author is absent from it. This putative absence of the author is what gives the narrative its 'power to tell the truth' (Marin 1978: 8). It enables the enunciative mechanism to be extracted from the field of vision so that 'the events seem to narrate themselves', achieving a kind of self-reference. History thus becomes a secular version of the Eucharist ceremony. There is the same pretended fusion of sense and reference in that the function of the historical narrative is assumed to be capable of bringing to light events that have taken place and of reflecting them in their purity.

As against the pretension of historians to tell events as they really took place, Marin emphasizes the performative nature of their undertaking. The mechanism of this performative ritual rests, according to him, on a complicity between the historian and his object. In the case of Racine this object is the absolute monarchy of Louis XIV – a point which lends more force to the theme which Marin broaches here and develops in more detail elsewhere (Marin 1981): that power is not a latent force or a hidden reality but the sum total of its representations (i.e. signs). The absolute monarch – or state power – requires the transformation of events into 'marmoreal signs thanks to which it can identify itself . . .' He requires discourse. The narrator effects this transformation by neutralizing the events as historical events, whilst at the same time effacing himself as narrator. Both moves contribute to the fostering of a belief in the power of the monarch or of the state to control historical destiny, and also to the illusion (the trap) that power exists as such, the historical narrative being merely the neutral medium of its epiphany.

History, however, only illustrates a contingent relationship between discourse and power, whereas Marin's contention is that the relationship is one of necessity. This arises from the conclusion that representations are everything – a conclusion which dispenses with the notions of truth and objectivity as well as with that of origin or essence. Since power has no reality beyond its representation, the representation of power is power itself, its very 'essence'. But power is also the exercise of force. Consequently since, like power, discourse is not a reflection of something immanent (because there is nothing immanent to represent), it is a product of force and desire and thus is linked to power. Power produces discourse, and discourse has the power to give representations to power. The casualty in all this is truth. Representational theory grounds the effectivity of discourse in truth. Following Pascal, Marin shows that the effectivity of discourse is the power that discourse can command to say that it says the truth (Pascal: 56). Conversely, power is 'the discourse that force has and will always have and which repeats that right is not right and that it is itself, force, that is right. Power is the right that force gives itself because it is force . . . : laws, institutions, customs, with all their mediations, rationalizations or imaginary justifications' (*Le Récit est un Piège*: 10).

The starting point of the Puss-in-Boots story follows from what has just been outlined. Force, that is, the discourse of power, cannot be gain-said. It is no use, for example, the discourse of right pitting itself against the discourse of might: might *is* right. The same applies to the discourse of truth. Only the discourse of power is able to insist that it is the discourse of truth. The question then is how to oppose the discourse of truth or of right which in reality is the only discourse of power. Inspired once again by Pascal, Marin suggests the use of irony, humour, and mockery – tactical devices which undermine whilst pretending to take seriously what is to be opposed. The important thing is to pretend to believe, 'to go on talking like an ordinary person' (Pascal: 91) but 'to think from the back of one's head' (*avoir une pensée de derrière la tête*). This is suggested as the only way to defeat the discourse of power and as the condition for the setting up of a move calculated to capture power by turning its force against itself.

To the discourse of power Marin therefore counterposes the power of discourse (the use of irony and duplicity). The power of discourse is its performative nature, a characteristic it hides under a professed obedience to the representative ideology of language. This is what the cat in Puss-in-Boots is aware of, and what explains its tactics. On the one hand, it appears to submit to existing representations whilst, on the other hand, it proceeds systematically to undermine them. Not only this, but as Marin observes, it re-enacts a mythical Eucharist, using language to effect a sort of transubstantiation through which words and representations are changed into real things (Marin 1977: 54). The fact that it does this through lies, that is, through using words outside their normally accepted frame of reference gives conviction to the theme; for, in the end, as in the sacrament, the words nevertheless end up being true. In the process, they even produce the consumable food the cat promised its master at the beginning of the story, thereby enabling it to fulfil its contract and taking its place alongside its master in a community in which both were, at first, marginals. Such is the power of language and the tricks that it places at one's 'disposal'. Such is the power of discourse that through the judicious exercise of linguistic tricks – but is the use of language other than this? – it is possible to overthrow established truths and replace them with one's own – that is to say, to capture power.

Marin's intricate analysis of how the cat achieves power for its master – the miller's son – need not be reproduced here. Two features, however, deserve mention. First, how through his analysis he erects the tale as a metaphor of socio-political themes: the question of contract at the origin of society represented by the micro-society of the cat and the miller's son; the question of nature and culture: how the cat leaves the realm of nature and enters culture through the use of discourse, and the question of how language, signs, and representations order and re-order social classifications and thus affect power distribution. Second, how in pursuing all these themes, Marin all the while continues his argument with representational theory – the same argument he started in the *Critique*. Here, however, the approach is one of levity and of the gratuitous pleasure of playing with the logic of representational theory.

This logic, relying on the existence of a 'fixed point' or centre, had already been called into question by the *Critique*. The results, the decentring of everything that the logic upholds (the subject, the object, origin and essence), is brought to the fore in Puss-in-Boots and distilled into the anecdote by Pascal about the lost king. This functions as conclusion to the *Critique*'s dismantling of representational theory, but it pervades the whole story even though it is only treated at the end. It certainly sanctions the cat's linguistic procedure, especially where this touches on 'nominal definitions. Indeed, if nominal definitions are arbitrary, as the *Critique* showed, then definitions are not centred on any fixed 'referents'. Therefore, one is free to change referents. This is the 'decentred logic' of what the cat practises in creating a referent (the Marquis de Carabas) for the miller's son. But in order to carry out such an undertaking and make it succeed, it has to flesh out the referent; and it does this, of course, not only by an act of representation, for then it would have to represent the miller's son *as* the miller's son, but by giving it a series of representations – the gift, the Estate – and having them accepted by those (for example, the king) whose very acceptance confers veracity on the pseudo-reference (the simulacrum).

Simulacra are, however, all important. 'It is really remarkable, I am supposed not to honour a man dressed in brocade and attended by seven or eight lackeys. Why? He will have me thrashed if I do not bow to him. His clothes represent power.' Thus Pascal (Pascal 1966: 53). Thus also the cat. The supreme humour of the piece consists of the way in which the cat bows to the wearer of the clothes that represent power (the king) whilst plotting to transfer the same clothes to the naked miller's son – naked both of clothes and of power – as he comes out of the river and is symbolically invested by the king, in anticipation of the final event when he will become the latter's successor – when he will wear his clothes in truth and in truth exercise power. But even this humour must take second place to the irony which suffuses Marin's project. A cat borrows items of clothing, 'a pair of boots and a sack', and becomes the medium for clothing his destitute master with the apparel of power. Everything depends for the success of this mission on simulation and dissimulation. But who is this cat? It is, I suggest, none other than Marin, who simulates it the better to catch the reader and trap him within a narrative which appears to be Perrault's but is, in fact, Marin's.

Indeed the sheer gratuitous pleasure of the cat is that of the author playing with the king-reader, absenting himself underneath the presence of the cat, in the same way as Racine seeks to remove himself from his historical narrative under the guise of an '*on*' (we) which is really an 'I' (Marin 1978: 76). Alternatively Marin transmutes himself into Pascal, issuing a warning. This is the deeper significance of the lost and found king anecdote. Pascal used it to warn a young prince of the fortuitous nature of his future power as king and thus of its fragility. Marin uses it to remind the reader, at the very moment when he hopes to have installed himself at the centre of the narrative, how fragile is his mastery of the signifying structure of the text: his grasp of the meaning of the story. In Marin's case, however, the warning is a ploy. In a book which is about deceits and traps, it is perhaps the most lethal of all. For the warning implies a reassurance which is in fact a lie: that the reader has somehow had a grasp of the meaning of the text, no matter how fragile, when, in truth, he has been led to a number of pre-determined conclusions by a king-author whose ultimate trick has been to engage in his own Eucharistic self-production and self-occultation. This is the most ironic aspect of the Puss-in-Boots story as recounted by Marin: the fact that the 'Eucharistic cannibalism' attributed to the cat, over and beyond what it tells us about discourse as representation, is the symbolic, performative act of an author, the impact of whose message requires the extinction-consumption of the reader, but also his preservation. Is this not, within the logic of 'postmodernism', the fate of the reader, preserved because he or she is required as *the* reader, but dispensed with as *a* reader? Is this not what the cat's last bow – Marin's final flourish – reduces a reader of this tale to: a function within a textual strategy?

References

Arnauld, A., and Nicole, P. (1662) *La Logique ou l'art de penser*, republished by Flammarion, 1978.

Lyotard, J.F. (1976) 'Que le signe est hostie et l'inverse; et comment s'en débarrasser', in *Critique*, 1112–26.

Marin, L. (1975) *Critique du Discours*, Paris, Editions de Minuit.

Marin, L. (1977) *Diacritics*, Vol. 7(ii), p. 54–63, Ithaca, Cornell University Press.

Marin, L. (1978) *Le Récit est un Piège*, Paris, Editions de Minuit.

Marin, L. (1981) *Le Portrait du Roi*, Paris, Editions de Minuit.

Pascal, B. (1966) *Pensées*, Harmondsworth, Penguin.

The narrative trap: the conquest of power

Louis Marin
Translated by R. Sanderson

> Deep down and for the first time, Wilson had doubts about the
> powers of his brilliant colleague. Why was he talking so much and
> doing so little? Why? Sholmes exclaimed in response to Wilson's
> innermost thoughts; because with this damned Lupin fellow, one is
> working in the dark, at random, and because, instead of extracting
> the truth from precise facts, one has to obtain it from one's own
> brain, in order to check afterwards if it fits in with the events.
>
> Maurice Leblanc, *Arsène Lupin versus Herlock Sholmes* (Livre de
> Poche, Paris: 1963, 127)

I will finish where I started. I come back to a tale, a fable, one about the
conquest of power – of absolute power – by a cat. However, this is not
completely the case since it was his master who conquered it. He was the
youngest son of a miller who, after losing his father, lost his mill and his
donkey but thanks to God and the law, inherited the cat. It was thanks to
this cat that he became a marquess, then married the king's daughter and
became a king himself – or so my story, Perrault's story, leads us to
believe. The cat's master, then, captures power, but in all this important
matter it will quickly be seen that in one form or another he is the instrument of the cat's cunning. It is the cat who gives him economic wealth,
erotic power, political power – who can say better than that? – and keeps
nothing back for himself, apart from the diversion, the gratuitous,
unending pleasure. This is a fine lesson in wisdom. Who was it that said
that power corrupts and that absolute power corrupts absolutely? Alas, it
only concerns a cat. Ah Racine, if only you had heeded, as fat Jean of
Château-Thierry did,[1] the lesson of the animals: staying in the depths of
the forest or on its edge and being subjected to the inexorable law of
nature – eat or be eaten, the law of simple necessity, 'without putting too
fine a point on it.'[2] Either exerting strength over another or being

subjected to the strength of the other. The strong or the weak, the law of life or death. However, the weak sometimes survives, often survives. That is because the strong stops exerting his strength for a moment, to eat when he is no longer hungry. Natural satiety and satisfaction. *Satis.* Enough is enough. There is a limit to strength. Nature may well leap forward but it does not countenance overindulgence or excess. There is a correction of the balance which has been momentarily upset. It is also because the weak evades the strength of the powerful: he disguises himself, he hides from the predatory eye, in burrows, in lairs, in gullies and narrow passageways. He flees by covering his tracks, goes round in circles several times, goes off into a stream and the keen bloodhound loses all trace of the scent. The weak stays stock still, more lifeless than a stone, quieter than a 'log' and no difference in sound reaches the pricked-up ear, busy listening. Furthermore, from time to time, the forces which confront each other in the life or death struggle are not of the same kind. The weak is strong through a strength which is other than that of the strong – the cat pounces swiftly on his prey but the mice flee even more swiftly and not in a straight line and our cat no longer knows where to strike with his claw. It is then that either one or the other resorts to trickery, to 'feats of agility' like hanging by their feet to feign death and then, 'he who is hanged comes to life again and landing on his feet/ Catches the slowest./ . . . It's one of the oldest tricks in the book'. Or else there is hiding in the flour, and this time it is the wisdom of the rat, 'an old campaigner who has more than one trick up his sleeve', that has an answer to this trick: 'It's no good being like flour/For even if you were a sack, I would not come near'.

It is no use the weak blaming force in rebelling against or demanding that it should yield to what is right; it is no good using the discourse of right against force since the latter, exerting itself all the same, will say that the just is in fact unjust and that it is the mighty that is just so that the righteousness of the just will not be able to overcome the righteousness of the strong. This discourse of might which one day said, once and for all, that it was right, is called *power.* However, it will always be possible for the weak to try to play tricks with the discourse of might, with the 'right of might', and to respond to its immutable discourse with cunning words. To take power using its own force is to use the language of cunning, since power is only the discourse of might, and Pascal taught me that this discourse was also the true one (a certain kind of truth) and also the just one (a certain kind of justice). Might can neither be opposed nor taken to task except by words which will always be pronounced by power to be false and unjust. To make a cunning use of language is really to seize power using its own might, or diverting and turning the might of power back against itself through discourse. To what purpose? There are two possibilities; either to seize power, i.e. taking one's own turn to use the discourse of might; there is a change of master but there is still a master; or to survive, to pull through one way or another. It even happens sometimes that there is an added bonus to pulling through safely, namely pleasure. That is what I read in *The Cat's Master (or Master Cat)* or *Puss-in-Boots*, as told by Charles Perrault at the time of Louis XIV's absolute power. The cat's master captures power, seizes the discourse of might, keeps it, holds on to it until the end, *thanks to his cat*. Is this an example of an animal being sublimely dedicated to his master? Of undying loyalty? Not at all. It is simply to save his own skin. Listen to his master's voice at the beginning of the tale. Down and out, excluded from all companionship, with his father dead and the inheritance divided up, the youngest son, the last of all, was unable to resign himself to such a poor deal: '"My brothers", he said, "will be able to earn their living honestly by pooling together; as for me, when I have eaten my cat, and made a muff out of his skin, I will of necessity die of hunger".' The cat is in danger of being eaten and that is what starts the story off; and even were he to be eaten, because his poor master himself is in danger of dying as well, the master's precedence over the animal is still there since he will not die of hunger until *after* he has eaten his cat. But read the end: the miller's son, having become a marquess, on the very same day marries the princess. There he is, the king's son-in-law, thanks to his cat who himself became a great lord. The hierarchy lives on in what is called the circles of power. However, what follows is what is important. He no longer chases mice except for sport. The power remains with the master. He has usurped absolute power and holds on to it. As for the cat, he is no longer needed, being neither eater nor eaten. But wait a moment, surely I seem to recall a version of the story from Brittany or Poitou where he ends up dying having known bliss and contentment?

What interests me in this story is this: How does the cat give his master power? Perhaps – to be completely realistic, some would use the word 'cynical' if it were not a cat that was involved – he only gives him power because within the framework of his own tactics, he cannot do otherwise? Perhaps that is where there is a tactical manoeuvre as opposed to a strategy? Using tactics would be the situation of he who has no force *per se*, who is not a subject of will or power because he has no force except in relation to another who, alone, either wishes to have or is able to have force. It is because his master, as poor, as wretched, as stupid as he is, has, right from the start, always been his master that the cat is able to save his own skin by giving him power. His master simply changes the locus and the situation of his mastership. In the beginning he is master of the cat and ends up by becoming the master of the king's daughter, future master of the kingdom, and the cat will always remain the servant. It is surely better, however, to chase after mice as a great lord than to end up as a muff and in the stewpot.

How then does the cat give his master power? How does he cause him to change position as a master? In the beginning they are both marginal characters, outcasts on the fringe of the civilised world. On the death of the father the two elder brothers build up an economic, socially viable, productive cell again, or at least they are capable of doing it, one with his mill, the other with his donkey. The youngest cannot achieve this with his cat. There is only one alternative left to him, a completely natural one: I am hungry, what can I eat? – my cat. I am cold, I will dress in his skin. This is the moment, but only a moment, for the satisfaction of basic needs, for a self-preservation which will not last, with no planning ahead, and death to follow. 'I will of necessity – hard natural necessity – die of hunger.' The master relationship carries on, but it will only operate once before vanishing, when the cat has been eaten. From the very outset this regression back to nature takes on the appearance of a transgression. You remember the unlucky hunter who, coming home empty-handed, gives his friends a cat done up as a rabbit to eat, to save face. For civilized man there is no going back to nature. There is only decline and fall. In this case, however, the infringement of the culinary taboo is a necessity and not a reaction of prestige. The cat's first trick arises out of this and is quite a negative one – pretending not to hear, not to understand, whereas the cunning animal, paying heed to everything, already understands everything. He hits back with a suggestion:

> 'Although you don't amount to anything, you are my master. Give me a sack, have me a pair of boots made so that I can go into the undergrowth and I will give you something.'

> 'What's that then?'

> 'You will see that what you believe yourself to be – left badly off, reduced to dying – is only superficial.'

There is a contract of exchange; instead of taking me (and eating me), give to me and you will receive. Let us look carefully, under the surface, at the reality of this contract. Give up the prey you have got in your hand for something unspecified, for another prey which I am promising you. But the cat does not promise anything. He lets him think that he is promising future sustenance, and in so doing, he introduces into the tight situation, into the imminence of mortal danger – for him anyway – a breathing space, an interval, an extension of time. The household pet is to revert to the wild beast, to the predatory animal; whilst acquiring the signs which categorize him as belonging to the order of men, whilst rising, in an ambiguous way, to the level of the masters with his aristocratic boots, and with the (knap)sack of the down-and-out, he reaches the level of the person who has sunk in the social scale. This is how he actually advances by going backwards. The master falls into the trap. Because he is *aware* of the tricks his cat uses to eat mice, he *believes* he will use trickery for his master's benefit. He does not eat his cat but on the contrary he gives him what he asks – the boots that his servant claims are useful in the undergrowth, and the sack.

We know the rest. The cat traps a 'young rabbit still ignorant in the wily ways of this world', as he had so many times before, when he trapped mice by pretending, by feigning the very death that he has just escaped from; two partridges follow, then some game. These are the normal tricks used by the domestic animal in dealing with the wild animal. The snare is set through cunning, a measure of the borderline between nature (wild) and civilization (humanity). The cat is a product of the latter because he constructs traps by outsmarting his opponent. The trap is a 'device', a machine which aims at catching, that is to say, at conserving the prey. Remember Hegel in this context, and his wisdom of animals who, in their lack of faith in the reality of sensible things, in the absolute certainty of their own nothingness, seize these things without further ado and devour them. The trap, the stratagem, allows for the seizure of that which the animal perhaps would not have seized and for putting off consuming it. That is in fact the sack's function, for capturing and for keeping. The sack is a sort of temporary larder as a deposit for food and in this way the cat could fulfil, three times over, the contract of exchange he suggested to his master. 'You didn't eat me, you gave me a sack and boots; I am giving you a rabbit, two partridges and some game to eat.' That then is what this couple of predatory outcasts, the master and his servant, could constitute; somewhere between the mill and the warren the 'civilized' parasites of the wild, the primitive form of society; in reality the disintegration of a social cell.

That would be to misunderstand the cunning animal that is Master Cat. His tactics have quite another dimension. He puts off fulfilling the contract, for him it is putting off the evil moment, and in one fell swoop he lays siege to the centre of power, the pinnacle of the social and cultural hierarchy. With his rabbit in his sack 'he went off to the king's palace and asked to see him.' From now on his tricks will be linguistic ones. Instead of giving his rabbit to his master, he gives it to the king: ' "there, Sire, is a wild rabbit which the Marquess of Carabas (that was the name that took his fancy to give to his master) has charged me to present to you on his behalf." "Tell your master", the King replied, "that I thank him and that he gives me great pleasure." ' The scene is repeated twice more in the narrative; two more partridges and the king 'had him presented with something for a drink', some game from time to time over two or three months that the cat brought the king on behalf of his master.

We must pause for a moment over the cat's cunning, which is really a double one and which brings about an essential change in the nature of things. His cunning is one of discourse. It consists on the cat's part in freely naming his master. He has not given him his rabbit, he gives him a name, but he gives him this name while giving the rabbit to another person, and not just any other person but the Head of State, Power itself, the hub and the pinnacle of power. From then on, as far as the miller's son is concerned, this designation is a denomination, a change of name, a pseudonym. He thinks he is called Pierre, Simon or Colin. However, in his position as someone isolated on the fringe of society, he only uses this name with himself. But do we call ourselves by our own names for our own benefit? Is not our *own* name for the benefit of others? Now as far as the others are concerned, as far as the king who eminently represents all the others is concerned, his name is something else. *He, however, knows nothing about it.* He does not know he has lost his name and received another. Suddenly, by losing his name without his knowledge, he has lost his identity. On the other hand, like the king, we too, as readers, we do not know the name of the miller who is dead, the 'real' name of the father and of the son. However, the difference between us and the king is that we suppose that this name exists. As far as the king is concerned, an anonymous person is, here, now, being called by a name which he thinks is 'real'. For us the readers, it is the same, except that we believe it to be false. Hence the textual and logical necessity of the interpolated clause; the utterance through which the narrator addresses himself to the reader to point out the cat's speech act.

In what way is the cat's activity a trick, and thereby the beginnings of a tactical manoeuvre? I may freely give a name to a thing, whether it already has a name or none at all. Nominal definitions are arbitrary and indisputable, provided, however, that I tell other people of them in advance and that I do not change them in the course of my discussion, and also provided that I do not confuse them with the definition of things by which I say *what the thing is.* Thus I can call a 'table' a chair and I would be understood by those to whom I am speaking if I let them know in advance of my decision; and provided that from then on in my discussion I do not call a 'chair' a table and that I do not surreptitiously attribute the characteristics of the table to the chair. In one sense the cat formulates a nominal definition of his master in the king's presence, but at the same time 'omitting' the basic requirement of its use. He does not make known to the king his act of denomination: '"From now on and throughout the whole of my conversation with you and with the others I will call my master the Marquess of Carabas"', so that the king understands, and cannot but understand that this name is the 'real' name of the cat's master. On the other hand he will in no way change definition during the course of his conversation and he does not confuse the name of the individual and what the individual actually is since it is a proper name, naming thus the individual who carries this name: 'The Marquess of Carabas is the name of the individual who is called the Marquess of Carabas.' However, this name, is it only a proper name? Yes in one sense, since it designates an individual, a particular individual, not only because there is none other than the miller's son who carries this name in and by means of the cat's discourse, but also since it is a 'false name', nobody has used it before him. No, in another sense, because it concerns a title of nobility, the 'Marquess of Carabas', since from then on not only does the cat use this name for his master but also through the title attached to the name he introduces him into a social hierarchy, into a cultural classification. Because of the name the cat's master belongs to the nobility, and within that nobility to one of the groups which is hierarchically the highest – the marquesses. From this point of view the name the cat has given the master is a false name, a pseudonym, and false in two ways since it is not the one that the miller's son carries through his paternal line – the attachment of the name is a detachment of name since it pushes the cat's master up into the nobility and within the nobility to the rank of marquess. Therefore it is not only a pseudonym – a false name – but it is also the misappropriation of a title – a false title. All the same, as far as the king is concerned, 'the Marquess of Carabas' refers to the man who has him presented with a wild rabbit, then two partridges, then some game with a regularity and frequency which imbue the pseudonym and the title with the consistency and weight of a custom and even with a certain legitimacy through the acts performed on their behalf. The king gets into the habit of receiving gifts from an individual called 'the Marquess of Carabas'. By accepting these presents he accepts, authorizes, without either willing it or knowing it, the use of a name and of a title. Given a little time, the most untrue things become true. There is a ruse in this, since the king is a power that names the individuals. It is he who confers the titles of nobility on his subjects to reward them for their merits. The cat traps the king in that he diverts the force of the power (the power of naming) from its customary use to his own personal *use*, whilst through repetition, he makes this particular use acceptable to the person who has the power of attributing names.

This initial strategy triggers off the whole story, that is to say a succession of complementary ruses, with the object of confirming the name which was attributed the first time. To call oneself, to be called the 'Marquess of Carabas' *means* to possess a marquess's clothes, property, an estate, a château. The cat's tactics will then be to bring into existence that which he stated (described) the first time by the appellative name. The false definition of the name will be a true definition of the 'thing'. In the end the miller's son will be the Marquess of Carabas, with the extra bonus of erotic pleasure – the king's daughter – which will be *at the same time* the conquest of power. He will take the King: check and mate.

For the time being, however, an essential transformation takes place, a simultaneous transformation of the act of designation. By presenting the king with the young rabbit, which the miller's son should have eaten, as a present from the Marquess of Carabas, the cat immediately transforms *the object which is good to eat into a sign*, a sign of the homage of the vassal towards the overlord, a sign of the acknowledgement of power brought about by the diversion and the reversal of the force of power. Power is caught in the trap since its own power, usurped by the cat, makes the usurpation legitimate, as it were. That is the circularity of the trap – it is by giving his master the false title of Marquess of Carabas that the cat is able to transform the edible wild rabbit into a sign of allegiance of his master to the king, but, by accepting this present from the marquess who is unknown to him, the king, without knowing it, authorizes the cat's master to bear this title. Thus by receiving the marquess's rabbit, the king does not receive an object but a sign and for the time being responds by giving the cat signs – words of thanks, of pleasure, money for a drink; it is the passage from nature to culture by virtue of a name. By the same token the marginals, the miller's son and his cat, are brought into the fold of society through linguistic signs. In language, they participate in the system, in its power, the master as a marquess and the predatory cat as a messenger, the means of communication between the vassal and the overlord.

The second episode of the narrative, the central episode, brings in a new stratagem and another trap.

> One day when he (the cat) knew that the King was due to go for a walk along the riverbank with his daughter, the most beautiful princess in the world, he said to his master:
> 'If you wish to follow my advice, your fortune is made. All you have to do is bathe at the river in the place I will show you and then let me do the rest.'
> (...) The Marquess of Carabas did what his cat advised him, without knowing what the point of it would be.

The cat, who, it must be pointed out, up to now has not fulfilled his first contract, suggests another one to his master: 'do what I tell you and your fortune is made.' This is a 'leonine' contract[3] because the master must obey his cat like a slave without knowing what this obedience will bring him. He becomes bound to a plan about which all he is told is that at the end of the day it will be to his advantage. Better still, everything seems in the cat's discourse as if, by blindly following his advice *in the future*, the master's fortune *was already made*, as if the *future* objective envisaged by the plan and suggested by promise and contract, *was already* achieved. What is required of the master is to strip himself of his clothes, to place himself naked in the river, to reduce himself to nothing (to this nothing which he already is but without knowing it – but then throughout the whole narrative does he ever know anything? – having lost his identity by losing his name), so as to become everything: to be nothing is to be everything. Impossible, a contradiction, would you not say? Certainly if it were not for the powers of a cunning discourse which will describe bathing as drowning and being in an undressed state as having one's clothes stolen. That is all well and good, but the pretence is worse than reality, it might be argued. However, *saying* drowning instead of bathing *means* calling for help; *saying* that clothes have been stolen instead of being undressed *means* having clothes to put on. Because he has received the marquess's gift of game, the king, who is passing by, is then placed under the obligation of returning this gift first of all with help, then with something to put on. The location of the river is the moment of opportunity, the favourable moment *kairos* (the proper time); the coming together of events in the present time.

> *At the very time* that he was bathing, the King passed by and the cat started shouting, 'Help!' *During the course of* getting the poor marquess out, the cat went up to the carriage and said to the King that, *during the time* that his master was bathing, some thieves had arrived who had carried off his clothes although he had shouted, 'Thief!' with all his might.

What is the cat doing? Lying, you will say – his master is bathing, he is not drowning. He got undressed but his clothes are not stolen, they have been hidden under a large stone. All right, but the lie he tells is not only a falsification of reality. He does not stop at saying what is not the case but he actualises what he says, or more precisely, in the context of the event he makes the opportunity happen by extracting all the possibilities from it. He only makes them obvious, however, because they are already there. In order to bring them out it was enough just to present them with an event. Being pulled out of the river by the guards at the King's behest, and wearing the coat of the King were possible only if the miller's son was bathing at the moment when the King was passing by, and only if he was completely naked at that very moment: the event. This possibility, however, was itself possible only if bathing was called drowning and only if the absence of clothes was called theft of clothes; only if the man who was drowning, who was robbed, had been called, had the title of Marquess of Carabas, who had given so much game to the king.

This stage in the career of the miller's son and that of his cat is essential. Up until now it was purely through signs that the marginal had gained entry into the seat of power, by delegation or representation – a name, a title, or gifts showing homage. From now on the marginal is actually in this place, 'in the flesh', clothed in one of the signs of power (the coat) and in turn is in a position to exercise power over the princess. Is it not at that moment when he is clothed by the king that he becomes handsome and lovable, 'when she falls madly in love with him'?

The third episode, after the name, after the clothes, is about procuring an estate. This episode is symmetrical to the previous one in respect of the event/opportunity of the bathing/drowning in the river. There is another trick of language, another cunning act, but quite different from the first ones. Here again the cat goes on ahead of his master. 'The cat, delighted at seeing that his plan was starting to succeed, took the initiative.' Everything happens in the narrative – and from now on it is a journey along a road, a path opened up from one place to another, as if the cat's speech acts, his discursive operations, had the function of programming the actions which his master will later carry out; as if what the cat says, in anticipation of the arrival of his master, posited the future actions of the latter as the inevitable consequences of the strategic calculation of his servant. It is remarkable, in fact, that compared to the first episode of the hunting of the wild animal, the cat no longer acts himself, or rather that his acts are linguistic ones whose calculated force engenders transformations which are themselves planned and fixed in advance, in the universe of discourse of the various protagonists in the story.

> Having met some peasants who were reaping a meadow, he [the cat]
> *said to them*:
> 'Good people who are reaping, if you do not tell the King that the
> meadow that you are reaping belongs to the Marquess of Carabas you
> will be made into mincemeat.'

There is a dialogue between the harvesters and the King who then comes by. The peasants reply with one accord that the meadow belongs to the marquess, 'for the cat's threat had frightened them'. The sequence, as in the first episode of the hunt, is repeated twice, and again as in the first episode, each repetition marks a quantitative increase in the marquess's property. Fields and corn follow on from the meadow and the hay and finally, without limit, all the products of nature under cultivation. At the end of the journey the marquess's material wealth is considerable, his rank of marquess, his title, is no longer a name, or clothes – it is a vast estate.

The question is quite obviously that of the power of the cat's discourse directed at the reapers, the harvesters, the peasants. Why is it so effective? The reply is twofold; the power of the discourse depends on the threat it contains: 'If you do not reply as I ask, if you do not lie, then you will be changed into cooked meals, you will be eaten in paté form', and this enigmatic threat takes on all its force from the signifying structure in which it is formulated – 'chopped up finely like paté meat' – the magical/poetic power of the sonorous signifiers, a 'music' which is instantly persuasive, which convinces straightaway. However, this reply is not enough. There is a much clearer, distinct reason for the effectiveness of the magic formula. This estate belongs to an ogre whose chief characteristic, that he shares with his fellow creatures, is anthropophagy, cannibalism. The peasants belong to the ogre both as producers of the products of agriculture and as articles of food, consumable, edible. They produce food in the form of vegetables and are products in the form of food as meat, and why not as cooked meat? The cat's formula 'traps' the peasants; they understand the reply which they must give to the king's question as an order from their master, the ogre. Expressed another way, the discourse they must use classifies them as belonging to the Marquess of Carabas but they only use it because they belong to the ogre. The cat's linguistic trick, in this case again, diverts the immediate and indisputable force of power – the monstrous appetites of the ogre – and turns it back against him. It is through the ogre's strength that the ogre is stripped of his possessions and that the Marquess of Carabas, just as he had usurped a title by diverting the king's power, now usurps the land, the estate which the title also gives a name to. In the narrative there are therefore two principles of power, the king and the ogre and two places of instituted power – the king's palace (first episode) and the ogre's castle (fourth episode); the narrative is the journey from one area to the other by the king, his daughter and the 'marquess' in their coach. The cat's tactics have been to exploit first one of the principles, then the other, aiming to reduce the second to the first, to the benefit of the third – his master. In a sense, the ogre can be considered as the anti-king: we will see in what way later. That is why the cat's journey, preceding his master's, will establish, through absorbing the second power, the power of the king as the absolute power, without exteriority, but here again let us reiterate, to the benefit of the marginal in the conquest of power.

It is no less remarkable that, if the cat's tricks are essentially linguistic tricks – leaving aside the very first one which allowed him to catch 'a young scatter-brained rabbit as yet unaware of the wily ways on this world' – nevertheless the spring for the traps that these tricks set, the motivation behind setting them up, the reason for their success, has something to do with immediate need, with hunger and the quest for food, the self-preservation of the individual by the assimilation of the object that is 'good to eat'; eat or be eaten is, or seems to be, the main theme *in basso continuo* which runs through the tale of the conquest of power. Speaking to another being in order to persuade him, in order to bring pressure to bear on him, is connected with food. At the beginning the cat is not eaten because he leads his master to believe that he will eat. The game – the wild animal – which he then hunts, thanks to the boots and the sack which his master gives him, is instantaneously transformed into a social sign through the act of giving a name to his master. His function then is no longer essentially as an article of food but initially to give meaning to, to prove to the king the false title of Marquess of Carabas which it took his fancy to give to his master. The episode of the meeting up with the peasants – symmetrical to the previous one beyond the river and the bathing/drowning – in turn brings about a remarkable transformation of the same theme. It is no longer a question, as it was in the other episode, of changing, by speaking falsely, the wild animal that is good to eat into a sign of social order and social hierarchy to receive in return other signs which this time are true, but of changing man, the social producer, the cultivator into an animal that is fit to eat, should he not speak falsely or should he not display certain linguistic signs. The cat, as a producer of signs, here gives way to other producers of signs. However, the rule governing their transmission includes a radical sanction – that of a regression to the savagery of nature, to the ferocity of urgent need. If you do not say what I tell you to say, then you will never say anything again, you will become the simple ingredient of a cooked dish.

The great importance of the fourth episode arises out of this; it is the one where the cat meets the ogre, the meeting of the power of discourse and of another power which is the alternative to the royal power. As we have already seen, the King is the master of signs; he is the one who fundamentally possesses their signifying force because he is the king, the power, the discourse which establishes force as just and good. Through him, because of him, objects, beings, the rabbit, the partridges, the game, the naked body of the miller's son, are imbued with meaning. But they are only like this, as we have already also seen, because our wily Grippeminaud, through his own discourse, has momentarily diverted and overturned the force of the king's power. With the ogre, the cat, really speaking, has to deal less with a power than with something powerful. The ogre is first of all the hyperbolic force of consumption; he eats a lot and he even eats the uneatable – man. A supernatural and infracultural force, the god-beast. Eating is transforming the foreign body, the other's substance into one's own substance – assimilating it. He possesses it totally and all at once. By eating him, not only does he transform the other – even man – into himself but also, conversely, he is able to transform himself into the other, even into a beast. Supernatural, infracultural, the ogre is the force which is the antithesis of established power. If established power is mastery of signs, of their rules of organisation, of the laws of their hierarchy, the ogre's powerful force is the anti-sign par excellence. It is raw strength with 'no refinements' – bodies and the transformation of bodies. The ogre is what force is without discourse; the powerful force of metamorphosis, at one and the same time within and beyond the world of signs. It is because he possesses this powerful force totally that he will be toppled, trapped, not by established power (the discourse of force, the king) but by that power which, as far as he is concerned, only has the force of discourse, the marginal, the cat. The ogre absorbs into his form the substance of others, but he *also* assimilates his substance into the form of others. He eats even the uneatable; he will be eaten – which is unbelievable – by the cat. The latter only makes clear what is the 'truth' of the power of metamorphosis – being eaten by the other, a truth which the cat brings about by transforming the reflexive into the passive and the temporary state into the permanent state. How does he do this?

The cat's trick, his competence, consists of drawing the anti-sign into the order of signs and in making it act only within this order. Listen to the introduction to this episode: 'The cat, who was careful to inquire who this ogre was and what he could do, asked to speak to him, saying that he had not wanted to pass by so close to his castle without having had the honour of paying him his respects.' Our cunning cat, because of his knowledge of the ogre – of the other – and the knowledge he has of his ability, establishes at once his relationship to him on the level of conventional signs of courtesy and politeness, on the level of that semiotics without semantics that Benveniste talks about – that is, of signs that have no meaning, of modes of behaviour without any other content and finality than that of producing signs. It is at that point and that point only that Master Cat asks the ogre to transform *himself*. At the level at which the dialogue has been pitched, that of signs at which the ogre is rather clumsy ('the Ogre received him as civilly as an ogre can'), the experiences of transformations can be no more than *a game*. The ogre *plays the part* of someone who has the power to transform himself, to show off his power to the cat. A pretence, if you like, at an activity which allows of no pretence. To make the other person in the conversation believe in his power, the ogre cannot resort to discourse, he can only demonstrate. The cat is willing enough to believe, but in order to believe, he must see. The ogre wishes to persuade the cat of his power, but to do that he has no other power than this very power itself. On the level of discourse, the ogre does not metamorphose himself, he is metamorphosed as a power of metamorphosis by the discourse of the cat. This is the first move in the cat's strategy – the reflexive has become passive. That is so true that not only does the ogre not eat the cat as an ogre, but does not eat him as a lion either. It is in this sense that he pretends to do it while all the time actually accomplishing his transformation. And the force of the cat's discourse has as its exact counterpart his weakness in reality: 'The cat was so frightened to see a lion in front of him that he went straight up onto the roof, not without difficulty or danger, because of the boots which were no good at all for walking on tiles.... Some time after, the cat, seeing that the ogre had abandoned his first change of form, came down and admitted that he had been well frightened.'

On to the cat's second move. On the level of argumentation and demonstration, on the level of what is believable and unbelievable, it is certainly more difficult for the ogre to transform himself into a mouse or a rat than into a lion or an elephant. That is what the cat says, irresistibly: 'I'll admit to you that I find that quite impossible.' The ogre's reply is by *deixis*. 'Impossible? You'll see,' and the cat pounces on the mouse and eats it. The metamorphosis game stops at a stroke. The ogre is metamorphosed into a cat, and that is permanent; he has lost his power. He has become, once and for all, the very substance itself of the cat. There again the trick works and succeeds only on account of the diversion and reversal of a force. There is diversion in that the cat ushers the ogre into the order of signs which is not his own order, and through this he makes him simulate the exercise of his power, all the time showing it for what it is, but to no end, to no purpose, without a sense of immediacy or necessity. There is reversal: at the *propitious moment,* on the occasion provided by the discourse of the cunning cat within the event which is presented to him, when the ogre plays at being the mouse to show off his power, suddenly the cat is no longer playing. In one fell swoop he leaves the order of signs to enter the order of bodies, the order of the ogre himself, which is that of force; but at that point the ogre is weak – he is a mouse – and the cat is strong, he eats the mouse. The ogre is eaten as a mouse only by his own force turned back on itself by the force of the cat's discourse. As Retz de Beaufort, who was executed politically by a *bon mot* and a burst of laughter, said, 'from this condition no one ever recovers'. The ogre has still not got over it.

Enter, however, the power of state in a coach; here is the king, here also is the moment of truth, the moment of the successful outcome – felicity – of the initial speech act of the cat that bestowed a false title on his master, a pseudoname. The young miller's son will not really be able to bear this title – and along with him neither will his descendants – unless the focal point of the estate, of the cultivated area, the castle, is to be occupied permanently by him; unless he replaces, for ever, its owner. The tactical problem which was resolved is this. How do you appropriate a name which is not your own? How can a name become a proper name? How can you bring together a name and an individual without any excess or residue without leaving any *traces*? Or furthermore how do you acquire a particular and proper being? How do you acquire a lost identity? The answer is by becoming indisputably, irrefutably the possessor of a title, of an appellation, that is of an area of land that 'yields abundantly every year', of a 'fine inheritance', and at its centre, of a residence – the castle from which the land derives its name. I say that the king's arrival in the castle is the moment of truth for all the cat's tactics, this is because he must communicate to his master, before the king asks any questions, the knowledge that he is, once and for all, a landowner – that he has, once and for all, a title, a name. And so once again making the first move, taking the initiative in speaking and placing his master and his king in a position where they can hear him, the cat says to the king: 'Your Majesty is welcome in the castle of the Marquess Carabas.' The cat is speaking to the king but in a way that he may be heard by his master, to communicate to him a piece of information which he does not as yet have and in giving it to him, to give him as well the right to bear the title which he has been usurping up until now. The cat speaks to the king so as to be heard by the marquess and the king replies to the marquess, giving him for the first time his title. 'Well then Marquess,' exclaimed the King, 'this castle as well is yours.' This property legitimises, permanently, the appropriation of the title. The King is trapped; the King believes everything and authorises everything while waiting for something to drink. The cat's false words have come true in this location, one might say, but that would not be going far enough. The cat's discourses have gone from false to true, not because before them there existed a reference which they gradually had to adapt to, but because, bit by bit, through a series of well articulated *moves*, they have created the reference which right from the first act of designation they had been signifying. The category of what is true and what is false is thus subordinated to the force of the discourse and to the tactics that this force has set in motion. Power, as we said, is the discourse that force *uses* and through which it sets itself up and makes itself just and true. The cat's stratagem consisted of taking over this discourse (which calls itself just and true in the mouth of power) and of making it strong. It is a discourse that respects neither law nor religion, a discourse that is deceitful and insolent, a daring discourse as well, which, being well expressed, at the right time, in the right place, diverted the force of power, captured it in its well constructed sentences in order finally, by turning it against the power, to seize the locus of justice and truth where power defines itself as such.

At that point the last phase of the game commences – the cat's last move. The King, without waiting for a reply from the cat's master, goes for a look round the property. 'Nothing could be finer than this courtyard and these buildings that surround it; let us see the inside please.' The cat has just named the ogre's castle by its 'true' name – 'that of the Marquess of Carabas', and the King, in replying to the miller's son, not only calls him marquess but indicates, points with his finger and points out with his words, the buildings and places them in their exterior reality as objects – *this* courtyard, *these* buildings – as the property of the man whom, without knowledge or volition, he has just elevated to the title of marquess by establishing the estate and the residence as a marquisate. The King goes round the property; as the absolute power – since the anti-power has been absorbed by the cat – is he not the distinguished owner of his kingdom? He is the symbolic owner and transmits the sign of this: he is the first to go up and find 'a magnificent meal' that the ogre has had prepared for his friends who were to come and see him that very day, but who had not dared to come in, 'knowing that the King was there.' Here is the unexpected, the unforeseeable event that the cat had not bargained for in his tactical plan. However, it is there, at the same time, after so many delays and extensions, that the contract proposed by the cat to his starving master is fulfilled. 'Don't eat me and I will give you something to eat.' At last the miller's son is going to eat for the first time. Not only have the cat's false words come true by actualising the referents which they signified, but they have also become just: Raminagrobis honours his commitments, as they say. He had simply put off doing it and he honours them a hundredfold. Instead of a young, quite small wild rabbit eaten alone on the edge of the woods and the cultivated lands, there are the sumptuous resources of a huge estate, re-created by culinary art, which he eats and offers to the King and princess to eat. The cycle of exchange at this point is redoubled. The cat gives back to his master, in the form of the meal, the rabbit which he had not given him in exchange for his own life; similarly the marquess gives back to the King in the same form the aid he has received, the clothes he was given and still more the title and the land which, unknown to him, he authorised the marquess to possess. This meal, which fortune (which, as everyone knows, smiles on the brave and even more on the cunning) has sent the cat to complete his venture with the most magnificent finale, is the meal of another, of the other, that the ogre prepared for the ogres, his friends; and I cannot help thinking that a few reapers and harvesters chopped up as mincemeat provided the choicest meats. In other words, it is his estate, his property that the marquess is offering the King, their distinguished landlord, with the sign of this meal which is as magnificent as it is symbolic. Fortune, events, the unforeseen and the unforeseeable, that is what makes contracts fair, promises genuine, and agreements reliable in the perfect reciprocity of exchanges, in the symbolic etiquette of giving and receiving gifts. The lesson of the sombre Pascalian irony on political justice and political truth is a terrible one. It would be a desperate lesson indeed if the whole social edifice and its exact functioning had not found themselves caught right from the beginning in the meshes of the cat's tricks with their clever, delicately set traps, succeeding each time through the diversion and the reversal of the force of power. The negative, desperate irony of Pascal, then, becomes humour, and the system of power in the imaginary representation it gives itself to justi-fy itself, to veri-fy[4] itself, in the ending to all this, falls into a final trap, due to an excess.

Here we have power being calculating in its infinite wisdom, in its omnipresent knowledge, 'the King, charmed by the Marquess of Carabas's good qualities, as was his daughter, who was crazy about him, and seeing the great wealth he possessed, said to him: "It only depends on you, Marquess, for you to become my son-in-law." '

The King is scheming; it would be better to integrate such a powerful vassal into the royal domain and the royal family. I will give him my daughter and the right to succeed me but in the same act I will absorb him, not to myself as an individual but to myself as the state. In return the marginal has conquered (in all senses of the term: polemical as well as seductive) power, but at the same time he has been conquered by power (in the strategic sense). Thus to capture power is to win and lose at the same time: winning and losing since all power is absolute and it cannot have exteriority. A subtle calculation on the part of the King, strategic wisdom on the part of the State; there is no exteriority, he must absorb everything for it to be total. He must devour everything. So be it.

Nevertheless, there again, I cannot help thinking that this conquest of power by the miller's son and his conquest by power are just a little mad and that this madness is the final stratagem, the cat's last trap, exploiting the event that fortune sends him to create an opportunity to get a good deal out of it. Power is calculating, as we have said, and that is certain. But you will have noticed that the King does not go as far as the solemn declaration 'It all depends on you, Marquess, for you to become my son-in-law', *until after he has drunk five or six glasses*; doubtless four or five too much. I cannot help thinking that the cat has got the King drunk and that his master is also a little light-headed from drinking. 'The Marquess, bowing deeply, accepted the honour which the King was bestowing on him.' The royal scheming involves an excess, the system of reciprocated gifts and counter-gifts rightly taken in turns, contains a surplus, a few extra glasses of wine which explain the final solution. There is a complete reversal of things: the young disinherited son on the edge of the wood had nothing to eat except his cat, nothing to put on his back except the animal's skin. In the end he marries the princess and will become king, perhaps because the King drank too much. If it is possible for a man to die of hunger because power and its laws are unjust, then it is possible for that power to eat and drink too much and the King gives his daughter to the first stranger. Justice between shortage and excess, justice by this reversal of one within the other – humour. It is true that a cat has journeyed between one side and the other, a cat who could talk well, and at the right moment, who had no other ambition, no other plan, no other scheme than to avoid being eaten by his master and who, in order to achieve this, little by little, from boots to a sack, from pretence to lies, from speech acts to discursive traps, conquered power, all power, absolute power, for his master. This power lost exteriority once the eater (the ogre) is eaten, once the princess is married, with the exception of the cat, who is its vestige – no longer of use. 'The cat became a great lord.' In the system of absolute power, he is the system's power of diversion devoid of appetites, without any needs, a finality without an end, gratuitousness and play, supplementary pleasure and in excess – 'who no longer chases after mice except for sport.'

The king who was lost and found again

Here is the counter-proof. You know the little story told by Pascal in the prelude to the *First discourse on the condition of men in high places*. A man is tossed by the storm onto an island whose inhabitants were having difficulty in finding their king, who has disappeared. As in Perrault's tale there is an event, a shipwreck, a marginal, the man tossed by the storm onto the coast, stripped of everything. However, there is a difference in this case: power is in abeyance, as they say. This is inexplicable but it is not the point. At the centre of the island, at the heart of the hierarchically constructed social system, closed off on all sides by the infinity of the sea, there is an empty space, the place of the king. However, since the shipwrecked man bodily and facially resembled the king who had disappeared, the inhabitants of the island take this man for him. The perfect resemblance is a new, inexplicable fact. The lost king is suddenly found again but in the form of his simulacrum, and the man who was lost by the storm on the island is found, only to be lost again, in an instant, since he is for the others something other than what he is in reality, neither the king nor the man in 'truth' but both, a simulacrum.

I say 'simulacrum' and not 'representation' since, as far as the people are concerned, the shipwrecked man is not the delegated representative of the absent king, in spite of, or rather because of his perfect resemblance. The king does not split into presence and absence in order to substitute, using the man, the presence of his absence for the absence of his presence, this being the structure and final aim of all representation. The man is not the natural sign of the king as my image in the mirror is of my body and my face. The man actually *is* the king for the subjects of the island, without the guarantee of a referent which would define the criteria and the tokens of validity and truth of his significance. Similarly, in the way the inhabitants of the island look at him and in the gestures they make towards him, in their respectful and obedient behaviour, the man is no longer in possession of himself, no longer identifies himself as the 'same', he discovers himself as another, saved from oblivion in the storm, to lose himself in difference. Power in its characteristic form is lost forever, a power which is supposed to be nothing but truth and justice, and in its place, in its deserted space, is its simulacrum. In one stroke, in one single stroke offered by chance, the man, the marginal has conquered power. Legitimacy, authority, the political base are all elements of chance. There is no effort of the will, no intelligent calculation, no tactics, no strategy, only the blast of a storm, the random element of a likeness which is so close that it instantly places a double on the throne.

At the outset the man does not know what to decide. Finally he resolves to let himself be treated as a king and to receive all the respects that the island's inhabitants pay him. At this point the discourse of truth and justice starts, discourse by means of which power establishes itself as power. The fact that the man allows himself to be treated as an *object* of admiration and respect is of no consequence. This inertia is the result of a hesitation and a resolution; this passivity is willed. The man decides to *act out the simulacrum*. Here fortune has turned into good fortune, the chance event has been transformed into the advent of a windfall. Such is the truth, the justice of the discourse of power, twice removed from Truth and Justice, which are forever lost; since no one knows which they are, or what they are or where the real king is, and since everyone except the man believes the real king has come back, everything happens as if there were no other truth, no other justice except those that the acting out of the simulacrum bestows on the forlorn inhabitants who are just as lost as their king.

Why does the man decide in this way? The inhabitants of the island are having difficulty in finding their lost king. Suddenly there is joy, a reunion. He who is (was and will be) Truth and Justice has returned to the island. Evohe! Evohe![5] Is it possible to deceive[6] those who are weeping and grieving when, all of a sudden, their distress vanishes with the return (of the king) and send them back on their search which will perhaps never end? Those who weep and grieve are consoled because they love his law; yes, the king has returned. Yet it is his double. If only all the messiahs, all the chiefs, all the leaders of peoples were never anything else but doubles (just as there were two Moses, according to Freud) whose role would be, whether they liked it or not, to ease the grief of men who have lost the king of Truth and Justice. Yes of course it would be better for the comfort of the distressed people without a king, without a father, to have that sort of power – the power of a double, of the simulacrum of truth and justice in the place that the other has vacated. For the castaway, the man, believes the inhabitants of the island and the whole of their story of a lost king when, cast onto the shore wretched and naked, he observes that they are greeting him as a king. He has no choice but to believe it since they feed and clothe him and, in procession, surrounded by chanting and dancing, they lead him onto the throne telling him that it is his, this throne that has been found again. And what if the king had been gone so long that nobody amongst the inhabitants could remember his facial features or the shape of his body? Their ancestors said that originally the island was governed by the king of Truth and Justice and that one day, in very ancient times, he disappeared, leaving no other traces than the empty throne and the deserted palace. From that moment, they have been watching for his return, scanning the sea's horizon every day. On this very day, for the first and only time perhaps, a man is cast by the storm onto the coast. It can only be him, returned. How can the castaway not believe their story to be true and think he is the king's double? Or even that he is the king but that he has forgotten that he was once king, the real king, king of Justice.

I, who read Pascal and fabricate around the fable he tells to a teenager, a future duke, a future master, I say this: do they exist 'in reality', this Justice and Truth, impregnable, the aims and ends of all our political ventures, except at the expense of an act of faith? Once upon a time there was an island whose king of Justice and Truth disappeared. Where is he then? In what place beyond the seas? Is it never anything else but his double that comes back? But how would I know this since he who is here now is indistinguishable from the other who was lost? This story once happened to the American Indians when they welcomed their demigods who had been prophesied; they were mounted on strange creatures and wore iron breastplates. We also know what this cost them.

Power, then, is this double trap. The man, by playing the role of the royal stand-in, traps the island's inhabitants into showing the obedience and the respect which legitimately they owe their master. But, conversely, by hailing him as their real king, they trap him into this kingness that he is not. Power is therefore exercised but it does not exist. It is the imaginary product of a double postulation, of a double belief. The man believes, as a necessary result of their acts and their behaviour, the inhabitants of the island (that their king has disappeared) and they believe, with the same necessity, that he has come back, since he is his lookalike. The trapped is the trapper and the trapper is trapped. We need to go even further. The inhabitants do not tell the castaway the story of the disappearance and their search since they think that the king who has disappeared is there in the flesh and therefore he knows the story as well as, or even better than themselves. He tells himself the story, he imagines it because he is, here and now, treated as a master. The same goes for his subjects, because the king who has returned alone knows the story of his loss and because he cannot say what has happened – the boat, the storm, and suddenly the unknown island; in short that he is not the one they are looking for – because they would not believe him. He traps the others, and the others trap him but without either him or the others setting the trap and without it being possible for either one or the other of them to escape from the trap. Power as a trap; that means that power does not exist and that it is a fundamental fact, an originary *factum*, and I really mean fundamental fact, *factum*:[7] there is no transcendental, no condition of legitimacy and authority, no proto-history, except in the narrative or the eternally repeated myth of the great sadness of the world from which Truth and Justice, the true and just force, have withdrawn and which is told only to state this originary (factum), this fact.

The power trap is not set by anyone; neither shipwrecked nor shipwrecker constructs it. Both parties find it already there – the trap of simulacrum that both parties are content to subscribe to and which they fall into of necessity. This is a simulacrum trap very different from the series of moves of Master Cat constructing Carabas and his marquisate through the force of speech acts, as a result of which the title, the estate and the castle are in the end without any lie, without deception or usurpation, legitimate, true and just.

Pascal's little story comes to an end. There is the double-think and the double behaviour of the man who became king. Some of these he uses to deal with the people, others to deal with himself. There is a split between public and private, between the master and the individual. On the one hand there are the deeds and words, the acts and deeds of the law whose edict is without appeal, the State which establishes itself and builds itself up, strategies and decisions, war and peace, the whole of existence, the whole of reality, the whole of history. On the other hand there is the insistent murmuring, the obsessional clamour, the formless repetition of the private and proper subject, the eternal, unchanging (de)negation – I am not who the others think I am; I am not what I am for the others; I am only what I am not and I can say so, repeat it to myself alone, only because I am the master, the king that I am not, having been established as such by the others whom I command, give orders to. Empty words, thought that is devoid of all meaning. The power on one side, all the power, and on the other, nothing. The State is me, and I, the residue of this identity, am nothing.

After others, I name this split 'irony' after the manner of the masters.

Well, one day the king who was lost and found again, was visited by a cat carrying a sack and wearing boots and who, having bowed deeply, said to him, 'There, Sire, a wild rabbit that the Marques of Carabas charged me to present to you on his behalf.'

Notes

1. i.e. Jean de La Fontaine.
2. *Sans phrases* – a possible pun: without discourse.
3. *Contrat léonin*: a one-sided contract.
4. These verbs are hyphenated in the original French, so that the ending 'fier' is separated, perhaps as a play on words. *Fier*, the adjective, means proud, while *fier*, the verb, means to have confidence in oneself, i.e. justi-fier, véri-fier.
5. The Bachanalian cry in honour of the god Bacchus/Dionysius.
6. *Décevoir* can mean to deceive, to delude, but can also mean to disappoint. It is probably used in both senses here.
7. '*Factum*' in Latin, perhaps even more than the French *fact*, carries the connotation of a fact as something done or made. Marin seems to be suggesting that power is 'made' by the sum of its 'representations'.

1987

Introduction to Deleuze

Graham Burchell

In *La vent Paraclet* (1977) Michael Tournier writes of his ambition to produce 'the literary equivalent of those sublime metaphysical inventions which are Descartes' *cogito*, Spinoza's three kinds of knowledge, Kant's transcendental schematism, Husserl's phenomenological reduction' (p. 179). But how? Having turned to literature from philosophy after failing the *agrégation*, Tournier set himself the task of effecting the passage from metaphysics to the novel. How to produce a novel from a philosophical writing machine? How to write the life of a theory, a cerebral adventure in classical novelistic form? His solution was to take a route which passed through the domain of myth. For Tournier, myth is first of all a fundamental story which is already known by its readers. It comprises an identical schema which is reproduced at different levels of increasing abstraction and which enables it to work simultaneously as a children's story and an ontological theory. Its heroes escape from the books in which they originated, they splinter, proliferate, and end up more famous than the authors who created them. Robinson Crusoe is clearly just such a mythological character. He has been taken up again and again in different guises and filled with economic, moral, educative, philosophical, literary and anthropological resonances. His solitary reproduction of an economic order has been taken as a model for a certain kind of economic theory. His art of solitary survival has been recommended for the edification of Rousseau's fictional pupil in an education 'according to nature'. And his encounter with Friday forms a central figure in the fundamental racism of the west. As a 'hero of solitude' Robinson finds his place as 'one of the constitutive elements of the soul of occidental man' (Tournier 1977: 221). Tournier's novel, *Friday, or the Other Island* (1974) is the successful outcome of a translation of philosophy into literature via the mythological. Since its publication in France in 1967 it has amply fulfilled its mythological vocation. It has been produced in a children's version, dramatized, and the most recent French edition includes the essay by Deleuze which we translate here.

Tournier has disclaimed any intention at formal invention in *Friday*. On the contrary, he works with many of the novel's 'givens', but in the sense in which one speaks of the givens of a problem and to which his story will be one possible solution. His experiment is to make a content with a philosophical form pass into already existing literary forms of expression, thereby giving a specific direction to the novel, or, making a specific *use* of it: to replenish the mythological domain, diverting its pre-existing lines, enriching it with the invention of new mythological images of ways of seeing, feeling, and thinking. From philosophy to the novel, and back to philosophy. Literature, art and science do not require that philosophy provide them with a foundation that they cannot provide for themselves. Deleuze's essay is not a reflection *on* literature, nor an attempt to produce a theory or philosophy *of* literature. It is an essay *in* philosophy which seeks to produce philosophical concepts, its own 'images of thought', as a way of expressing what is expressed elsewhere by other means and in other kinds of images. Philosophy and literature exist *alongside* each other and as distinct means of invention which may nonetheless enter into productive relations with each other and even converge to the point of indiscernibility.

Colin Gordon has aptly described those works by Deleuze devoted to other philosophers as 'anatomies' which produce the effect of 'making a philosophy walk off the page, like a kind of abstract animal' (Gordon 1981: 28).[1] The same could be said of his books and essays devoted to literature. There is, for example, a strange kind of formal resemblance between his book on Kant, a master of philosophy's legislative ambitions (Deleuze 1963), and his book on Proust, which picks out an anti-philosophical image of thought (Deleuze 1973). They are anatomies which resonate through the effect of a simultaneous movement of dismemberment and composition. The resultant lack of friction, the complicity between the life/work under consideration and its rendering in a philosophical form of expression is so striking that very often what Deleuze says of an author he loves can also be said of himself. For example, the account Deleuze and Guattari give of Kafka's procedure of simultaneous *démontage* and composition seems particularly appropriate for a description of certain features of his own works (cf. Deleuze and Guattari 1975: 96). In a Deleuze book each chapter is distinct, but at the same time it is possible to trace lines of connection between each chapter and each of all the other chapters which are both specific and cumulative. This formal structure or method reaches an extreme, culminating point of achievement in *Mille Plateaux*, written with Felix Guattari (1980). It is a book composed of plateaux:

> so many 'specific regions of intensity', each sufficient unto itself but also connected and connectable to others. . . . Each plateau may be read in no matter what order, and related to any other part of the

book. If it is a success, it should function, not only in relation to itself, but in relation to the outside. (Patton 1981: 47)

In those works devoted to an individual life/work, Deleuze's procedure involves a kind of dismantling into meticulously and scrupulously discriminated component parts *of different kinds* and, at the same time, their assembly according to a formal, almost deductive, plan of functional connectivity. One effect of this is a kind of novelistic, narrative momentum as the lines of an immanent or compositional plan are traced, along with their incline or 'line of flight', which bears them along and opens out on to the outside. In *Proust and Signs* (1973) the plan of an experience of signs is plotted according to a number of different but interlocking dimensions: the different regimes of signs distinguished by the narrator of Proust's work; the different relations of these signs to meaning, truth, and time; their role in a literary apprenticeship to signs which result in the discovery of the signs of Art expressing a world of essences as Viewpoints; the role of different kinds of signs in the forced mobilization and disjunct use of different faculties in an activity of sign-interpretation; the different modes of the incarnation of signs in substances; and the creation of an artistic unity of a multiplicity of transversally connected regimes of signs, dimensions of time, and mental faculties. And bearing all of this along there is traced the line of a Search which culminates in the invention of a 'literary machine' – the book itself – for the capture, translation, emission, and *production* of signs: a 'literary machine' which produces effects on itself and on its readers, a book-machine which works and which can function as an instrument. *In effect*, the construction of a non-logical, anti-philosophical image of thought.

Most of Deleuze's books and essays either include a proper name in their titles, or they are concerned with something designated by a proper name: Spinoza, Hume, Kant, Nietzsche, Bergson, Sacher-Masoch, Sade, Proust, Kafka, Francis Bacon, Tournier, Klossowski, Zola, and so on. They are attempts to capture thought as an event, they are cases, experiment-lives, examples without models or, as Claire Parnet puts it, 'acts of thought without image' (Deleuze and Parnet 1977: 32). Deleuze has written of a certain usage of the proper name that it effectuates an individuation by *heccéité*,[2] that it designates an assemblage (*agencement*), or an effect (in the sense in which one speaks of a 'Doppler effect' in physics). The proper name does not identify an author or a subject, even if it is from lives and works that the assemblage-event is disengaged. Deleuze has described the procedure for this kind of individuation as involving the strict blending of the 'critical' and the 'clinical' (Deleuze and Parnet 1977: 142–147). Already in *Sacher-Masoch, An Interpretation* (Deleuze 1971) he had linked the theme of the proper name with that of the blending of the critical and clinical. A brief consideration of some of the topics treated in this book may help to guide us in reading the essay on Tournier.

The subject of perversion which is taken up in the Masoch book and in the essay on Tournier is discussed in a number of places in Deleuze's work (cf. especially the essay on Klossowksi in Deleuze 1969, the discussion of homosexuality in Deleuze 1973, and, of course, Deleuze/ Guattari 1977). However, perversion may be of less interest for its own sake than for the leverage it might provide for prising open the field of desire and for devising a way out of psychoanalytic, Oedipalizing interpretation. And, as a step along this road, Deleuze may be seen as operating a kind of perversion of psychoanalysis, as making a perverse use of psychoanalytic theory.

Sacher-Masoch, An Interpretation is, amongst other things, a use of the literary works of Sade and Masoch to interrogate Freudian theory for its borrowing of the names of these authors to postulate the existence of a sado-masochistic clinical entity. Such an entity would supposedly combine the two perversions within a complementary and dialectical unity based on the association of pleasure and pain. Whilst largely remaining within the terminology of Freudian (and Lacanian) theory – including a brilliant and not unsympathetic discussion of *Beyond the Pleasure Principle* – Deleuze combines 'critical' and 'clinical' forms of analysis to take apart the supposed unity of sadism and masochism and to question the very concept of a sado-masochistic entity.

> The critical (in the literary sense) and the clinical (in the medical sense) may be destined to enter into a new relationship of mutual learning. Symptomatology is always a question of art; the clinical specificities of sadism and masochism are not separable from the literary values peculiar to Sade and Masoch . . . we should aim for a critical and clinical appraisal able to reveal the truly differential mechanisms as well as the artistic originalities. (p. 13)

Sade and Masoch 'present unparalleled configurations of symptoms and signs' (16). It is not, however, a question of a psychoanalytic interpretation of Sade and Masoch, nor indeed is it a question of textual signification. Rather, it is a kind of clinical phenomenology which on the one hand attends to the concrete forms of sadistic and masochistic experience which are depicted, and on the other is a critical analysis of the literary forms invented for the expression of this experience. Throughout his 'presentation' Deleuze insists on the necessity of taking into account the concrete formal conditions from which a particular association of pleasure and pain results (cf. 40, 65, and 88). A consequence of this is that something 'foreign' is introduced into the discussion of perversions, to the extent that perverse desire, in the form of its active assembly of these formal conditions, is shown as immediately plugging in to the outside, in to mythical, historical, political, juridical, aesthetic, metaphysical and even comical dimensions and forms of expression. These concrete formal conditions and forms of expression are not derivatives from some more primary, material level which can be interpreted in turn by reference to a supposed sado-masochistic entity. They are elements combined and transformed in the *invention* of 'new forms of expression, new ways of thinking and feeling and an entirely original language' (16).

A similar effect is produced in the book on Kafka (Deleuze and Guattari 1975) where, by a kind of magnification *ad absurdum*, Oedipal triangulation is made to appear as a particular state or figure of desire and no longer as the model or code for the interpretation of desire. Deleuze and Guattari seek to show how, in Kafka's *Metamorphosis*, the familial-Oedipal triangle is magnified as under a microscope and projected onto a map of the world; how other triangles, from which the family derives both its powers and its fragilities, are made to appear behind and branching out from the family; how one term of the family triangle is replaced by another term from outside, thereby defamiliariz- ing the Oedipal triangle, 'deterritorialising' it (cf. pp. 17–23). This 'perverse use of Oedipus' results in a kind of 'molecularisation' of the forms or terms of the Oedipal structure in the opening out of desire on an immanent plan: 'desire is not then internal to a subject, any more than it tends towards an object: it is strictly immanent to a plan which it does not pre-exist, a plan which it must construct' (Deleuze and Parnet 1977: 108). Such also might be the description of Robinson at the end of Tournier's novel: 'Robinson become elemental in his island itself rendered into the elements.' The attainment of a level beyond subjective or organic forms, a Spinozist eternity.[3]

In *Sacher-Masoch*, as in the essay on Tournier and in so many of Deleuze's books, there is a kind of 'ascent to the impersonal'. The sadist's victims and the masochist's tortures are not subjects or persons. They are essential 'elements' required by the structure of the perversion. It would be stupid, according to Deleuze, to imagine that the sadist requires a masochistic victim or the masochist a sadistic tortures. Both require no more than the incarnation of an element essential to the impersonal perverse situation: 'The woman torturer of masochism cannot be sadistic precisely because she is *in* the masochistic situation, she is an integral part of it, a realization of the masochistic phantasy ... the woman torturer belongs entirely to masochism' (Deleuze 1971: 37). This imper- sonality, this 'Spinozism', describes the terrain of the Death Instinct. Yet it is a strange Death Instinct in which desire immediately invests a style of thought, a politics, an art and the entire history of mankind. It is a Death Instinct on the way to being replaced by a positive conception of desire. In more recent writings, the Death Instinct disappears to the profit of an entirely positive, machinic conception of desire, and to the profit of the impersonal element of an immanent plan wherein desire functions in immediate connection with the Outside *from which it arises*.

But how is it done? How does desire attain its plan of immanence or composition? It is here that the cases Deleuze presents acquire their value as *experiments*. Whether it is a question of desire or language, Deleuze's approach characteristically presents 'examples' of conditions and forms of effectuation, of the form of the event, of the movement of becoming in encounters between things external to each other. For example, in recent books written jointly with Guattari, attention is directed on language in its 'pragmatic' dimension. Pragmatics, often expelled by modern linguistics to the periphery of the study of language, tends to invade and occupy the whole of the language domain (cf. Deleuze and Guattari 1975: ch. 3, and Deleuze and Guattari 1980: ch 4). Language is to be thought of in terms of the conditions and forms of its effectuation as utterance-event. It is thereby brought into an immediate relation with, and conceived of as a direct intervention in, the outside. As in Kafka, the juridical utterance (the verdict, the judgement) provides the model for a form of expression valid for every utterance (Deleuze and Guattari 1975). And what is true for language is true for literary art. Deleuze and Guattari insist on the collective character of the utterance, on the way in which it picks out a collective assemblage of enunciation (*agencement collectif d'énonciation*). And Kafka is seen as putting literature in direct contact with a Jewish-Czech minority in his construction of a new collective assemblage of enunciation for the German language, one which is produced by way of a dismantling or *démontage* of bureaucratic, fascist, capitalist, or Stalinist assemblages of enunciation. In the same way, the 'original languages' invented by Sade and Masoch are produced by way of a taking apart, by a putting into pieces and a transformative composition of distinct component forms of expression. The impersonal and immediately violent language of rationalist demonstration in Sade is counterposed to the equally impersonal language of disavowal and suspense in Masoch's dialectical imagination. The former is described as working in an ironic, institutional fashion by means of its imperative force and its multiplied and condensed descriptions of sadistic activities. The latter works in a humorous, contractual manner through the force of its persuasive and educative rhetorical strategies.

This emphasis on the active force of the utterance, in which conception always 'comes after' – like intelligence in Proust, goaded into action by the violent force of an encountered sign – suggests a certain kind of 'expressionism'.[4] 'Only expression gives us the *method (procédé)*' (Deleuze and Guattari 1975: 29). Deleuze and Guattari have taken up and used to their own effect the distinction between forms of expression and forms of content introduced into linguistic theory by Louis Hjelmslev. The distinction refers to two independent and heterogeneous planes of formalization. Their co-ordination in a given 'regimes of signs' determines the collective assemblages of enunciation on the plane of expression and machinic assemblages of desire on the plane of content. In this use of Hjelmslev's distinction, whilst the two formalizations reciprocally presuppose each other, there is no structural correspondence between the two and a certain primacy is given to expression. In literature, for example, or at least in the literature valued by Deleuze and Guattari, it is the 'machine of expression' which is always in advance and which precedes content, drawing the latter along in its wake. In Kafka, pure sounds disorganize the forms of expression and at the same time blend with new contents in a single, non-formal material which announces a becoming: a becoming-man of an ape through a 'cry', a becoming-animal of man through a 'mournful whining'.

The primacy accorded to expression may also be seen at work in the primacy of conceptualization in scientific thought and experiment. *'To form concepts is a way of living . . .'* (Foucault 1980: 60). Deleuze's work succeeds in capturing thought in flight, the activity of thinking, in rendering thought as an event and in inventing corresponding concepts which create new possibilities for thought. And in so far as thinking implies a way of living, or even an art of life, it provides what he himself finds in Kafka: experimental 'protocols of experience', socio-political protocols for life as experiment. Images of thought: Deleuze's description of David Hume's philosophy as a kind of science fiction in the domain of abstraction and conceptual invention (Deleuze 1972: 65) could be applied with equal justice to his own philosophical style.

The essay on Tournier is a fine example of Deleuze's rendering of thought as an experiment-event opening out onto a strange new world which is still somehow recognizably our own. It is hoped that the reader will persevere through the initially unfamiliar scenery of this essay in order to reach the result of the adventure it records.

Notes

1. Gordon's essay remains by far and away the best introduction to Deleuze's thought in English and remains indispensable as a corrective to the somewhat fearful responses to Deleuze's work that have made it better known by reputation than through direct acquaintance. This reputation is largely based on his work with Felix Guattari and in particular their *Anti-Oedipus* (1977). This book may have appeared less strange had English readers been able to become familiar with Deleuze's earlier work. Prior to *Anti-Oedipus*, the only other books available in English translation were *Sacher-Masoch, An Interpretation* and *Proust and Signs* (1967 and 1973). One might have expected from the dates of their English publication, their titles and the topics to which they are devoted, that they would have excited considerable interest and attention from certain quarters. However, they seem to have met with almost complete silence and are now out of print.
2. The concept of *heccéité* is taken by Deleuze and Guattari from Duns Scotus. It is used by them as a concept for a mode of individuation different from that of a

thing or a subject. For example, the mode of individuation of an event, of an hour or a season. It suggests a quality of 'thisness' (cf. Deleuze and Guattari 1980: 318–24).

3. The concept 'plan of immanence or composition' and its opposition to a transcendent 'plan of organization' are developed by Deleuze in his work on Spinoza. See especially 'Spinoza et nous' in Deleuze 1981a: 171–7. For useful treatments of these and other concepts in Deleuze, see Gordon (1981) and Patton (1981). Tournier has explained that *Friday* was written according to a plan of progression through stages corresponding to Spinoza's three kinds of knowledge: despair and retreat to the mire/knowledge based on sensation and feelings; the administered island and production/knowledge based on the sciences and *savoir*; the solar island and solar Robinson/intuition of the essence of the Absolute in artistic and philosophical creation.

4. The concept of expression occurs throughout Deleuze and most notably in the books on Spinoza and Proust (1968 and 1973). In a different context, there is an interesting discussion of expressionism in painting in his recent study of the English painter Francis Bacon (1981b).

References

Deleuze, G. (1963) *La philosophie critique de Kant*, Paris, P.U.F.

Deleuze, G. (1965) *Nietzsche*, Paris, P.U.F

Deleuze, G. (1968) *Spinoza et la problème de l'expression*, Paris, Editions de Minuit.

Deleuze, G. (1969) *Logique du sens*, Paris, Editions de Minuit.

Deleuze, G. (1971) *Sacher-Masoch, An Interpretation*, trans. J. McNeil, London, Faber & Faber. (First published 1967.)

Deleuze, G. (1972) 'Hume' in Francois Chatelet (ed.) *Histoire de la philosophie*, Vol. 4, Paris, Hachette.

Deleuze, G. (1973) *Proust and Signs*, trans. R. Howard, London, Allen Lane. (First published 1964.)

Deleuze, G. (1981a) *Spinoza, philosophie pratique*, Paris, Editions de Minuit.

Deleuze, G. (1981b) *Francis Bacon. Logique de la sensation*, Paris, Editions de la Différence.

Deleuze, G and **Guattari, F.** (1975) *Kafka, pour une littérature mineure*, Paris, Editions de Minuit.

Deleuze, G. and **Guattari, F.** (1977) *Anti-Oedipus*, trans. M. Seem, R. Hurley, H.R. Lane, New York, Viking Press.

Deleuze, G. and **Guattari, F.** (1980) *Mille Plateaux*, Paris, Editions de Minuit.

Deleuze, G. and **Parnet, C.** (1977) *Dialogues*, Paris, Flammarion.

Foucault, M. (1980) 'Georges Canguilhem: philosopher of error' in *I&C*, No. 7, *Technologies of the Human Sciences*.

Gordon, C. (1981) 'The subtracting machine in *I&C*, No. 8, *Power and Desire: Diagrams of the social*.

Patton, P. (1981) 'Notes for a glossary' in *I&C*, No. 8, *Power and Desire: Diagrams of the social*.

Tournier, M. (1974) *Friday, or the Other Island*, Harmondsworth, Penguin.

Tournier, M. (1977) *La vent Paraclet*, Paris, Gallimard.

Michel Tournier and the world without others

Gilles Deleuze

> The goat abruptly stopped grazing and looked up with a stalk of grass hanging from its lips. Then it seemed to grin and reared up on its hind legs; and thus walked several paces towards Friday, waving its forefeet and nodding its immense horns as though acknowledging the applause of a crowd of spectators. This astonishing performance turned Friday rigid with amazement. When it was within a few yards of him the goat dropped its forefeet to the ground and suddenly charged like a battering ram – or a great arrow with a flight of fur – with its head lowered and its horns aimed at Friday's chest. Friday flung himself sideways a fraction of a second too late. A musky smell filled his nostrils.[1]

These very beautiful pages recount Friday's struggle with the goat. Friday will be wounded, but the goat will die – 'the great goat is dead.' And Friday announces his mysterious project: the dead goat will fly and sing, a flying and musical goat. For the first part of the project he makes use of a piece of plucked, cleaned and rubbed skin, stretched on a wooden structure. Tied to a fishing rod, the goat amplifies every single movement of the line, assuming the function of a gigantic celestial float, transcribing the water on the sky. For the second stage of the project, Friday uses the head and intestines, making an instrument of them that he puts in a dead tree in order to produce an instantaneous symphony in which the only player will be the wind: it is in this way that the earth's rumour is transported likewise into the sky and becomes an organized celestial sound, a pansonority, 'music that was truly of the elements'.[2] In these two ways the great dead goat liberates the Elements. One will notice that the earth and air play less the role of particular elements than that of two completely opposed figures, each bringing together the four elements on its own account. But the earth is what holds them in and constrains them, and contains them in the depth of bodies, whereas the sky, with the light and sun, raises them to a free and pure state, freed from their limits to form a cosmic surface energy, single yet peculiar to each element. There is thus a fire, water, air and earth, all of which are terrestrial but also an aeriel or celestial earth, water, fire and air. There is a struggle between earth and sky in which the stake is the imprisonment, or liberation of all the elements. The island is the frontier or focus of the struggle. This is why it is so important to know on which side it will come down, whether it is able to disgorge its fire, earth and water into the sky to become itself solar. The hero of the novel is the island as much as Robinson and Friday. The island changes its figure in the course of a series of doublings, just as much as Robinson changes his form in the course of a series of metamorphoses. The subjective series of Robinson is inseparable from the series of the states of the island.

The final term is Robinson become elemental in his island itself returned to the elements: a Robinson of the sun in the island become solar, uranian in Uranus. It is not therefore the origin which matters here, but on the contrary the result, the final goal revealed across all kinds of avatars. This is the first major difference from Defoe's Robinson. It has often been remarked that the theme of Robinson in Defoe was not only a story, but the 'instrument of an investigation': an investigation whose point of departure is the deserted island and which claims to reconstitute the origins and the rigorous order of works, and the conquests which will follow from this over time. But it is clear that the investigation is doubly flawed. On the one hand the image of the origin presupposes what it claims to produce (cf. everything that Robinson salvages from the wreck). On the other hand, the world which is re-produced on the basis of this origin is the equivalent of the *real*, that is to say, of the economic world, or the world as it would be, as it should be if there were no sexuality (cf. the elimination of all sexuality in Defoe's Robinson).[3] Must one conclude from this that sexuality is the only fantastic principle capable of making the world deviate from the rigorous economic order assigned to it by its origin? In short, in Defoe, the intention was good: what becomes of a man who finds himself alone, without the Other, on a deserted island? But the problem was badly posed. For, instead of leading a desexualized Robinson to an origin which reproduces an economic world analogous to our own, an archetype of our world, it is necessary to carry a desexualized Robinson to *ends completely different and divergent* from ours, in a fantastic world which has itself deviated. In posing the problem in terms of ends and not of origin Tournier prevents himself from allowing Robinson to leave the island. The end, the final aim of Robinson is 'de-humanization', the encounter of libido with free elements, the discovery of a cosmic energy or of a great elemental Health which can only arise in the island and, then, only to the extent that the island has become aeriel or solar. Henry Miller has referred to these 'new-born wailings of the fundamental elements, helium, oxygen, silica, iron'. And doubtless there is something of Miller and even Lawrence in this Robinson of helium and oxygen: the dead goat already organizes the wailing of the fundamental elements.

But the reader also has the impression that this great Health of Tournier's Robinson hides something which is not at all Millerian or Lawrentian. Might it not be that what it implies is this wholly essential *deviation*, inseparable from the sexuality of the desert? Tournier's Robinson is opposed to Defoe's but three traits which are rigorously interlinked: he is related to ends, to aims, rather than to an origin; he is sexualized; and the ends represent a fantastic deviation from our world, under the influence of a transformed sexuality, rather than an economic reproduction of our world under the action of a continuous labour. This Robinson does nothing perverse strictly speaking; and yet how does one rid oneself of the impression that he is perverse himself, perverse in the sense of Freud's definition, of one who deviates with respect to the aims of the sexual instinct? It was the same thing, in Defoe, to relate Robinson to the origin, and to make him produce a world in conformity with our own; it is the same thing in Tournier to relate him to aims, and to make him deviate, diverge with respect to aims. Related to origins, Robinson must necessarily reproduce our world, but, related to aims, he of necessity deviates. A strange deviation which is, however, not of the kind Freud speaks of, since it is solar and takes the elements for its objects: such is the meaning of Uranus.

> If this is to be translated into human language, I must consider myself feminine and the bride of the sky. But that kind of anthropomorphism is meaningless. The truth is that at the height to which Friday and I have soared difference of sex is left behind. Friday may be identified with Venus, just as I may be said, in human terms, to open my body to the embrace of the sun (*je m'ouvre à la fécondation de l'Astre Majeur*).[4]

If it is true that neurosis is the negative of perversion, will not perversion for its part be the *elemental* of neurosis?

Perversion is a bastard concept, half-juridical and half-medical. But neither medicine nor law gains from the concept. In the renewal of interest in such a concept today it seems that the reason for its possible relation with medicine as much as with justice − a very ambiguous relation − is sought for in a structure of perversion itself. The point of departure is this: perversion is not defined by the force of a desire in the system of drives; the pervert is not someone who desires but someone who introduces desire into a completely different system and makes it play there the role of an interior limit, of a virtual source or a zero point (the famous Sadian apathy). The pervert is not an ego who desires; nor is the

Other (*Autre*) for him a desire object endowed with real existence. Tournier's novel, however, is not a thesis on perversion. It is not a novel with a thesis. Nor is it a novel of characters, since there are no others. Nor a novel of interior analysis, Robinson having little interiority. It is, astonishingly, a comic novel of adventures, and a cosmic novel of avatars. Rather than a thesis on perversion it is a novel which develops the thesis of Robinson itself: the man without others on his island. But the 'thesis' acquires the more meaning as, rather than being related to a supposed origin, it promises adventures: what will happen in the insular world without an Other? One will seek then first of all for what the Other signifies by its *effects*: one will seek for the effects of the absence of an Other on the island, one will seek to induce what the effects of the presence of Others in the habitual world are, one will conclude what the Other is and what its absence consists of. The effects of the absence of Others are the true adventures of the mind: an inductive experimental novel. Now philosophical reflection can record what the novel shows with so much force and life.

The first effect of others is the organization of a marginal world around each object that I perceive or each idea that I think, a setting, a background, from whence other objects, other ideas can arise, according to laws of transition which regulate the passage from one to the other. I look at an object, then I turn away leaving it to re-enter the background at the same time as a new object arises from the background for my attention. If this new object doesn't hurt me, if it doesn't happen to strike me with the violence of a projectile (as when one bumps against something that one hasn't seen), it is because the first object had an entire margin where I already felt the pre-existence of subsequent objects, of an entire field of virtualities and potentialities that I already knew were capable of being actualized. Now such a knowledge or feeling of marginal existence is only possible through other people:

> He discovered that for all of us the presence of other people is a
> powerful element of distraction, not only because they constantly
> break into our activities, but because the mere possibility of their
> doing so illumines a world of matters situated at the edge of our
> consciousness but capable at any moment of becoming its centre.[5]

The part of the object that I do not see, I simultaneously posit as being visible to others; so much so that when I have gone round in order to reach this hidden part, I have rejoined the others behind the object in order to reach a foreseeable totalization of it. And I feel the objects behind my back as joining up and forming a world precisely because they are visible and seen by other people. And this *depth* for me, according to which objects overlap and merge with each other, and are hidden one behind the other, I experience as being also a *possible breadth* for others, a breadth where the objects fall into line and are pacified (from the point of view of another depth). In short, the other makes possible the margins and transitions in the world. It is the gentleness of contiguities and resemblances. It regulates the transformation of form and ground, the variations of depth. It prevents assaults from behind. It peoples the world with a benevolent rumour. It makes things incline towards each other, and from one to another find natural complements. When one complains of the cruelties of other people one forgets that even more deadly cruelty that things would have if there were no others. Other people relativize the not-known, the not-perceived, since, for me, other people introduce the sign of the not-perceived into what I perceive, causing me to grasp what I don't perceive as perceivable for others. In all of these meanings, it is always through others that my desire passes and receives an object. I desire nothing which may not be seen, thought, possessed by a possible other. That is the foundation of my desire. It is always other people who fasten my desire down onto the object.

What happens when the Other is absent in the structure of the world? Only the brutal opposition of sky and earth reigns with an insupportable light and an obscure abyss: 'the summary law of all or nothing'. The known and the not-known, the perceived and the non-perceived confront each other absolutely in an unconditional combat. 'My vision of the island is reduced to that of my own eyes, and what I do not see of it is to me a total unknown. Everywhere where I am not total darkness reigns.'[6] Raw and black world, without potentialities or virtualities: it is the category of the possible which has collapsed. Instead of relatively harmonious forms arising from a ground and entering the world to inhabit it in accordance with an order set by space and time, nothing more than abstract lines, luminous and wounding, nothing more than a without-ground, rebellious and grasping. Nothing but the Elements. *The without-ground and the abstract line have replaced the model and the ground.* Everything is implacable. Having ceased to stretch and bend towards each other, objects rise up menacingly; we then discover cruelties which are no longer those of man. It is as if each object, having surrendered its model, reduced now to its hardest lines, slaps us or strikes us from behind. The absence of others is when one bumps into things and when the stupefying speed of our movements is revealed to us.

> Nakedness is a luxury in which a man may only indulge without peril to himself when he is warmly surrounded by the multitude of his fellows. For Robinson, while his soul had not yet undergone any change, it was a trial of desperate temerity. Stripped of its threadbare garments – worn, tattered and sullied by the fruit of civilized millenia, and impregnated with human associations – his vulnerable body was at the mercy of every hostile element.[7]

There are no longer any transitions; gone is the softness of contiguities and resemblances which allow us to inhabit the world. Nothing subsists except unbridgeable depths, absolute differences and distances, or even the opposite, unbearable repetitions, like so many exactly superimposed durations.

In comparing the first effects of its presence with those of its absence, we can say what the Other is. The error of philosophical theories is to reduce the Other sometimes to a particular object, sometimes to another subject (even a conception like Sartre's in *Being and Nothingness* is content to bring together these two determinations, making of the Other an object under my gaze, even if he gazes at me in turn and transforms me into an object). But the Other is neither an object in the field of my perception, nor a subject who perceives me: the Other is first of all a structure of the perceptual field without which this field, in its totality, could not function as it does. That this structure may be effectuated by real persons, by variable subjects, me for you and you for me, does not prevent it from pre-existing, as a condition of organization in general, the terms which actualize it in every organized perceptual field – yours, mine. Thus, *The Other-a priori* as an absolute structure is the foundation of the relativity of other people as terms effectuating the structure in each field. But what is this structure? It is that of the possible. A frightened face is the expression of a possible world which is frightening, or of something frightening in the world, which I have not myself yet seen. Let it be understood that the possible is not here an abstract category designating something which does not exist: the possible world which is expressed exists perfectly, but it does not exist (actually) outside of that which expresses it. The terrified face does not resemble the terrifying thing, it implies it, it envelops it as something other, in a kind of torsion which puts the expressed in that which does the expressing. When I in my turn and for myself grasp the reality of what the Other was expressing, I do nothing except explicate the Other, develop and realize the corresponding possible world. It is true that the Other already gives a certain reality to the possible that it envelops: in speaking, precisely. The Other is the existence of the enveloped possible. Language is the reality of the possible as such. The ego is the development, the explication of possibles, their processes of realization in the actual. Of Albertine glimpsed, Proust says that she envelops or expresses the beach and the unfurling of waves: 'If she had seen me, what could I have represented to her? From the depths of what universe did she discern me?' Love, jealousy, will be the attempt to develop, to unfold this possible world called Albertine. In short, the Other as structure is *the expression of a possible world*, it is the expressed grasped as not yet existing outside of that which expresses it.

Each of these men was a *possible* world, having its own coherence, its values, its sources of attraction and repulsion, its centre of gravity.

And with all the differences between them, each of these possible worlds at that moment shared a vision, casual and superficial, of the island of Speranza, which caused them to act in common, and which incidentally contained a shipwrecked man called Robinson and his half-caste servant. For the present this picture occupied their minds, destined very soon to be returned to the limbo from which it had been briefly plucked by the accident of the *Heron*'s getting off course. And each of these possible worlds naively proclaimed itself the reality. That was what other people were: the possible obstinately passing for the real.[8]

We are now better able to understand the effects of the presence of the Other. Modern psychology has perfected a rich series of categories which explain the functioning of the perceptual field and of the variation of objects in this field: form–ground; depth–length; theme–potentiality; profile–unity of object; fringe–centre; text–context; thetic–non-thetic; transitive states–substantive parts, etc. But the corresponding philosophical problem is not perhaps so well posed: it is asked whether these categories belong to the perceptual field itself and are immanent to it (monism), or whether they refer to subjective syntheses exercised on a substance of perception (dualism). It would be wrong to reject the dualist interpretation on the grounds that perception is not achieved by a judging intellectual synthesis; one can evidently conceive of passive sensible syntheses of a completely different type being exercised on a substance (Husserl never renounced a certain dualism in this sense). But, even so, we doubt whether dualism is well defined so long as this definition is established in terms of a substance of the perceptual field and pre-reflexive syntheses of the ego. True dualism is to be found elsewhere: between the effects of the 'The Other-as-structure' in the perceptual field, and the effects of its absence (what perception would be if there were no Other). It must be understood that the Other is not one structure amongst others in the field of perception (in the sense that, for example, one might think of it as naturally different from objects). *The Other is the structure which conditions the whole field* and the functioning of this whole, in making possible the constitution and application of the preceding categories. It is not the ego, it is the Other as structure which makes perception possible. The authors who badly interpret dualism are therefore the same ones who fail to abandon the alternative according to which the Other is either a particular object in the field or another subject of the field. In defining the Other, following Tournier, as the expression of a possible world, we make it, on the contrary, the *a priori* principle of organization of every perceptual field according to the categories, we make it the structure which makes possible the functioning as well as the 'categorization' of this field. True dualism then appears with the absence of the Other: what happens to the perceptual field in this case? Is it structured according to other categories? Or, on the contrary, does it open on to a very special material, causing us to penetrate a particular informalism? This is Robinson's adventure.

The thesis, the Robinson-hypothesis, has one great advantage: it presents to us the progressive effacement of the Other-as-structure as the result of the circumstances of the desert island. To be sure, it still survives and functions, long after Robinson ceases to encounter on the island any actual terms or persons to effectuate it. But there comes a moment when the structure is finished: 'Those lights have vanished from my consciousness. For a long time, fostered by imagination, they continued to reach me. Now it is over, and the darkness has closed in.'[9] And when Robinson encounters Friday, we will see that it is no longer as an Other that he grasps him. And when a ship lands at the end, Robinson will know that he can no longer restore men in their function as Others since the structure that they might thus fulfil has itself disappeared:

> That was what other people were: the possible obstinately passing for the real. All Robinson's upbringing had taught him that to reject the affirmation was cruel, egotistical and immoral; but this was an attitude of mind that he had lost during the years, and now he wondered if he could ever recover it.[10]

Now this progressive but irreversible dissolution of the structure, is this not what the pervert achieves by other means in his interior 'island'? To speak like Lacan, the 'forclusion' of the Other means that others (*autres*) are no longer apprehended as Others (*des autruis*), since the structure is lacking which would be able to give them this place and function. But is it not just as much the whole of our perceived world which collapses? To give way to something else . . .?

Let us return to the effects of the presence of Others such as they derive from the definition of 'the Other as expression of a possible world'. The fundamental effect is the distinction of my consciousness and its object. This distinction derives in effect from The Other-as-structure. Populating the world of possibilities, grounds, fringes, transitions – registering the possibility of a frightening world when I was not yet frightened, or even to the contrary, the possibility of a reassuring world when I am myself really frightened by the world – enveloping under other aspects the same world which remains developed completely differently before me – constituting in the world so many nodules which contain possible worlds: this is what the Other is.[11] Consequently, the Other makes my consciousness fall of necessity into an 'I was', into a past which no longer coincides with the object. Before the Other appears there was, for example, a reassuring world from which one did not distinguish my consciousness; the Other arises, expressing the possibility of a frightening world which is not developed without making the previous world pass away. I myself am nothing other than my past objects, my ego is only made of a past world, precisely the one which the Other causes to pass away. If the Other is a possible world, I am a past world. The whole mistake of theories of knowledge is to postulate the contemporaneity of the subject and object, whereas the former is not constituted except by the annihilation of the latter.

> Then, suddenly there was a click. The subject breaks away from the object, divesting it of a part of its colour and substance. There is a rift in the scheme of things, and a whole range of objects crumbles in becoming *me*, each object transferring its quality to an appropriate subject. The light becomes the eye and as such no longer exists: it is simply the stimulation of the retina. The smell becomes the nostril – and the world declares itself odourless. The song of the wind in the trees is disavowed: it was nothing but a quivering of the tympani. . . . The subject is the disqualified object. My eye is the corpse of light and colour. My nose is all that remains of odours when their unreality has been demonstrated. My hand refutes the thing it holds. Thus the problem of awareness is born of anachronism. It implies the simultaneous existence of the subject with the object, whose mysterious relationship to himself he seeks to define. But subject and object cannot exist apart from one another since they are one and the same thing, at first integrated into the real world and then cast out by it.[12]

The Other, then, ensures the distinction of consciousness and its object as a temporal distinction. The first effect of its presence concerned space and the distribution of the categories of perception; but the second effect, perhaps more profound, concerns time and its dimensions, of the before and after in time. How could there still be a past when the Other no longer functions?

In the absence of the Other, consciousness and its object are one. There is no longer any possibility of error: not merely because the Other is no longer there, constituting the tribunal of all reality, disputing, invalidating or confirming what I believe I see, but because, its structure being missing, my consciousness is left to join or coincide with the object in an eternal present.

> And it is as though, in consequence, my days had re-arranged themselves. No longer do they jostle on each other's heels. Each stands separate and upright, proudly affirming its own worth. And since they are no longer to be distinguished as the stages of a plan in process of execution, they so resemble each other as to be superimposed in my memory, so that I seem to be ceaselessly re-living the same day.[13]

Consciousness ceases to be a light cast on objects in order to become a pure phosphorescence of things in themselves. Robinson is only the consciousness of the island, but the consciousness of the island is the consciousness the island has of itself, it is the island in itself. One now understands the paradox of the desert island: the castaway, if he is alone, if he has lost the Other-as-structure, does not make the island any less a deserted island; instead, he seals it. The island is called Speranza, but who is I? 'The question is far from being an idle one, nor is it even unanswerable. Because if it is not *him* then it must be *Speranza*.'[14] Thus Robinson gets progressively nearer to a revelation: he had experienced the loss of the Other first as a fundamental perturbation of the world; nothing continued to exist except the opposition of light and darkness, everything made itself wounding, the world had lost its virtualities and transitions. But (slowly) he discovers that it is rather Others who perturbed the world. *They* were the perturbation. The Others having disappeared, it is not only the days that rise up anew; things also, which are no longer pressed down on top of each other by the Others. Desire also is no longer tied down to an object or a possible world expressed by the Other. The desert island rights itself up again, in a generalized erection.

Consciousness has become not only a phosphorescence interior to things, but a fire in their heads, a light over each thing, a 'flying I'. In this illumination *something else* appears: an aeriel double of each thing: 'I seemed to glimpse *another island* hidden . . . Now I have been transported to that other Speranza, I am fixed in a moment of innocence.'[15] It is this that the novel excels in describing: in every case the extraordinary birth of the erected double. Now, what exactly is the difference between the thing as it appears in the presence of Others and the double which tends to release itself in their absence? The point is that Others preside over the organization of the world into objects, and over the transitive relations between these objects. Objects only existed through the possibilities with which the Other populates the world; none are closed on themselves nor opened onto other objects except as a function of the possible world expressed by the Other. In short: it is Others who imprisoned the elements within the limits of bodies and, at the furthest point, within the limits of the earth. For the earth is itself only the great body which retains the elements. The earth is only earth when populated by Others. It is Others who manufacture bodies from elements, objects from bodies, as they manufacture their own faces from the worlds they express. The liberated double, when otherness collapses, is not then a replica of things. The double, on the contrary, is the re-erected image in which the elements are free and recover themselves, all the elements having become celestial, and forming a thousand capricious elemental figures. And first of all, the figure of a solar and dehumanized Robinson:

Sun, are you pleased with me? Look at me. Is my transformation
sufficiently in the manner of your own radiance? My beard, which
pointed earthwards like a cluster of earthbound roots, has vanished
and now my head carries its glowing locks like a flame reaching
upwards to the sky. I am an arrow aimed at your heart.[16]

Everything happens as if the whole earth attempts to escape through the
island, not only reinstating the other elements that it held unduly under
the influence of the Other, but tracing by itself its own aeriel double
which renders it celestial in its turn, and makes it complete for the solar
figures with the other elements in the sky. In short, Others, enveloping
possible worlds, are what prevent the doubles from uprighting themselves. Other people were the great reducers. So much so that the de-
structuration of the other is not a disorganization of the world, but an
upright-organization in opposition to a supine organization, the uprising,
the release of an image which is at last vertical and without depth; then
of a pure element finally liberated.

Catastrophes were necessary for this production of doubles and
elements: not only the rituals of the great dead goat, but a formidable
explosion in which the island throws up its fire and vomits itself out of
one of its grottoes. But through these catastrophes, upright desire
discovers what is its true object. Did not nature and the earth tell us
already that the object of desire is neither the body nor the thing but only
the Image? And when we desire the Other himself, on what is our desire
focused if not on this little possible world that it expressed, that the Other
was wrong to envelope in himself, instead of allowing it to be free to float
and fly above the world, developed as a glorious double? And when we
contemplate this butterfly which pollinates a flower exactly replicating
the abdomen of its female, and which comes out of the flower bearing on
its head two horns of pollen, it appears that bodies are only detours for
reaching Images, and that sexuality realizes its aim so much better and so
much more promptly if it dispenses with this detour, if it addresses itself
directly to the Images, and finally to the Elements liberated from bodies.
The conjunction of libido with the elements, such is Robinson's deviation;
but the entire history of this deviation of aims is also the 'uprighting' of
things, of the earth, and of desire.

What efforts were needed in order to reach this point and what a story
of adventures! The first of Robinson's reactions was despair. This despair
expresses exactly that moment of neurosis when the Other-as-structure
still functions, even though there is no-one to fulfil or accomplish the
structure. In a certain way it functions that much more rigorously when
it is no longer occupied by real beings. The others (*autres*) are no longer
adjusted to the structure; the latter functions in an empty state and is
accordingly all the more exacting. It ceaselessly drives Robinson back into
an unrecognized personal past, into the traps of memory and the pains of

hallucinations. This moment of neurosis (where Robinson finds himself 'repressed' in his entirety) is incarnated in the wallow that Robinson shares with the hogs:

> Only his eyes, nose and mouth were active, alert from edible weed and toad-spawn drifting on the surface. Rid of all terrestial bonds, his thoughts in a half-stupor pursued vestiges of memory which emerged like phantoms from the past to dance in the blue gaps between the motionless foliage.[17]

The second moment, however, shows that the Other-as-structure begins to crumble. Tearing himself from the wallow, Robinson seeks for a substitute for the Other, capable nevertheless of maintaining the habitual shape that the Other gave to things: order, work. The ordering of time by the water-clock, the installation of a superabundant production, the establishment of a code of laws, the multiplicity of official titles and functions which Robinson entrusts himself with, all of these testify to an effort to repopulate the world with Others who are nonetheless himself, and to maintain the effects of the presence of the Other when the structure is lacking. But the anomaly makes itself felt: whereas Defoe's Robinson prohibits himself from producing beyond his needs, thinking that evil begins with excess of production, Tournier's Robinson launches himself into a 'frenetic' act of production, the only evil being consumption, since one always consumes alone and for oneself. And, parallel to this activity of labour, as a necessary correlate, a strange passion for relaxation and sexuality develops. Stopping his clock sometimes, descending to the bottomless night of a cave, covering the whole of his body with milk, Robinson ensconces himself right in the interior centre of the island, and finds a cavity to curl up in which is like the larval envelope of his own body. A regression more fantastic than that of neurosis since it goes back to the Earth-Mother, to the primordial Mother: 'He himself was that supple dough, caught in the hand of all-powerful stone. He was the bean, caught in the massive, indestructible flesh of Speranza.'[18] Whereas labour conserved the form of objects as so many accumulated vestiges, this involution renounces every formed object for the benefit of an interior of the Earth and a principle of burial. But one has the impression that these two conducts, so different, are singularly complementary. On both sides there is a frenzy, a double frenzy defining the moment of psychosis, and which evidently appears in the return to the Earth and the cosmic genealogy of the schizophrenic, but no less so already in labour, in the production of unconsumable schizophrenic objects, proceeding by piling up and accumulation.[19] Here is then the Other-as-structure which tends to dissolve itself: the psychotic attempts to obviate the absence of real others by installing an order of human vestiges, and to obviate also the dissolution of the structure, by organizing a superhuman filiation.

Neurosis and psychosis – this is the adventure of depth. The Other-as-structure organizes depth and pacifies it, renders it liveable. Thus the troubles of this structure imply a disruption, a turmoil of the depth as an aggressive return of the lost-ground that one can no longer conjure away. Everything has lost its meaning, everything becomes *simulacrum* and *vestige*, even the object of labour, even the beloved, even the world in itself and the ego in the world. . . . Unless, however, there be a salvation for Robinson. Unless Robinson invents a new dimension or a third meaning for the expression 'loss of the Other'. Unless the absence of the Other and the dissolution of his structure doesn't merely disorganize the world but opens up a possibility of salvation. Robinson must return to the surface, discover surfaces. The pure surface, this is perhaps what the Other hides from us. It is perhaps on the surface, like a vapour, that an unknown image of things emerges and, from the earth, a new energetic figure, a superficial energy without any possible Other. For the sky does not at all signify a height which is only the inverse of depth. In their opposition with the deep earth, the air and the sky are the description of a pure surface and the flight over the field of this surface. The solipsistic sky has no depth:

> It is strange prejudice which sets a higher value on depth than on breadth, and which accepts 'superficial' as meaning, not 'of wide extent' but 'of little depth', whereas 'deep', on the other hand signifies 'of great depth' and not 'of small surface'. Yet it seems to me that a feeling such as love is better measured, if it can be measured at all, by the extent of its surface than by its degree of depth.[20]

On the surface there arises, first of all, these doubles or aeriel Images; then, in the celestial flight over the field, these pure and liberated Elements. The generalized erection is that of surfaces, their rectification, the Other vanished. The simulacra arise and become *phantasms* at the surface of the island and the flying over of the sky. Doubles without resemblance and elements without constraint are the two aspects of the phantasm. This restructuration of the world is Robinson's great Health, the conquest of the great Health, or the third meaning of 'loss of the Other'.

It is here that Friday intervenes. For the principal character, as the title says, is Friday, the young boy. Only he can guide and achieve the metamorphosis begun by Robinson, and reveal to him its meaning and aim. All this with innocence and superficiality. It is Friday who destroys the economic and moral order installed on the island by Robinson. It is Friday who kills Robinson's attachment to his little valley, having on his own initiative made another species of mandrake grow by taking his own pleasure there. It is he who blows up the island by smoking prohibited tobacco near a barrel of powder, and who restores the earth, as well as water and fire, to the sky. It is Friday who makes the great dead goat (= Robinson) fly and sing. But it is Friday above all who presents the image of a personal double to Robinson, as necessary complement of the image of the island:

> Robinson turned the question over in his mind. For the first time he was clearly envisaging the possibility that within the crude and brutish half-caste who so exasperated him another Friday might be concealed – just as he had once suspected, before exploring the cave or discovering the combe, that another Speranza might be hidden beneath his cultivated island.[21]

Finally, it is Friday who leads Robinson to the discovery of free Elements, more radical than the Images of Doubles since they are what forms them. What can one say of Friday if not that he is mischievous and playful, but only superficially? Robinson will not cease having ambivalent feelings with regard to him, having saved him only by chance, firing and missing his target, when he wished to kill him.

But the essential thing is that Friday does not function at all as a rediscovered Other. It is too late, the structure having disappeared. Sometimes he functions as a strange object, sometimes as a strange accomplice. Robinson sometimes treats him like a slave whom he attempts to integrate into the economic order of the island, a poor simulacrum, sometimes as the possessor of a new secret which threatens order, a mysterious phantasm. Sometimes he treats him almost like an object or an animal, sometimes as if Friday was a beyond of himself, a beyond of Friday, the double or image of self. Sometimes falling short of Other-ness, sometimes beyond it. The difference is essential. For the Other, in his normal functioning, expresses a possible world; but this possible world exists within our own world and, even if it is not developed or realized without changing the quality of our world, it still conforms to the laws which constitute the order of reality in general and the succession of time. Friday functions completely differently, he indicates an *other (autre)* world supposed as true, an irreducible, solely true double. And on this other world, a double of the Other which he is not, which he cannot be. Not an other, but a completely-other (*autre*) than the Other. Not a replica but a Double: the revealer of pure elements, the one who dissolves objects, bodies, and the earth.

> It seemed indeed that he belonged to some quite other order, wholly opposed to that order of earth and husbandry, on which he could only have a disrupting effect if the effort were made to confine him within it.[22]

That is why he is not even an object of desire for Robinson. For all that

Robinson enclasps Friday's knees, and gazes into his eyes, he can only apprehend his luminous double which retains scarcely more than the free elements escaping from his body.

> As to my sexuality, I may note that at no time has Friday inspired me with any sodomite desire. For one thing, he came too late, when my sexuality had already become elemental and was directed towards Speranza.... It was not a matter of turning me back to human loves but, while leaving me still an elemental, causing me to change my element.[23]

The Other *reduces*: reduces the elements to the earth, the earth to the body, the body to objects. But Friday innocently resurrects the objects and bodies, he carries the earth to the sky, he liberates the elements. To resurrect, to rectify, is also to shorten. The other person is a strange detour, he brings my desires down on objects, my loves on the world. Sexuality is not bound to the act of generation except by such a detour which makes the difference of the sexes pass first of all through the Other. It is firstly in the Other, through the Other that the difference between the sexes is founded, established. To institute a world without Others, to resurrect the world (as Friday does, or rather as Robinson perceives him as doing), is to avoid this detour. It is to separate desire from its *object*, its detour through a body, in order to attach it to a pure *cause*: the Elements.

> there . . . also perished the framework of institutions and myths which permits desire to become *embodied*, in the twofold sense of the word – that is to say, to assume a positive form and to expand itself in the body of a woman.[24]

Robinson can no longer apprehend himself or Friday from the point of view of a differentiated sex. Psychoanalysis is free to see in this abolition of the detour, in this separation of desire's cause from its object, in this return to the elements, the sign of a death instinct – an instinct become solar.

Everything owes its being to the novel here, including the theory which merges into a necessary fiction: a certain theory of the Other. First of all we must attach the greatest importance to the conception of the Other-as-structure: not at all a particular 'form' in a perceptual field (distinct from the 'object' form or 'animal' form), but a system conditioning the functioning of the whole of the perceptual field in general. We must then distinguish *the Other a priori*, which designates this structure, from *this* or *that Other*, which designates the real terms effectuating the structure in such and such a field. If this other is always someone, me for you, you for me, that is to say, in every perceptual field the subject of another field, The Other *a priori*, in return, is no one, since the structure transcends the terms which effectuate it. How then to define it? The expressivity which defines The Other as structure is constituted by the category of the possible. The Other a priori is the *existence* of the possible in general: in so far as the possible only exists as expressed, that is to say in an expressing which does not resemble what is expressed (torsion of the expressed in the expression). When Kierkegaard's hero demands: 'possibilities, possibilities, or else I suffocate', when Henry James demands 'the oxygen of possibility', they do no more than invoke The Other a priori. We have attempted to show in this sense how the Other conditions the whole of the perceptual field, the application to this field of the categories of the perceived object and of the dimensions of the perceived subject, and finally the distribution of other people in their particularity in every field. Indeed, the laws of perception for the constitution of objects (form/ ground, etc.), for the temporal determination of the subject, for the successive determinations of worlds, have seemed to us to depend on the possible in the guise of The Other-as-structure. Even desire, whether it be desire of the object or desire of the Other, depends on this structure. I do not desire any object except as something expressed by the Other in the mode of the possible; I do not desire anything in the Other except the possible worlds it expresses. The Other appears as that which organizes the Elements into the Earth, the earth into bodies, bodies into objects, and which simultaneously regulates and measures the object, perception and desire.

What is the meaning of the 'Robinson' fiction? What is a robinsonade? A world without the Other. Tournier supposes that through a lot of suffering Robinson discovers and conquers a great Health to the extent that things end by being organized completely differently than they are with the Other, because they free an image without resemblance, an ordinarily repressed double of themselves, and that this double in its turn frees ordinarily imprisoned pure elements. It is not the world which is disturbed by the absence of Others; on the contrary, it is the glorious double of the world which is found to be hidden by their presence. Here is Robinson's discovery: discovery of the surface, of the elemental beyond, of the other (*Autre*) than the Other (*Autrui*). Then why the impression that this Great Health is perverse, that this 'rectification' of the world and of desire is also deviation, perversion? For Robinson has no perverse behaviour. But every study of perversion, every novel of perversion is forced to manifest the existence of a 'perverse structure' as principle from which perverse behaviours eventually derive. In this sense the perverse structure may be considered as that which is opposed to The Other-as-structure and is substituted for it. And in the same way that concrete other people are actual and variable terms effectuating this Other-as-structure, the behaviours of perverts, always presupposing a fundamental absence of the Other, are only variable terms effectuating the perverse structure.

Why does the pervert have the tendency to imagine himself as a radiant angel, of helium and fire? Why has he this hatred that is already to be found systematized in Sade simultaneously for the *earth*, for fecundation and for the objects of desire? Tournier's novel does not seek to explain but shows. In this way it is linked, by completely different means, to recent psychoanalytic studies which seem destined to renovate the status of the concept of perversion, and first of all to extricate it from that moralizing uncertainty where it has been kept by the alliance of psychiatry and law. Lacan and his school insist with great force on the necessity of understanding perverse behaviours on the basis of a *structure*, and of defining this structure which conditions behaviours themselves; they insist on the manner in which desire undergoes a kind of *displacement* in this structure, and in which the *cause* of desire is thereby detached from the *object*; on the way in which the *difference of the sexes* is disavowed by the pervert, in favour of an androgynous world of *doubles*; on the annulment of the other in perversion, on the position of a 'beyond the Other', or of an Other (*Autre*) than the Other (*autrui*), as if the Other in the eyes of the pervert releases his own *metaphor*; on the perverse 'desubjectification' – for it is certain that neither his victim nor his accomplice functions as an Other for the pervert.[25] For example, it is not because he wishes to or desires to make the Other suffer that the sadist dispossesses him of his quality as an Other. The opposite is the case, it is because he lacks the Other-as-structure, and lives under a completely different structure serving as conditions of his living world, that he apprehends Others either as victims or as accomplices. But in neither case does he apprehend them as other people but always as Others (*Autres*) rather than Others (*autrui*). Here again, it is striking to see to what extent in Sade the victims and accomplices, with their necessary reversibility, are not at all grasped as Others: but sometimes as detestable bodies, sometimes as doubles or allied Elements (above all not as doubles of the heroes, but as doubles of themselves, always out of their bodies in the conquest of atomic elements).[26]

The fundamental misinterpretation of perversion consists, through a hasty phenomenology of perverse behaviour, as well as on account of the exigencies of law, in referring perversion to certain offences done to other people. And everything persuades us, from the point of view of behaviour, that perversion is nothing without the presence of the Other: voyeurism, exhibitionism, etc. But from the point of view of the structure the contrary is the case: it is because The Other-as-structure is lacking, replaced by a completely different structure, that the real 'others' are not able to play the role of terms effectuating the first disappeared structure, but only, in the second structure, the role of victim-bodies (in the very particular meaning that the pervert attributes to bodies), or the role of accomplice-doubles, accomplice-elements (there again in the very particular sense of the pervert). The world of the pervert is a world without the Other, therefore a world without the possible. The Other is that which possibilizes. The perverse world is a world where the category of the necessary has completely replaced that of the possible: a strange Spinozism where oxygen is lacking replaced by a more elemental energy and a rarefied air (the Sky-Necessity). Every perversion is an othercide (*autruicide*), an altruicide, and so a murdering of possibles. But altruicide is not committed by perverse behaviour, it is presupposed in the perverse structure. All the same, the pervert is perverse not constitutionally but at the end of an adventure which has surely passed through neurosis and bordered on psychosis. This is what Tournier suggests in this extraordinary novel: it is necessary to imagine Robinson perverse; the only robinsonade is perversion itself.

Translated by Graham Burchell

Notes

This is a translation of Gilles Deleuze's 'Michel Tournier et le monde sans autrui', which is published as an appendix to his *Logique du sens*, Editions de Minuit, Paris, 1969, 350–72. Translations of Tournier follow the Penguin English translation – Michel Tournier, *Friday, or The Other Island*, Penguin, 1974. I would like to thank G. Salemohamed for help with this translation. (GB)

1. Michel Tournier (1974: 159–60)
2. Tournier (1974: 171)
3. On Defoe's Robinson, cf. Pierre Macherey's remarks which show how the theme of the origin is bound to an economic reproduction of the world, and to an elimination of the fantastic in favour of a pretended 'reality' of this world: P. Macherey (1978: 240–8).
4. Tournier (1974: 180)
5. Tournier (1974: 33)
6. Tournier (1974: 48)
7. Tournier (1974: 28–9)
8. Tournier (1974: 187–8)
9. Tournier (1974: 49)
10. Tournier (1974: 187–8)
11. Tournier's conception evidently contains Leibnizian echoes (the monad as expression of the world) but also some Sartrean echoes. Sartre's theory in *Being and Nothingness* is the first great theory of the Other because he goes beyond the alternative: is the Other an object (which would be a particular object in the perceptual field) or subject (which would be another subject for another perceptual field)? Sartre is here the precursor of structuralism, for he is the first to have considered the Other as structure proper to, or specificity irreducible to object or subject. But as he defines this structure by the 'gaze' he falls again into the categories of object and subject by making of the Other the one who constitutes me as object when he gazes at me, free to become object when I come to gaze at him. It seems that the Other-as-structure precedes the gaze; the latter rather marks the instant when *someone* comes to fulfil the structure; the gaze only effectuates, actualizes a structure which must be defined independently.
12. Tournier (1974: 81–2)

13. Tournier (1974: 174)
14. Tournier (1974: 74)
15. Tournier (1974: 175)
16. Tournier (1974: 173)
17. Tournier (1974: 35–6)
18. Tournier (1974: 91)
19. Cf. the pages of Henri Michaux describing a table fabricated by a schizophrenic, *Les Grandes épreuves de l'esprit*, Gallimard, 156 sq. Robinson's fabrication of a non-transportable boat is not without analogy.
20. Tournier (1974: 58)
21. Tournier (1974: 148)
22. Tournier (1974: 153)
23. Tournier (1974: 180)
24. Tournier (1974: 97)
25. Cf. Perrier, F. *et al.* (1967). The article by Guy Rosolato, 'Etude des perversions sexuelles à partir du fétichisme', presents some very interesting remarks, albeit too short, on 'the difference of the sexes' and on 'the double' (25–6). Jean Clavreul's article, 'Le couple pervers', shows that neither the victim nor the accomplice occupies the place of the Other. (On 'desubjectification', cf. 110, and on the distinction between Cause and Object of desire, cf. 'Remarques sur la question de la réalité dans les perversions' by the same author in *La Psycho-analyse*, no. 8, 290 sq). It seems that these studies, founded on the structuralism of Lacan and his analysis of *Verleugnung*, are in the process of being developed. The article by Clavreul, 'The Perverse Couple', appears in English translation in S. Schneiderman (ed.) (1980).
26. In Sade, the constant theme of molecular combinations.

References

Deleuze, G. (1969) *Logique du Sens,* Paris, Editions de Minuit.
Macherey, P. (1978) *A Theory of Literary Production,* London, Routledge & Kegan Paul.
Michaux, H. (1966) *Les Grandes Epreuvres de l'Esprit et les innombrables Petites,* Paris, Gallimard.

Perrier, F. *et al.* (1967) *Le désire et la perversion,* Paris, Seuil.
Schneiderman, S. (ed.) (1980) *Returning to Freud: Clinical Psychoanalysis in the School of Lacan,* New Haven, Yale University Press.
Tournier, M. (1974) *Friday, or the Other Island,* Harmondsworth, Penguin.

1984

CHAPTER 5

Borges/Menard/Spinoza[1]

Mike Gane

A close friend of mine, Huguette A., recently lent me some books and magazines. In one of them, Spinoza's *On the Improvement of the Understanding*, I discovered some manuscript pages. It was a fragment of an autobiographical essay written, it seemed, in Huguette's hand. The first page has a piece missing from the top half so the fragment begins in mid-sentence.

... circumstances at Leiden in 1969. I had become friendly with an American undergraduate called George Lewis. When I met him in November 1969 I was delighted, since I hadn't seen him for some time. He told me that he had come in to the University to give a paper, a paper which had involved difficulties of an unusual kind. He told me that some weeks before he had parted with his friend Wiclif. (I never knew whether this was a surname or Christian name: if it was a nickname how had it been acquired, I wondered?) He had 'replaced' Wiclif with a new girlfriend, but his troubles were far from being resolved, for, from the first, the new girlfriend seemed, in many curious respects, 'identical' with Wiclif, he said. She even sat, for instance, in exactly the place Wiclif had habitually used in the library.

Almost from the start, however, said George, there was something odd about her: she seemed to possess a secret book. He swore he had seen her reading it, but whenever he approached her the book would slip out of sight. He confessed that he had searched through her things at the flat but could not locate it. She, for her part, denied that such a book existed. From a certain moment he had become, he admitted to me, obsessively interested in the possible nature of the book: was it an autobiography in which details of their lives were inscribed? Was it a novel written by her? Was it a diary containing a series of frank comments about him? Was it perhaps a work of private fiction written for her by someone else: who was this someone? Was it, he speculated, a sacred book?

Since she continued to deny its existence, he tried all kinds of stratagems to get her to reveal it. His latest was to take up the theory of authorship and to discuss this with her in a provocative manner. On one occasion her response was one of disdainful concern, on another mild amusement tinged with sadness. He now discovered that a response was never repeated. He was never able to 'recreate' exactly a previous mood, and therefore could never make progress. He became aware that each time he looked at her some detail was always different: eyes, hair, expression . . . One night he admitted, he had woken at four and had used a magnifying glass to check the authenticity of the conclusion. Was her face some strange, enchanted mask? He himself changed. He became frightened to let her out of his sight. He marvelled at the subtleties of such barely perceptible transitions.

Then came an important but enigmatic event. He had dreamt in the very paper he had written on the theory of authorship he had discovered just what the secret book was, but, in some distress, could not recall it, nor, on re-reading the paper he had written, could he decipher it. He had, he said, re-read his paper many times, searching without success. He then became frightened that to change the paper in any way might risk the loss of the secret. In a calm voice he asked me if I would help him by coming to his seminar in the afternoon. I replied that I would, and later that day I went to the appointed room. George, looking slightly uneasy, began his paper.

Borges's story 'Pierre Menard, Author of the *Quixote*',[2] could be taken, I suggest, as a fertile text in four overlapping areas in sociology: sociology of religion, sociology of knowledge, sociology of literature, and socio-logical theory. In all four areas it would have a similar function – to raise the question of the nature of reflexivity and authorship and the question of reading. That it does so in a striking and unusual way only serves to increase its value.

First of all let me quickly outline the story. Its form is clear. The critic of the story (first-person narrator) writes to rectify a fallacious inter-pretation of the work of Menard. He refers to 'eminent testimonies' (literary ladies) who will authenticate his authority to speak on Menard. He then gives a complete list of Menard's 'visible' work, some nineteen items. The other part, the 'invisible' but 'interminably heroic' aspects of Menard's work are discussed with reference to parts of *Don Quixote* and a letter dated 30 September 1934. The rest of the piece presents extracts of this letter, a quotation from *Don Quixote*, and commentary from the critic.

The argument of the story is as follows: Menard refuses complete identification (in the manner of Novalis) with Cervantes in writing *Quixote*, or to present an equivalent of *Hamlet* on the Cannebière (as do 'parasitic books'), or to reduplicate Daudet's idea of presenting two figures in one. He chose not to copy it, transcribe it, nor to alter it in free paraphrase. He wanted to 'produce a few pages which would coincide' with those of Cervantes. He thought of two methods of doing this: the first, to be Cervantes, which he rejected; and the other, to be Menard 'and reach the *Quixote* through the experiences of Pierre Menard'. This latter choice has implications for his choice of sections of the work. To attempt this feat, he leaves out the autobiographical sections. Menard says that writing the *Quixote* in this way makes the work realize its inevitability, whereas Cervantes had the aid of chance and 'the inertias of language and invention'. Menard's writing is governed by two rules: first, try out variations, and second, sacrifice them to the original and account for this 'in an irrefutable manner'. The existence of the *Quixote* itself acts as a natural hindrance. For Menard the *Quixote* deliberately neglects local colour thus he begins a 'new conception of the historical novel'. He treats isolated chapters: in Chapter XXXVII where Quixote speaks of the relative virtue of arms and letters, the critic remarks on the remarkable identity of Cervantes and Menard and four possible reasons are entertained. A psychological account suggested by Mme Bachelier (the authoress of the fallacious catalogue), or Menard in transcribing, or it may be the influence of Nietzsche, or Menard may deliberately have proposed an idea contrary to his own. The critic supports the third and fourth suggestions. Then two quotations from the work of Cervantes and Menard are cited (they are identical phrases) by the critic, who concludes that Menard's is superior, because richer. Finally, Menard concludes that 'every man should be capable of all ideas', the critic concludes that Menard has 'enriched the . . . rudimentary art of reading: this new . . . technique . . . of . . . erroneous attribution.'

It is possible at this point to take up the idea of suggesting alternative authors for this essay other than Borges. For example, the idea that the objective meaning of the text, an event, or a life, can be lost only indicates a purely secular conception of history and time. If the essay proposed the idea that a life might be thought of as unforgettable 'even if all men had forgotten it . . . it would point to a requirement not satisfied by man and, simultaneously, to a realm in which it could be satisfied: the memory of God.'[3] This quotation from Walter Benjamin's early work is a possible coincidence with Borges' intent.

The insistence on the 'identity' of words in Cervantes and Menard contrasts sharply with the narrative technique of Raymond Roussel. Roussel developed an unusual technique whereby a work would begin with a specific set of words (expression, quotations) and through the work make a rational transition towards another set which was virtually identical. The logic is thus purely imprisoned in the original language of composition. The essay here, however, plays on identity and in one possible interpretation could be seen as an anarchic response to Roussel which plays securely but humorously on the infirmity of repetition. Such a response to Roussel may have been imagined by Foucault, who wrote a study of Roussel.[4]

Or it could be read as an indulgent gesture which questions from a position of superiority the emptiness of contemporary culture. Culture is reproduced but has become 'richer' only in the mode of irony. One

Marxist critic has written of Eliot's *The Waste Land:* 'The reader who finds his or her access to the poem's "meaning" baulked by its inscrutable gesturing off stage is already in possession of that "meaning" without knowing it. Cultures collapse, but Culture survives, and its form is *The Waste Land:* this is the ideological gesture of the text. . .'[5] The suggestion that the story is by T.S. Eliot would support the critical reading of Menard's project as essentially philistine. The ambiguity of Borges' own position is then thrown into relief.

It is clear, then, initially, and perhaps naively, that reading and authorship are linked. But what of actual readings of the story? It is clear that a considerable variation may be found here. I present a brief account of some of them, and then will provide one of my own.

Silverman

David Silverman's eclectic essay on this story can be found in *Reading Castaneda* (1975). (The revelation that Castaneda's own works might be fictional [and not the anthropology he claimed][6] does not deter Silverman. Castaneda's doctoral thesis poses an acute question of the relevance and value of fictional discourses for social science but 'it does not matter in the least whether any or all of the "events" reported by Castenada ever "took place".'[7] Silverman is interested in the Menard story because it plays on the irony of 'the historical character of our production (of texts, of selves) . . . as we read . . . we locate ourselves in time.' Menard in one sense is Castaneda as he poses the question of historicity, and the retrieval of tradition.[8]

Macherey

The essay by Macherey on Borges (1964) forms the subject of a comment on the fictional theory of narrative in *A Theory of Literary Production* (1978). Although the story of Menard, says Macherey, plays with the problem of identity and difference, the main thrust of the story is to suggest that reading is always directly related to writing. 'The meaning of Menard's apologue is now obvious', he says, 'reading is in the end only a reflection of the wager of writing (and not vice versa); the hesitations of reading, reproduce, perhaps by distortion, the modifications inscribed in the narrative itself. The book is always incomplete because it harbours the possibility of inexhaustible variety.'[9] Thus Macherey, who himself wishes to break the religious myth of reading, finds in Borges a reflection on this break: the work is read while it is written.

Steiner

Steiner (1976) notices that Menard's 'visible' work, the bibliography, is not accidental. It reveals that Menard is very much aware of the problem of developing a universal language. Even the chapter which Menard himself selects for his work is concerned with the *Quixote* translated from Arabic into Spanish. Not a copy but a translation, and Menard, like the translator, seeks to negate time and distance. In opposition to Macherey, Steiner argues that when Menard comes near to succeeding he enters a crisis of identity, for Menard is a mystic. The story is, says Steiner, the 'most acute commentary anyone has offered on translation.'[10] Steiner's own book is subtitled 'Aspects of language and translation', and in an attempt to reflect on the issues of translation of meaning, reading Cervantes and Borges to this end.

Sturrock

For John Sturrock, the story is an illustration of a philosophical problem of dialectics. The bibliography again is invoked as it contains references to chess. Menard constitutes himself as an adversary in a game which strictly parallels that of chess, written, though, by a philosopher (who demonstrates the 'immateriality of fictional objects') in a fictional mode. The writer has to find a 'principle of division', since only then can the production of fiction occur. But in Menard's case the 'ambition is so perverted that the synthesis he eventually produces is identical with the thesis plan which he first began. The dialectical process seems to be short-circuited. The identity is purely textual . . .'[11] Sturrock's general argument is that Borges's themes are principally philosophical, and he finds this confirmed in this story.

Borinsky

Having outlined enthusiastic and laudatory readings, this one is hostile (Alicia Borinsky: 'Repetition, museums, libraries: J. Borges'). She takes an image, from Borges, of a monkey, who sits while the writer writes and when he is finished drinks the remaining ink. She uses this as an image for the anonymity of that other which is active alongside the author: 'the monkey *is* the writer if every writing is a rewriting.' Pierre Menard is 'the most obvious embodiment of the monkey's work'. Understanding the difference between the two passages of *Quixote* is possible only through understanding their authors, she suggests. The critic regards Menard's as superior because it is a 'higher level of artifice . . . displacement and anachronism.' But there is an obvious flaw in Menard's position, for he believed that the Cervantes work was an act of spontaneous invention whereas it is clear from the text that Cervantes was rewriting a work by the moor Cid Hamete Benengeli. So Menard has *not* understood 'the status of the piece he has written . . . his rewriting is, in fact, a misreading. But the form of the error . . . is a simulacrum of the "original" situation which is, already, devoid of the kind of anteriority conveyed by a fixed producer.' The critic, who evidently sides with Menard in the Nimes literary circle, takes the place of Menard and takes the opportunity to make an intervention in these circles. The underlying struggle therefore concerns the meaning of literature and culture as against barbarism. The laughter generated by the story is focused against 'ignorance' which succeeds only to the extent that there is a complicity between 'good readers'. The laughter is aimed at both Menard and the critic, since the latter shares Menard's shallowness. This implies a complicity behind the text between actual writer and reader: the Nimes enterprise is to be scorned because it involves a basic misunderstanding of what good literature is all about '. . . our laughter is the effect of that conspiracy overdetermining the reading.' Literal repetition is naive. The idea of anonymous literature is brought into doubt. Far from the mirror creating a great value in literary endeavour it produces nothing. The whole fabricated story of Menard is only possible because of the specular corroborations of the complicit reviewer.

Borinsky now invokes a class analysis as the basis for an understanding of the Menard story: to locate the intellectual aristocracy in the political history of Argentina. The 'neutrality' of the text acquires significance against that national background. The initial struggle in Argentina involved an antagonism between the culture of Beunos Aires and the backward provinces. The struggle for literacy, a neutral truth, is a struggle for Europe. The dividing lines are drawn and redrawn: a left and a right tradition develops. Borges hears a different lineage from Perón, but the appearance of a third term, the left based on the working class, effects a change in the space of the re-enactment so that the two former lines unite against the left. She concludes: 'By thinking of some of the humorous effects of his texts as the result of a complicity among good readers we have found a *place* for the exchange which would otherwise remain unmarked, neutral, universal. Our reading opens up puzzling analogies between the Borges we encountered and a Perón eager to dilute any direct reference to class antagonism.' In effect, therefore, Borges is able to support a 'neutral' cultural drive which finds its eventual agents are fascists, which continues, paradoxically, a task begun by Perón, whom Borges opposed. Borinsky concludes: 'All this cataloguing and exhibiting is rendered possible . . . by the suspicion that "neutral" discourses work against themselves.'[12]

Monegal

This account claims to provide a biographically based analysis of the genesis of the Menard story in Borges's own development. The idea apparently grew out of another project whereby Borges was attempting to drawn up a document left by an obscure master. A young French writer

discovers the document is a list of things a writer should not do. One of
these is that a writer should shun praise or censure. Thus the origin of the
idea lies in Borges's attempt to write about fame and vanity. But in the
developed idea 'Menard's mad pursuit becomes the centre of the story.'
The young French writer becomes the narrator. 'The story is presented as
a parody of the kind of article written in defence of a misunderstood
genius by one of his followers. . . . It becomes a brilliant parody of French
literary life, with its touches of bigotry, anti-semitism, and adulation of
the upper classes.'

Monegal notes that the phrase Borges gives as the successfully
'reconstructed' Cervantes was already satirical and contained a parody of
the literary model Cervantes was attempting to discredit; since the story
was already in existence, *Quixote* is already a reconstruction. But the
critic does not develop this, rather he turns to the possibility that this
project, unknown to Menard (and here there is a contradiction perhaps),
has opened up the possibility of a 'new poetics, based not on the actual
writing but on its reading'. Monegal cites Borges: 'that imminence of
revelation that is not yet produced is, perhaps, the aesthetic reality'.[13]

Lewis

Finally, I come to my own reading. I suggest that the positions of Menard
and the critic are not identical and the differences between them should
be made the focus of a reading of the story. Menard's letter fragments, if
read together, reveal a striking position: the first implies that the product
of his labour is God, the second that his project is only possible if he
becomes immortal, the third that Cervantes had the collaboration of the
devil, and the fourth that he intends or understands (Sturrock) that in
the future everyman will 'be capable of all ideas'. Clearly a theological
position. What the critic does with these fragments is to turn them into
their opposite, to secularize them. He says, for example, 'Menard
(perhaps without wanting to) has enriched . . . the art of reading.' And in
suggesting the attribution of the *Imitatio Christi* to James Joyce, he
remarks ironically and sarcastically 'is this not a sufficient renovation of
its tenuous spiritual indications?' What Menard proposed was a new
order of writing; the critic proposes a new technique of reading by
erroneous attribution.

Menard wants to eradicate contingency and realize – in an absolute
sense – the text's necessity. He refuses to be Cervantes, thus poses the
question of reading in the most active possible manner: writing. The
critic on the other hand translates this into a technique of reading where
contingency (choice of erroneous author) is given free licence, and the
outcome is perhaps unserious. The meaning of the story now becomes
clear: the choice presented concerns a rigorous theology of the author or
a frivolous game of attributions.[14] Menard's position is superior because

his rigour includes the critique of inertias of spontaneous invention, so that in the process of the sacrifice of the variation to the original and its rationalization of the effect is the fullest possible knowledge of necessity, even though this may not be achieved in practice. On the other hand, the author's account alters Menard's rigorous position, for it reads Menard's *Quixote* as if Menard was the erroneously attributed author (hence the contrast with William James and Russell etc.). For Menard, it is clear, these questions were only ancillary within a deeper project. The critic is suggesting that he puts the possibility of a theological position of understanding textual determination in doubt, though the project to attain it produces a by-product, a new technique of reading – hardly what was sought by Menard. (How Borges would read this story is an open question.)

The meaning of the Menard story has been constructed with reference to authors who have 'quoted' sections of it and have selected various paths across it. Indeed, they quote Menard just as the critic himself has selected passages from Menard. The three 'imaginary' authors constructed earlier are understood in relation to the text in exactly the same way. One author constructs with reference to a selection, another author constructs by providing an extension to the text. In quoting from the story, however, none of the readers have understood the text in a Menardian manner (and realized its necessity), they have all simply used the 'final term of a demonstration' (a reference no doubt to Spinoza's critique of 'conclusions without premises') but whereas Menard produced then destroyed his premises, our readings use only unproduced conclusions (whose necessity is barely grasped). It is not surprising that even closely related readings result in differing judgements: Sturrock sees in Menard's dialectic a 'perverted ambition', whereas my own reading sees his ambition as 'divine'.

Finally, in the light of the Menard story and its readings, I want to turn now to the relation between author, text, and reader. Instead of the laughter at Menard arising out of a complicity of 'good readers' defined in terms of degree of civilization (Borinsky) the laughter arises out of an embarrassment at the realization of his 'divine' ambition and its implication. His position suggests that to know a text, that is *to be able to reproduce it*, to know its necessity, is to acquire divinity. His task is not undertaken naively (to be Cervantes), it is undertaken 'critically' (remaining Menard). He challenges the fact of Cervantes's superiority not as a writer but as a theorist, for Cervantes remains profoundly unconscious of his sources, which perhaps are the true creators of his work – language, other 'inertias' – though he is aware that he is translating something, as is evident in his references to the moor's text.[15] The reduction of chance in the production of conscious knowledge of the text is the aim of the project. But this is posed by Menard in profligate manner, since he destroys it. His theoretical productivity remained personal, private, subjective. There exists the testimony of the author-critic as the sole source of any real authenticity, though this again is indirect and provides no actual theoretical knowledge, indeed this witness betrays the very effort.

Much of the evident interest which Borges has evoked stems from the fact that his project seems to involve an extra-literary element. All of the readings I have quoted have argued that the Menard story provides commentary on tradition, time, translation, dialectics, God, reading, or politics, etc. In this sense Borges is taken as providing the instance of fictional theory, either beyond literature or, most notably reflexively on literature – writing. The problem of the specificity of this instance, in its difference with other modes of theoretical discourse, is provoked, not answered. But Borges does not seek to move to other modalities, though he is not mute on them. The literary mode is for him the chosen mode of the imagination, since the force of the imagination is necessary to speak at one level removed from its object: the image is the product of a censor. A paradox is apparent at this point, since Borges appears a pedantic realistic or documentor. The aim of this referential illusion is to produce a literary effect, an intellectual aesthetic and indirect philosophy. It would entirely ruin the Menard story as literature had the theoretical knowledge attained by Menard been presented. It is sufficient that Borges has produced the story as the effect of such imagined knowledge (and its destruction and betrayal).

The Menard story can therefore be taken as a provocation to theory. Menard himself poses the Spinozist question of the Intellect and the Imagination. In so far as the ontological link between author and text is the site of a question, Menard takes the link in its strongest and most critical reflection. Understanding the text cannot simply mean to comprehend it. It is to understand the conditions of its determinate reproduction. The problem is pointed up clearly in a different, though relevant, articulation by Althusser (another Spinozist) in talking of Solzhenitsyn and the 'Cult of Personality' in Russia: 'a novel of the "cult", however profound, may draw attention to its "lived" effects, but it cannot give an understanding of it; it may put the question of the "cult" on the agenda, but it cannot define the means which will make it possible to remedy these effects.'[16] This theoretical knowledge which literature can indicate it can never provide in a direct manner. Menard's 'reasoning' was burnt, we learn from the critic, but we gain an impression of the space which this knowledge would occupy, and this is enough to divert the sceptical author to another path. In this respect the story, in so far as the author's view is adopted, closes off the path to non-fictional theorizing.

The path that is indicated (by the critic) is that of erroneous attribution. This challenges the ontological link from author position, and because secularized, is perhaps more acceptable? For example, could not the apparent regression in Althusser from a position of giving primacy to theoretical knowledge to an ontotheology of Marx be countered and criticized? The function of this idea in theory more generally could produce interesting and instructive results because it would force open a number of conventionally closed doors. Returning, as Althusser does, to Marx's experiences merely acts to resurrect the sanctity of authoriality. It is indeed naive to imagine the imminent end of sterile artifices that are enshrined in the 'great men', or the emergence in the forms envisaged by Shelley or Wöllflin of a communism of culture presaged by communist oral culture. This should be based on a fatal confusion of personal and private.[17] In fact erroneous attribution is parasitic on such culture, though that is not necessarily a good reason to suppress it. One of the fundamental issues which this idea raises is that of the role of popular or even esoteric presentations of social analyses. Marxism is popularly presented in forms quite remote from those of Marx and in conditions quite different from those envisaged by Marx, yet forcibly defined in a Marxist image nonetheless.

The important translation of European sociology into the Anglo-Saxon cultures in the interwar years by such figures as Talcott Parsons could in many respects be said to have produced the erroneous reality of correct attribution. More than one thesis has been devoted to a problem produced entirely as an effect of translation inadequacies; and more recently the tide has turned so that theses are now being written which restore the originals to their rightful place.

Max Weber's advocacy of fictional history as a theoretical device is reported by Parsons, via von Schelting. It must be said, however, that the device, though outlined after Weber's suggestion that use of the hypothetical alternative outcome to the battle of Marathon might throw light on the analysis of social structures of antiquity, was never developed by Parsons or any major sociologist as a more general method. Six steps were involved in the procedure. They can be summarized as follows: in a social process of any complexity each element which can be established as law-governed is identified, then hypothetical elimination or alteration of these can be attempted and a new outcome constructed: comparison between actual and hypothetical is then possible with the eventual objective of drawing causal conclusions.[18]

Fiction, for Weber, is not limited to historical conjecture, for the 'ideal-type' itself is regarded as a utopia, and not a reconstruction of reality. Ideal types are produced by logical purification: the elements, the raw material are abstracted and recombined into an ideal form. The sociology of knowledge of Karl Mannheim developed, for instance, in *Ideology and Utopia*, uses the notion that ideal types are active in society as world-views playing a dynamic or regressive role in the social process. Sociology appears in this perspective in the following curious form. 'Ideas which correspond to the concretely existing and *de facto* order are designated as 'adequate' and structurally congruous. These are relatively rare and only a mind that has been sociologically fully clarified operates with situationally congruous ideas and motives.' So sociology may play the role here that is, in some respects, an inversion of that proposed by Weber.

A Marxist variation on this problem is the Lukács-Goldmann approach to the literary work. Goldmann, producing a structuralist continuation of Lukács, came to view the great literary work as an 'ideal-typical' fictional expression of a class fraction's world vision: the 'non-conscious' structured unity of the great work is homologous with the unity of the world vision. Again, a series of 'natural' pure types are produced, and this is the object of the sociology of literature: the great text is 'saved' (Goldmann: 1969). A Goldmannesque reading of *Don Quixote* would of course be possible (Pierre Vilar has indeed put forward the view that the work represents the Spanish tragic vision.[19] It is a small step to regard Marx's work as a theoretical utopia expressing the world view of the proletariat in the age of scientific forms.

Borges of course is interested in utopias.[20] In a piece called 'Utopia of a tired man' (1979: 64–70) he describes a meeting with a man called Someone, who lives, *sub specie aeternitatis*, in a land where printing has been abolished. The utopia appears as a bleak communism. Borges describes the piece as 'honest and melancholy' (1979: 93).

It is therefore not novel to suggest a connection between fiction and theory. The whole of this connection is polarized towards the role of fiction as knowledge. Knowledge assumes the form of rationally unified structures: ideal forms, pure types, etc. Borges, however, offers a fictional challenge to this, as Foucault has perceived. Initially stimulated by the idea of the theme of reflexity, infinity, and death, he proposed the project of classifying the dominant forms of reflexivity in European culture: 'a general analysis of all the forms of re-duplication of language . . . these forms . . . are of a limited number and it should be possible to list them in their entirety' (1977: 57). And *The Order of Things* has a Preface which again takes up Borges as stimulant, but this time as critic of the idea of utopia and as proponent of what Foucault calls 'heterotopias': which disturb 'because they make it impossible to name this *and* that, because they shatter or tangle common names, because they destroy "syntax" in advance, and not only the syntax with which we construct sentences but also that less apparent syntax which causes words and things (next to and also opposite one another) to "hold together" . . . heterotopias (such as those to be found so often in Borges) desiccate speech, stop words in their tracks, contest the very possibility of grammar at its source; they dissolve our myths and sterilize the lyricism of our sentences.'[21] Foucault's example is taken from the essay by Borges called 'The analytical language of John Wilkins'.[22] Wilkins's classifications of the universe produce ambiguities which recall the *Celestial Emporium of Benevolent*

Knowledge. 'On those remote pages it is written that animals are divided into (a) those that belong to the Emperor, (b) embalmed ones, (c) those that are trained, (d) suckling pigs, (e) mermaids, (f) fabulous ones, (g) stray dogs, (h) those that are included in this classification, (i) those that tremble as if they were mad, (j) innumerable ones, (k) those drawn with a very fine camel's hair brush, (l) others, (m) those that have just broken a flower vase, (n) those that resemble flies from a distance.' Borges goes on to explain why some such classification cannot be other than arbitrary: 'there is no universe in the organic, unifying sense inherent in that ambiguous word . . . if there is, we must conjecture the words, the definitions, the etymologies, the synonymies of God's secret dictionary.' The general line of theoretical commentary and theoretical fiction provoked Foucault, at least, to theory, in another mode, in *The Order of Things.*

The heterotopia of the Menard story concerns the relation: author–text–reader–context. The (religious) utopia-myth of reading, which is conventional, postulates the effect of the creative writer and the consuming reader, where the text retains its 'external' message. The dialectic at work here in Borges's critique suggests that textual 'identity' under changing conditions becomes 'difference'. (The logic of this dialectic in Borges is uneven and complex (heterotopic): for 'who is Borges?' is a fundamental issue. For Borinsky he is a confused anti-democrat. For some others the fact of Borges's right-wing political affiliation is sufficient reason for censorship: not reading his works.) The dialectic is also active in the reflexive paradox: the mirror in Cervantes[23] becomes the problem of knowledge which Menard attempts to attain (of the necessity of textual production) which, as Menard knows, is not a mirror in the same sense, if it is a mirror at all. Here Macherey is right: theoretical knowledge of the text is not 'in' the text, it is alongside it. In this way it is possible to see Menard, like Macherey, as a Spinozist. The theology of the ontological author is a product of the imagination: the work of the intellect works in a different mode. In so far as this is successful the 'author' 'knows' the 'necessity' of 'his' 'work'.

At this point, George's paper at an end, he said he had one final remark to make. A few minutes before giving the paper he had come across a remarkable new story by Borges which had caused him some anguish. It was a story about a monstrous book, a book without a beginning or end, which had created a monster out of the reader. He began to quote:

The text was closely printed, and it was ordered in versicles. In the upper corners of the pages were Arabic numbers. I noticed that one left-hand page bore the number (let us say) 40,514 and the facing right-hand page 999. I turned the leaf; it was numbered with 8 digits. It also bore a small illustration . . . an anchor drawn with pen and ink. . . .

I noticed my place and closed the book. At once I reopened it. Page by page, in vain, I looked for the illustration of the anchor . . .

I went to bed and did not sleep. At three or four in the morning, I turned on the light. I got down the impossible book and leafed through its pages. On one of them I saw engraved a mark. The upper corner of the page carried a number which I no longer recall, elevated to the ninth power.

I showed no one my treasure. To the luck of owning it was added the fear of having it stolen . . . A prisoner of the book, I almost never went out anymore. After studying its frayed spine and covers with a magnifying glass, I rejected the possibility of a contrivance of any sort . . . At night in the meagre intervals my insomnia granted, I dreamed of the book.

Summer came and went, and I realized that the book was monstrous. What good did it do me to think that I, who looked at the volume with my eyes, who held it in my hands, was any less monstrous?[24]

He put the book down.

What shocked him most of all, he said, was something purely contingent. This book had taken the place, in the life of the author, of a Wiclif bible.

I knew at that instant he knew the secret his dream had revealed to him.

I did not see George very often after that. He mentioned to me at one of our subsequent meetings that he had become a hermit, devoting himself to a 'reconstruction' of the Latin original of Spinoza's works after reading Elwes's criticism that Spinoza's Latin lacked 'the niceties of scholarship'.

For my part I simply wish I could see more of him.

At this point the manuscript broke off. I must return to reconstructing Spinoza.

G.L.

Notes

1. Ideally at this point the reader should read the 'story' 'Pierre Menard, Author of the *Quixote*' by J.L. Borges. The paper here puts into play certain Borgesian techniques, and the effect of pastiche is entirely intended. (Roy Gottfried [1978] has developed a diagrammatic representation of another Borges story; it would be quite feasible to develop a similar one for this paper.) A version of this paper read at the Leicester University Department of Sociology Staff Seminar was preceded by circulation of the Borges story but without attribution. I would like to thank members of the Department for the lively and helpful discussion which followed my paper.

2. J.L. Borges (1970).

3. Quoted by G. Steiner (1976: 63).

4. Now in translation, entitled *Death and the Labyrinth* (1987), Athlone.

5. Terry Eagleton (1978: 149).

6. Richard de Mille, *Castaneda's Journey* (1978), London: Sphere Books.

7. D. Silverman (1975: xi).

8. D. Silverman (1975: 100).

9. P. Macherey (1978: 250).

10. G. Steiner (1976: 67–73).

11. J. Sturrock (1977: 167).

12. Borinsky's argument appears to overlook the fact that *Don Quixote* is not 'neutral', or that its neutralization has to be realized by Menard. Though this terminology appears remote from the whole project.

13. E. Monegal (1978: 327–331).

14. This is not altogether unambiguous. The theology of the author is possible in at least two modes: an onto-theology which regards the author as subject, and a natural theology which, in its Spinozist form, attacks the idea of subject-author. It is the latter which is suggested as appropriate here.

15. Though Borinsky and Monegal argue that Menard is naive here, since they regard Menard as being ignorant of *Quixote* as translation and of Cervantes's parody, it is quite possible to argue that they have not understood the difference between Cervantes's conception of spontaneity as reproduction and Menard's conception of the intellectual understanding of necessity as determinism.

16. L. Althusser (1971: 205).

17. Another important dimension here is the question of public responsibility of texts. This issue is discussed with reference to Marx and Engels in 1850 by Jeffrey Mehlman (1977: 5–6). Unfortunately Mehlman gets in to pseudo-profundities such as 'what is *umheimlich* about the *unheimlich* is that absolutely anything may be *unheimlich . . .*'

18. T. Parsons (1964: 610-24).

19. Pierre Vilar, 'The Age of Don Quixote', in *New Left Review* 68, July–August 1971.

20. J.E. Irby, 'Borges and the Idea of Utopia', in L. Dunham and I. Ivask (1971: 35–45).

21. M. Foucault (1970: xviii).

22. J.L. Borges (1964: 101–5).

23. J.L. Borges (1970: 228–31).

24. J.L. Borges (1979: 88–91).

References

Alazraki, J. (1971) *Jorge Luis Borges*, New York, Columbia University Press.

Alter, R. (1975) *Partial Magic*, Berkeley, University of California Press.

Althusser, L. (1971) *Lenin and Philosophy*, London, New Left Books.

Borges, J.L. (1964) *Other Inquisitions*, London, Souvenir Press.

Borges, J.L. (1965) *Fictions*, London, John Calder.

Borges, J.L. (1970) *Labyrinths*, Harmondsworth, Penguin.

Borges, J.L. (1976a) *Ficciones* (in Spanish), London, Harrap.

Borges, J.L. (1976b) *Doctor Brodie's Report*, Harmondsworth, Penguin.

Borges, J.L. (1979) *The Book of Sand*, Harmondsworth, Penguin.

Borinsky, A. (1977) 'Repetition, museums, libraries: J.L. Borges', in: *Glyph* 2, 1977, Baltimore, Johns Hopkins University Press.

Christ, R.J. (1969) *The Narrow Act. Borges' Act of Allusion*, London, Univers of London Press.

Dunham, L. and Ivask, I. (1971) *The Cardinal Points of Borges*, University of Oklahoma Press.

Eagleton, T. (1978) *Criticism and Ideology*, London, New Left Review Editions.

Foucault, M. (1970) *The Order of*

Things, London, Tavistock.

Foucault, M. (1977) *Language, Counter Memory, Practice*, Ithaca, NY, Cornell University Press.

Goldmann, L. (1969) *The Human Sciences and Philosophy*, London, Cape.

Gottfried, R. (1978) 'Jorge Luis Borges' "The garden of forking paths"' In: *Structuralist Review* 2, 1. Winter 1978. City University of New York.

Macherey, P. (1978) *A Theory of Literary Production*, London, Routledge & Kegan Paul.

Mehlman, J. (1977) *Revolution and Repetition*, Berkeley, University of California Press.

Monegal, E.R. (1978) *Jorge Luis Borges*, New York, E.P. Dutton.

Parsons, T. (1964) *The Structure of Social Action*, New York, Free Press.

Silverman, D. (1975) *Reading Castaneda*, London, Routledge & Kegan Paul.

Stabb, M.S. (1970) *Jorge Luis Borges*, New York, Twayne Publishers.

Steiner, G. (1976) *After Babel*, Oxford, Oxford University Press.

Sturrock, J. (1977) *Paper Tigers*, Oxford, Clarendon Press.

1980

CHAPTER 6

A rose is a rose is ... Umberto Eco, the double agent

Pasi Falk

The labyrinth of *The Name of the Rose* by U. Eco[1]

The Name of the Rose stands amid a labyrinth. It can hardly be at the heart of a classical Greek labyrinth, alongside the Minotaur, at the point to which the traveller always and inevitably returns. It may possibly lie near the exit of a manneristic baroque labyrinth, chanced upon only after numerous attempts and errors, unless one happens to be holding Ariadne's thread. Nor can we exclude the possibility that *The Name of the Rose* was planted along a path in the rhizome labyrinth described by Deleuze and Guattari, where the wanderer may either come across it because 'each path connects to every other path' (Eco/Rosso 1983) – or become irretrievably lost.

It is probably best to begin by eliminating at least a few certain dead ends. To begin with, it is futile to stray along the paths of 'old' literary criticism to seek explanations in the biography and psychology of Umberto Eco (maybe he grew tired of his eternal semiotics and perhaps everything reverts back to his relationship with his mother?), to place the work in literary genres and assign it to its own pigeonhole in the history of literature. No. I am quite ready to accept Eco's own reasons for writing the book: 'I began in March 1978, possessed by an indefinite idea: I was troubled by an obsession to poison a monk . . .' (Eco 1983a). This is as good a reason as any. Pigeonholing the work in turn proves to be a thankless task, because it can with equal justification be placed in several compartments – detective novel, historical novel or 'key novel' – and especially since *The Name of the Rose* does not fit innocently into any given category. The work is characterized by a strange calculating element and an awareness of its own multiplicity of level and meaning. It is an artificial construction and makes no attempt to conceal the fact. As Eco himself described it, *The Name of the Rose* is in any case a 'postmodern' novel in which irony occupies a central role both in the journey into the past and in the construction of the metalinguistic play of the textual world (Eco/Rosso 1983).

But the road of new critics also seems to stop short. Examination of the work as an autonomous entity (forgetting The Author and The Correct Interpretation) that can be broken down into structures and a number of possible interpretations ultimately leads only to tautology. For *The Name of the Rose* (non-innocent) lays its structures bare. The structure and hierarchy of the work is not 'absent' (*la strutture assente*): it is just as much in evidence as the buttresses supporting the walls and vaults (the content) of a Gothic church. Eco himself describes the visibility of the structures of *The Name of the Rose* as follows: in the work 'the scaffolding is so ironclad, so evident, as to leave one suspecting that it may be made of *papier-maché* . . ., like the facades of Las Vegas' (Eco/ Rosso 1983). The work simply contains a (self-)analysis of its own structure. It is both a novel and a story about the construction of a novel, and thus also a semiotic project.

It could even be claimed that *The Name of the Rose* is primarily a semiotic project, in which the deconstruction elements of Eco the semiotician have been turned into the structural elements of a novel. The conspicuousness and the certain artificiality of the structures are part of the semiotic calculatingness: the adaptation, illustration, and playful experimenting with semiotic principles.

Does Eco's semiotic calculatingness extend as far as the world success reaped by the work? Was Eco consciously planning a 'semiotic jackpot'? The question is further made interesting by the fact that while putting the finishing touches to *The Name of the Rose* Eco was also writing the introduction to his collection of articles on 'the role of the reader' (Eco 1979), in which he put forward the following thesis: 'If there is a "jouissance du texte" (Barthes), it cannot be aroused and implemented except by a text producing all the paths of its 'good' reading (no matter how many, no matter how much determined in advance).'

If *The Name of the Rose* is a best-seller in many countries not merely or primarily because it is of a suitable thickness or it has an attractive cover, but because the text provides 'enjoyment', its popularity can at least partly be explained by Eco's successful attempt to build a number of predetermined 'paths of good reading' into his work. To put it crudely, *The Name of the Rose* falls among two categories of 'model readers' (Eco), or rather it creates them. Eco characterizes these two categories from a 'postmodern' angle as the 'naive readers' who, being devoid of any sense of humour, fail to appreciate the duality of level and meaning, and the (civilized) readers, who have lost their innocence, who understand the multiplicity of level and the irony. The former read the novel as a simple tale – as a cross between a detective novel and a historical novel – while the latter understand the joke, the irony and the whole 'metalinguistic and meta-narrative game' (Eco/Rosso 1983). It is precisely on the basis of this duality that Eco describes his work as a postmodern experiment, placing it alongside Joyce's *Ulysses* (which he had studied). Joyce, too, plays with language and breaks the rules of unilevel narrative – but not with the calculatingness of a semiotician.

One unique feature of Eco's postmodern experiment is that he has not forgotten the naive reader (who nevertheless proves to be a mere fiction in his ideal-like purity). And although Eco himself does not consider the naive manner of reading 'fruitful' – and not therefore as a good path of reading – it is in any case one possible approach. Many probably read just the story, charmed, perhaps, by the excitement of the detective story or the romanticism of the past. And this cannot be called false reading or a false interpretation: it is simply one, we could say the first, manner of reading.

The matter is not quite as simple as this. The division into naive and non-naive is no clear dichotomy that may without any problem be likened to the distinction between simple and civilized. Eco himself referred indirectly to this. In the correspondence mentioned (Eco/Rosso 1983) he tells about a young boy, a naive reader, who did not understand a word of the theological reasoning of the work but who nevertheless 'sensed that he was up against a story of labyrinths and not just spatial labyrinths either'. The naivest interpretations – Eco presumes – possibly do not easily get caught up in the philosophical, political or religious *content*, nor in the metalinguistic play of references, but founder over the bare *structures* of the narrative. These interpretations have a notion that the tale is not enclosed within an iron frame – as the less naive reader may be led to believe – but that it is open (*opera aperta*), a tale of several tales. The naive reader possibly does not appreciate the irony but he reads without any necessity for interpretation. The less naive (clever?) reader may catch the irony, but he may at the same time be possessed by an obsession for interpretation. As long ago as the mid-1960s Eco cast doubt on the juxtaposition of avantgarde and conventional entertainment and referred to the (clever) people he met 'who doubt the value of a work because it pleased them too much' (Eco 1983a).

The paths of reading contained in *The Name of the Rose* are thus neither right nor wrong, neither better nor poorer interpretations: they are simply different. It is also clear that there are at least two paths of *good* reading, for the success of the novel cannot be explained by the clever interpreter and the understander of irony alone, nor by the emphathetic naive reader, but by both together and all the types in between. And this is clearly what Eco was consciously striving towards: the creation of a novel always involves the 'creation of the reader' too (Eco 1983a).

No. Eco's *The Name of the Rose* cannot be examined from the point of view of a literary critique. Eco is not a Great Creator of text, nor is he a mere textual effect or noxious appendix. *The Name of the Rose* is indeed part of an uninterrupted 'intertextual' process, but at the same time it is a conscious playing with tales that always turn out to be variations, combinations, mutations or images of other tales. Provocatively, one could say that the third path in the labyrinth of a literary critique, Derrida's deconstructionism and the post-structuralist 'textual strategy' does not seem possible either, simply because *The Name of the Rose* is hardly *text* at all. According to one formulation by Derrida, 'text is text only if on first glance it conceals (. . .) the law of its composition and the rule of the game' (Derrida 1972), and this is precisely what Eco's 'novel' does not do: it provides the keys to its deconstruction and is at the same time a demonstration of intertextuality. Viewed from the perspective of literary critique, analysis of the work becomes a triviality: the explicit must be made even more explicit. I would thus prefer to speak of *the explication of Umberto Eco's semiotic project*, layer by layer from the naive reader's story to the secrets of semiotics.

The Detective Story

The reader does not need to be particularly postmodern to observe that the detective story does not seem familiar merely as an orthodox representative of its genre but also as a compilation of literary borrowings. At this point the 'more civilized' reader, for whom the 'jouissance du texte' is primarily the joy of discovery, steps forward. Naturally, William (of) *Baskerville* is strongly reminiscent of Conan Doyle's Sherlock Holmes and Adso of his assistant Dr. Watson.[2] There is almost no end to the borrowings from and variations on Doyle's works (such as *A Scandal in Bohemia* and *The Adventure of the Devil's Foot*) – as from many other classics. The whole work is in fact built around literary thefts – conscious ones, of course. The stories always tell about other stories, such as Agatha Christie's 'Ten little Indians' (not seven monks), which is a version of an African fairytale or a story about 'ten little Indians'.

Locating the original sources may, of course, be fun in the same way as solving crosswords is, but the paths of good (?) reading contained in *The Name of the Rose* do not end here.

The following paths of reading in the detective story do, however, lead to Eco's semiotic labyrinths.

In the postscript of *The Name of the Rose* Eco speaks of the 'metaphysics' of the detective novel, surmising that readers are captivated by this genre of literature, by no means because there are murders and crimes and because good and evil generally gain their just reward, but because these tales are stories based on inference in their purest form. The adventure is built round the gradual solving of a seemingly inexplicable state of affairs or strange findings by means of inference – also a fundamental method used in medical diagnosis, scientific research or the framing of metaphysical questions.

Eco calls the method of hypothetical inference characteristic of the detective story, in which clues or traces (cf. Derrida) are the basis for assumptions and inference *abduction* – to distinguish it from the two other models, deduction and induction. Abduction, like induction and deduction, has its origin in none other than Aristotle, but the concept of abduction was introduced in a semiotic context by the other classic in the field (alongside Saussure), Charles S. Peirce. Aristotle, the detective novel, and semiotics are thus the fixed points marking out the central magic triangle of *The Name of the Rose*.[3]

These three models of reasoning are distinguished by how the relations between the (general) rule, (its special) case and the (manifest) outcome are determined. Without going further into the differences between these rules of reasoning, abduction may be described as the least mechanical of the three, the most dynamic and in a certain sense also the most creative: there is no given rule in abduction (as there is in deduction), but on the other hand neither is the outcome interpreted mechanically as a case of the rule (as in induction). In abduction results (traces/clues) are the starting point for solving the mystery of both rule and the case by reconstruction of a number of alternative 'possible worlds' and constant testing of their conformity with reality (meta-abduction). And once the relations between the outcome, the rule and the case are clear, the murderer and the motives for the murders have been solved.

But what has this got to do with Eco's semiotic project? Demonstrating the connection does not call for any great detective reasoning, since it is all stated in Eco's semiotic writings, especially those published since *The Name of the Rose* (Eco 1983b, 1984a and 1984b). The year 1983 saw the publication of a work (*The Sign of Three*) edited by Umberto Eco and Thomas A. Sebeok, the theme of which is precisely the logic of detective reasoning, the main characters being Dupin, Holmes and Peirce. In his own article Eco examines the 'three forms' of abduction and uses Voltaire's Zadig as an illustration of overcoded and undercoded abductions (see also Eco 1984b). In this tale Zadig concludes from traces – clues – the whereabouts of the king's runaway horse and dog, and also the outward appearance and behaviour of the animals. A fragment of this tale is included in slightly varied form in *The Name of the Rose* as an indication of William Baskerville's splendid and creative power of abduction (23). But this story, too, has its home in the old Middle East.

The idea of abduction is central both to *The Name of the Rose* and to Eco's semiotic thinking in general. The third type of abduction, 'creative abduction', in which no explanatory rules are stated even as probable alternatives *a priori* but in which this rule has to be discovered *ex novo*, is equally fundamental to the solving of a crime and to the handling of a poetic text (Eco 1984a). And ultimately abduction turns out to be a central element of Eco's 'theory of meaning'.

According to Eco there is an organic link between the theory of meaning and the theory of evidence. Their difference lies not in the duality of semiotic and scientific inference. Semiotic plausibility is based on social conventions, scientific plausibility on other criteria of verifiability. But both are concerned with signs and the processes of inference surrounding them, which are at the same time interpretations. Understanding is never just the recognition of a sign, it is always an interpretation.

Creative abduction also has a role in another story in *The Name of the Rose*, in the reconstruction of Aristotle's lost text on comedy or the comic. Out of the traces left by Aristotle, the extant texts (which are in fact traces of traces, an 'intertextual' continuum of copies, translations, and editions), Eco constructs a 'philosophy of laughter'. But now the principle behind creative abduction and the reconstruction of a 'possible textual world' is by no means a striving towards authenticity, but rather a deliberate falsification explained by the striving to reinforce two interconnected 'rules'.[4] On the one hand the 'dangerous' content of the philosophy of laughter acts as the basic background to the whole detective story, but on the other hand, from the point of view of Eco's semiotic project, it represents criticism and testing of the limits and universal application of the theory of meaning in a way reminiscent of post-structuralist conceptions from Foucault to Lyotard[5] and Derrida to Kristeva.

Creative abduction is responsible to 'reality' – however that is defined – as only part of scientific discourse. This being so, it inevitably takes in a certain 'meta-abduction' (Eco 1984a: 42), in which the possible world of creative abduction is compared in some way or another with reality. But meta-abduction is not essential in fiction, even though it be constructed on the unity of true ('historical facts') and fictive elements, as in *The Name of the Rose*. The reconstruction does not need to be true or even probable, but it may nevertheless be 'textually verisimilar', in keeping with some outcome of trace, as in Borges's 'Babylonian lottery'. And furthermore, the distinction between 'scientific' and 'fictive' abduction may in practice prove very diffuse: is the reconstruction made on the basis of plaster casts of the footprints of the abominable snowman true or fictive? A similar question could be raised in connection with the third abduction theme in *The Name of the Rose*: since we know from the traces (of traces) left by Aristotle that a tract on comedy did once exist but has subsequently been lost, surely it could have been destroyed in the way described in *The Name of the Rose*?

The Historical Novel

The above question may also be extended to *The Name of the Rose* as a historical novel, in which reality and fiction are woven into an unbroken entity. Creative abduction functions in this case too, for the rules act as the common denominator. Whether the world for (re)construction be real, possible or fictive, it must in any case fiction in accordance with certain rules. The textual world created by Eco '*also* includes real history' (Eco 1983a), and so it is also a historical novel: the story of Pope John XXII of Avignon and his quarrel with the ruler of Rome, the story of the dispute between the Pope and the Franciscan, the story of the mediaeval theological and philosophical – scholastic – debate and dispute over the contrast between nominalism and realism, and so on. *The Name of the Rose* is not only a historical novel, it is also a novel about the history of thought.

But why a historical novel? To this one could, to imitate Eco, reply: why not? Or trivially refer to the fact that Eco is not only a semiotician but also an expert on the philosophy of the Middle Ages, and has been since the mid-1950s. But on the other hand Eco himself says that he originally planned to set the story in a modern monastery, and the monk-detective was to have been a faithful reader of *Il Manifesto,* the independent left-wing paper for which Eco himself wrote in the early 1970s. This may act as encouragement to those interpreters who have viewed *The Name of the Rose* as a key novel in the Italy of the 1970s, beset by terrorism, where 'inquisition-trials' were everyday occurrences: *The Name of the Rose* (Le Nom de la Rose) as a great allegorical-satirical novel in the manner of the mediaeval 'rose novel' (*Le Roman de la Rose*)?

Maybe it is so that Eco's only relationship with the present day is one transmitted by television, whereas he has 'first-hand knowledge' of the Middle Ages, as he once said in an interview. Be that as it may, *The Name of the Rose* does, as a novel about the history of thought, seem to launch a new type of 'linguistic game' concerned not simply with hunting out nameless quotations but also with revealing the anachronism of philosophical and theological statements. The well-read reader notes that the idea spoken in the novel by some contemporary mystic of the 'instrumental value of a step ladder in the search for truth' is taken from Wittgenstein (492), or that the episode on the non-existence of God is a direct borrowing from the seventeenth-century mystic Angelus Silesius (501). The anachronism is laid bare. But almost immediately there appears on the scene the even better-read reader, who may perceive the continuum between Wittgenstein's ladder and the neoplatonic mystics, who were using the metaphor of 'Jacob's ladder' as an illustration of a related idea even before the days of *The Name of the Rose.* The quotation from Silesius goes back to a contemporary of *The Name of the Rose,* to Master Eckhart, who put forward the same idea in a less poetic form. The anachronisms thus prove to be intertextual traditions, the roots of which lie in the Middle Ages or even further back in the past. Perhaps Eco is right in describing the Middle Ages as 'our' (= the modern western) childhood, to which we must return again and again to make our anamnesis (Eco 1983a).

The Conversation of Books

Intertextuality is, along with abduction (Eco 1984b), the second organizing principle of *The Name of the Rose*. It is the common denominator uniting the metalinguistic play with quotations and loans, the historical dimension and also the contextual theme on the fate of Aristotle's texts. 'All books always talk about other books: and every tale tells a story told long ago' (Eco 1983a).

The game of literary thefts and nameless quotations could, of course, be played indefinitely, and it need not be limited to literary sources: the 'civilized' reader familiar with art and its history may well note that the monastery librarian paints a detail from a painting (of 1559) by Pieter Breughel (the older) in speaking of pies growing on the roof (80). But this tale, too, has already been told before, in the Flemish proverb tradition. There is indeed a certain charm about the intertextual game by way of illustration, but let us leave future readers the joy of discovery – such as the realization that the cliché-like beginning to the First Day ('it was a beautiful day at the end of November ...') (21) is in fact a tribute to Snoopy (of Peanuts fame) embarking on his career as a writer.

The idea of intertextuality also appears in the frame story of the work 'Naturally, a manuscript', in which Eco the Author does a vanishing trick and frees his text for its intertextual role: the manuscript's many generations of 'family history' as an almost endless series of copies, translations, editions and interpretations. Through the frame story the work is turned into a labyrinth in which the reader and the author are made to lose one another. Here, too, there is of course something strangely familiar. In his vanishing trick Eco in fact describes the historical adventures of Aristotle's texts, and especially *Poetica*, a good picture of which is provided by, for example, the introduction to D.W. Lucas's English version of *Poetica* (1968). In this story manuscripts – the copies, translations, translations of translations, and editions (interpretations) placed in their historical points in time – become subjects which have their own family roots and which fight among themselves for validity and authenticity. A textual adventure that is at the same time family and military history. The effect of intertextuality is complete. Aristotle no longer features as the Author, but as something between an initial explosition and the initiator of a chain letter. The texts live their own lives . . .

The Philosophy of Laughter

The problem of *laughter* is certainly no new theme, for it has been attacked from various angles by such as Henri Bergson, Friedrich Nietzsche of course, Mihail Bakhtin, Sigmund Freud, and Georges Bataille and the so-called post-structuralist thinkers influenced by him. 'The laughing animal' – laughter as a feature of the human species – was mentioned not only by Johan Huitzinga but also by Aristotle, so why not grant him the magic cloak of 'the philosophy of laughter' (even if it is not an authentic reconstruction of the second book of *Poetica*)?

It is therefore not in the least surprising that in one interview Eco said he had always wanted to write about 'the important philosophical problem of laughter' – just as in his work on Rabelais Bakhtin refers to A.J. Herzen's dream of writing 'a history of laughter'. What is interesting and fascinating in this case is that the desire is expressed by the *semiotician* Umberto Eco. For it could be claimed that in the last story of the semiotic project called *The Name of the Rose* the writer Umberto Eco in a certain sense casts doubt on, or at least relativizes, the life's work of semiotician Umberto Eco. In his novel Eco deals with the philosophy of laughter but also with a semiotic problem in a way that is difficult to fit into his semiotic system. The systematic examination of laughter within the confines of semiotic theory may even prove impossible, for the transition of the philosophy of laughter is a transition beyond the confines of semiotics – at a critical distance – just as laughter is the transition from the organized world of signs and meaning (language) to the deconstruction of signs and the reversal of meanings. Laughter exists on the borders of obscurity, in the domain where semiotics became 'semioclasm'. Laughter is born in 'the other world', infringing the borders of meaning and order, in the topsy-turvy world of the festival, the uprising, and the carnival.

In *The Name of the Rose* the philosophy of laughter chiefly comes up in the discussions between William and Jorge, the blind old librarian who turns out to be the murderer, culminating in the apocalyptic finale. Jorge defends *Order*, which extends from the hierarchy of power in society and the authority of the Church to books and the structures of language. The unambiguity and 'naturalness' of the relationship between master and servant are combined in the explicability of meanings. Fear of the Lord and the power of the Word are two sides of the same coin (prologue: 'In the beginning was the Word and the Word was with God, and the Word was God . . .' (11).

Laughter is a violation of order and it thus contains the seed of revolt. When the subordinated laugh at their subordinators, these in turn become subordinated as objects of laughter. Laughter is a threat to order, whether this be called God, the Lord, the Word or Reason.

Jorge had to hide, and finally destroy, 'the philosophy of laughter' because the very fact that it was 'written by a philosopher' made harmless and innocuous laughter serious and dangerous. As Jorge says at the end: '. . . here/in this book/the function of laughter is reversed, it is elevated to art, the doors of the world of the learned are opened to it, it becomes the object of philosophy, and of perfidious theology . . .' (474). The philosophy of laughter points out the close affinity between the festival and the uprising and tells how the former becomes the latter. The philosophy of laughter is the philosophy of revolt.

Has Umberto Eco finally discarded his structuralist-semiotic orthodoxy and gone over to the post-structuralist camp, where the social and semiotic philosophies of revolt are often intertwined (e.g. Deleuze, Foucault, Lyotard and Baudrillard)? Indeed he has not. Eco has not denied his structuralist-semiotic past (herein lies the difference between Eco the semiotician and Eco the writer), but on the other hand his semiotic framing of questions has approached the positions of post-structuralism. In the field of literary critique he has moved towards a 'textual strategy' (the main figure hovering in the background is the post-structuralist Derrida), but in the domain of the 'general theory' of semiotics, too, he is seeking a way out of the structuralist metaphysics of the sign. Eco is no longer content with the structurally sterile object-framing of semiotics, the speaking subject having been eliminated as the most troublesome impurity, thus arriving at a pure (given) system of signs. Questioning the autonomy of the sign and the sign-system reinstates the 'speaking' subject, but as a post-structuralist and not a pre-structuralist theme. It is indicative that Eco ends his 'theory of semiotics' that appeared in 1976 (which is in a way a revised and developed version of the 'absent structure' that appeared in 1968) with a chapter on 'the subject of semiotics'. In it he points out the importance of the 'threshold-trespassing semiotics' represented by Julia Kristeva (*sémanalyse*), even though Eco does not, as he himself says, venture into this field in his work.

Post-structuralist critique of the metaphysics of the sign and the autonomy of the sign system is not concerned with reinstating the transcendental subject, but a subject whose dimensions are both corpo-reality and the historical–social orders binding corporeality. Envisaged thus, the post-structuralist revolt provides a setting in which the structures of meaning and power merge and in which Laughter could well play the main role as the principle combining both the maintaining and the overthrowing of the meanings/order binding the subversive contents of corporeality (Falk 1985).

But Umberto Eco has not become a radical post-structuralist or a philosopher of revolt since 1976. He did not set out to write 'a philosophy of laughter', but a story about its possibility and impossibility. *The Name of the Rose* is a story about the philosophy of laughter and also about its disappearance: an interpretation supported by Eco's recent essay concerning 'The frames of comic "freedom"' (Eco 1984c).

Eco is, after all, reminiscent more of William than of a philosopher of laughter, but on the other hand both have a common opponent: Jorge, a man of Order and one Reason. Eco – like William – dissociates himself from one Reason and one Truth, but sets up the heterogeneous principle of 'sensibility' instead. Neither is there just one Order: William lives in a world that is 'structurable but not completely structurised' and Eco has in turn shifted from the structuralist orthodoxy of semiotics towards a Peirce-inspired 'unlimited semiosis' founded on endless abduction.

'The philosophy of laughter' simply had to be destroyed because it was not possible. Had it been possible, the philosopher-semiotician Umberto Eco would have written it and the writer Eco would never have told the story of how it was destroyed.

Notes

1. Umberto Eco, *The Name of the Rose* (trans. William Weaver), New York: Harcourt & Brace, 1983. (Orig. *Il nome della rosa*, Milano: Bampiani, 1980).

2. We could, of course, stop to 'decode' these names. Baskerville naturally refers to Doyle's well-known Holmes story *The Hound of the Baskervilles* and William (of) could well refer to William of Moerbeke, whose subscript to the Latin version of Aristotle's *Poetica (Primus Aristotelis de arte poetica liber explicit)* dated 1278 supports the theory that a second book of poetics originally existed ('the philosophy of laughter', dealing with comedy). The version 'Adso' may in turn be derived from Watson by the same code transformation by which the keyword 'quatour' opened up the way to the most secret library (finis Africae) and the ultimate solution of the mystery (458) – as has been suggested by Michael P. Carroll (1984).

3. The story of the two angles of a triangle – Aristotle and the detective story – has already been told: Dorothy Sayers found the recipe for the modern detective story in Aristotle in the 1930s. (The article is included in her collection of essays *Unpopular Opinions* of 1946.)

4. Attempts have indeed been made to reconstruct the second book of Aristotle's *Poetica* on authentic scientific criteria. The reconstruction by Lane Cooper (*An Aristotelian Theory of Comedy*) published in 1922, based primarily on the *Poetica* and the strange fragment 'Tractatus Coislinianus', thought to be a summary of Aristotle's theory of comedy, is many times 'less dangerous' than Eco's 'philosophy of laughter' approaching Nietzscheanism. But on the other hand Cooper's reconstruction, too, is only an interpretation.

5. Furthermore, *The Name of the Rose* contains a reference to this French post-structuralist philosophy. In his carnival dream (434) Adso sees 'the great Lyotard', the beast of the book of Job, which could playfully be a reference to Lyotard's earlier (1973) Leviathan-like concept of 'the energy devil of capitalism'.

References

Carroll, M.P. (1984) 'Review of *The Name of the Rose*', *American Anthropologist* 86, 2, June.

Derrida, J. (1972) *La Dissemination*, Paris.

Eco, U. (1976) *A Theory of Semiotics*,

Bloomington, Indiana University Press.
Eco, U. (1979) *The Role of the Reader,*
Bloomington, Indiana University Press.
Eco/Rosso, (1983) *Correspondence.*
Boundary 2, 12, 1, Autumn.
Eco, U. (1983a) Postille a *Il nome della
rosa.*
Eco, U. and **T.A. Sebeok** (eds.) (Eco
1983b) *The Sign of Three,* Bloomington,
Indiana University Press.
Eco, U. (1984a) *Semiotics and the*

Philosophy of Language, London,
Macmillan.
Eco, U. (1984b) 'Intensional Man v.
Extensional Man: A Difficult Dialogue',
in *Cognitive Constraints on
Communication,* eds. L. Vaina & J.
Hintikka.
Eco, U. (1984c) 'The frames of comic
"freedom"', in *Carnival!* ed. Thomas A.
Sebeok, Berlin.
Falk, P. (1985) 'Corporeality and its
fates in history', *Acta Sociologica,* 28, 2.

1985

PART III

Two Manifestos

After representation: recent discussions of the relation between language and literature

Ian Hunter

Introduction

Recent discussion of literary representation has been centred in debates over the question of realism. This discussion remains divided between an *aesthetico-moral criticism* and attempts to install an historically sensitive *formal analysis*. While this division may threaten to obscure important differences between work done on either side, there is no doubting its capacity to organize the field of discussion. We are well prepared to accept that aesthetico-moral approaches will found literary represent-ation in a conception of consciousness or the experiencing subject. From the formalist point of view such a foundation tends to obscure the role of textual rules and conventions. It reduces language to a purely expressive medium whose representational power and moral value derive from a 'humane consciousness'. We seem equally willing to accept that formal analysis can be characterized by its refusal to found literary represent-ation in the experiencing subject, and by its deployment of some concept of 'structure' instead. It is well known that this concept is particularly protean, changing its form and content depending on whether it is specified by linguistic, psychoanalytic, or Marxian discourses. However, in each case it is agreed that, far from founding the representational power of literary texts, the experiencing subject is nothing more than an effect of the structures that make the text possible, be these structures linguistic, psychical, or historical, or some combination of all three.

Of course there is disagreement about the intellectual and political appropriateness of these two positions, and this is reflected in counter-posed valorizations. The achievement of a 'realistic' or 'unforced' representation will be valorized in the aesthetico-moral approach as a realization of experience that transcends sectional norms and technical rules. Meanwhile, the same achievement put under the scrutiny of a formal analysis will be regarded as a mere disguising of formal rules and conventions; a textual sleight-of-hand in which structure is the hidden stage-manager of a performance that produces both the effect of experience and its subject. But, despite these different valorizations, there is a surprising degree of agreement about how to characterize the division of the field itself. It is accepted on both sides that each is attempting to account for the same thing – literary representation – and that the differences in approach can be crudely marked by the opposition between 'humane consciousness' and linguistic (etc.) structure.

In this paper I give some reasons for thinking that this characterization of the field is spurious. In particular I argue that representation is not a concept or process which can be the object of a single account or theory and is instead only a topic heading for a loose collection of practical activities and social artefacts. Generally speaking, the 'aesthetico-moral' and 'formalist' approaches name different bodies of techniques and uses of texts inside this collection. Their overlap is not the result of competing for the same theoretical object (literary representation) but of their recent gravitation to the same social organization: the reformed apparatus of literary pedagogy. If we wish to understand the new relations being formed inside this apparatus then we must give up the idea that we are dealing with two different accounts of literary representation, the one founded in experience and the other in structure.

Experience

Paradoxical as it may sound, at the centre of modern English literature we find a rigorously anti-didactic pedagogical apparatus. Focused in a set of texts (the realist canon) and a body of techniques (those of the seminar of conscience), this apparatus apparently allows students to learn from experience without the imposition of norms, save those embodied in the 'tradition' of language itself. No doubt we are confronted by a *staging* of experience here. We can be equally sure that this staging is one that ties the student's knowledge of the text to the formation of his or her secular conscience. But this does not mean that this experience is staged by irreducibly linguistic or psychical structures. There is no need to think that the practical exercises involved – for example, the exercise of character analysis in which the rhetorical analysis of fictional characters is tied to the introspective scrutiny of the student's character – have foundations any deeper than those provided by the practical deployment of the exercises themselves. Furthermore, it is quite possible to give an account of how such exercises succeed in the staging of educative experiences without making them dependent on the participant's failure to recognize the off-stage structures.[1]

Consider Ian Watt's *The Rise of the Novel*, fairly representative of the aesthetico-moral approach in its account of the advent of literary realism. Briefly, Watt argues that realism is the end-point or goal of a linear history of the novel. His account is structured by the opposition between conventional and expressive techniques. Conventional techniques such as those found in eighteenth-century picaresque novels are, for Watt, simply the enemy of expressive or realistic representation. Hence his history of the novel is a history of the progressive elimination of the conventional and the normative in favour of the realistic. The realist novel of the nineteenth-century is not so much a technical achievement as a reduction of the technical to a form of representation able to represent the inner life of the author and the outer life of society. In Watt's account *techniques* of representation give way to *voice*.

This account may seem to be contradicted by Watt's own disclaimer that 'Formal realism is, of course, like the rules of evidence, only a convention,' (Watt 1957: 33) However, as soon as we read what this convention is, the apparent contradiction dissolves.

> Formal realism, in fact, is the narrative embodiment of a premise that Defoe and Richardson accepted very literally, but which is implicit in the novel form in general: the premise, or primary convention, that the novel is a full and authentic report of human experience . . . presented through a more largely referential use of language than is common in other literary forms. (33)

In other words, the 'primary convention' of the novel is to transcend convention. Watt's 'full and authentic report of human experience' is by definition absolute and transhistorical. It does not concern historically installed techniques and protocols of literary verisimilitude, but 'the study of the particulars of experience by the individual investigator, who, ideally at least, is free from the body of past assumptions and traditional beliefs.'

It is for this reason that Watt's account of the emergence of novelistic realism cannot but be linear and teleological. A disparate array of historical developments – technical (the spread of printing and literacy), economic (the rise of publishing and the middle-class novel market), and moral (the spread of puritan techniques of self-scrutiny and individuation, the reorganization of personal identity around sexuality) – receive a retrospective unity as so many midwives attending the birth of authentic authorial experience. As a result, the possibility that these developments are amongst those determining what *counts* as experience at a particular time cannot be fully taken into account. Neither can the possibility that literary experience may be nothing more than a temporary and contingent outcome of such collective and material transformations. Once the techniques of novelistic verisimilitude have been identified with an epistemologically full and authentic individual experience, then the history of literary realism must be written backwards from a point which cannot be surpassed. The novel finds its true voice with the discovery of a form of representation that imposes no convention or norm on the author's experience save those implicit in the tradition of 'English' itself, which is to say, conventions and norms so close to being universal that they lose their linguistic and technical character and pass for experience itself in the long march towards 'humane consciousness'.

Of course, Watt's is only one version of the aesthetico-moral history of realism. Lukács's Hegelian Marxism provides us with a more openly political transcendence of politics. In this version the obstacle that delays the meeting of the inner world of 'man' and the outer world of 'society' is not the conventionalized and normative machinery of the novel as such. It is this machinery in so far as it expresses an economically determined fragmentation of social consciousness. Novelistic techniques are aligned with stages in the development of capitalism in so far as they represent the partial and instrumentalized forms of consciousness appropriate to a particular phase of economic relations. So, according to Lukács (1977: 30–6), the development of disjunctive anti-narrative techniques in the modernist novel is in fact a distorted or inverted representation of the increasingly unified form taken by social relations in mature capitalism.

It might seem from this that Watt's account cannot be made to square with Lukács's. After all, in the former technique is reduced to the lone voice of the novelist, while in the latter technique is transcended through a totalizing synthesis of the forms of consciousness, and the bearer of this synthesis is a whole class. But these differences are not as important as they first appear. In Lukács's scheme the objective totality of social relations imposed by capitalism is heading towards a historical rendezvous with a form of representation that is a synthesis of all the partial forms, that is, a rendezvous with consciousness. It is no accident, then, that this synthesis and rendezvous should be anticipated by individual authors, the major realists. At this point Lukács's transcendence of technique through historical synthesis is indistinguishable from Watt's reduction of technique to expressive voice. Neither should we be surprised when Lukács (39) says that the great realist must 'artistically conceal' the 'abstract' techniques used in the production of his representation.

The upshot is that Lukács endorses the techniques of character writing used by Gorky, Balzac, and Mann for exactly the same reason that Watt praises those used by Jane Austen. In both cases ideas and norms are relayed to the reader in the form of a staged experience – the deployment of techniques for securing introspection, identification with characters, etc. – 'without the need for any external commentary' (Lukács 1977: 34). In both cases what is invoked is a non-normative pedagogics. Moral values and political analysis can ostensibly be 'perceived' implicitly, without the need for imposing definite criteria and techniques, in the novelistic recreation of experience. Lukács could thus attack modernism for the abstract violence it perpetrated on our (allegedly) organic and continuous experience of story and character *and* for its failure to reach that point of abstract distance from experience where a political judgement of the social tonality becomes possible. The realist novel, on the other hand, apparently allows moral and political judgements to grow organically from its synthesizing recreation of experience.

Literary representation is thus placed in a transcendent position in relation to all those knowledges that work by imposing technical criteria and norms, the social sciences in particular. This means that literary realism does not name a set of historical techniques but the point where history anticipates its ultimate goal: the formation of a consciousness which synthesizes and thereby transcends all merely technical knowledge, recovering everything lost to fragmented and instrumentalized ideologies along the way. It is hardly surprising that in this universalized consciousness Watt's notion of the march of humane consciousness or culture should merge with Lukács's conception of the development of proletarian class consciousness.

> For a writer to possess a living relation to the cultural heritage means being a son of the people, borne along by the current of the people's development. In this sense Maxim Gorky is a son of the Russian people, Romain Rolland a son of the French and Thomas Mann a son of the German people. For all their individuality and originality, for all their remoteness from an artiness which artificially collects and aestheticizes about the primitive, the tone and content of their writings grow out of the life and history of their people, they are an organic product of the development of their nation. That is why it is possible for them to create art of the highest quality while at the same time striking a chord which can and does evoke a response in the broad masses of the people. (Lukács 1977:54)

Regardless of Lukács's talk of essences and appearances and despite recent claims to the contrary,[2] neither the realist novel nor Lukács's account of it is based on a theory of knowledge. Yes, Lukács does say that it is the political role of literature to penetrate ideological appearances and reveal the underlying social relations; and he does make this revelation dependent on society's capacity to secure its own representation through its historical synthesis of a universalized class consciousness. But the *criteria* for this happy event having occurred are not in fact epistemological. They are provided by 'culturalist' or aesthetico-moral conceptions of the uniqueness of literary language: we can tell when writing anticipates the formation of true consciousness, says Lukács, because it is writing in which linguistic technique and political interest are totalized and gone beyond in the synthetic immediacy of literary language.

The problem with this strategy, as Brecht was quick to point out, is that it is not consciousness that is being universalized but a particular set of literary techniques. According to Brecht, these techniques (for example, those involved in producing 'rounded' characters) remain instrumentalities wedded to limited and specific moral and political interests (the interest in maximizing audience identification with a character type). Representation, says Brecht, does not have an essential form, provided by literary language, through which political judgement can anticipate the emergence of a universal consciousness. We can be sceptical, then, about such attempts to provide general criteria for deciding whether or not a piece of writing is on the path down which the humane consciousness is progressing towards its historical rendezvous with experience. It is no easy matter to distinguish between writing in which ideas and norms are being technically imposed on experience and writing in which they flow from it. If it were, then one would be hard pressed to explain why modern literary criticism is so thoroughly preoccupied with securing just this distinction. Steven Marcus's *The Other Victorians* provides a convenient exemplification.

Marcus sets himself the task of distinguishing pornographic writing from literary realism. Pornography is given a dual specification. On the one hand, it is too removed from experience, too abstract and self-contained. This leads to a relation to the world in which norms and fantasies are coercively imposed, the paradigmatic case being the coercive objectification of women in male fantasies. On the other hand, it is insufficiently detached in relation to the experiences that it deals with. Pornography reduces the complex intentionality of literature to a single function – sexual arousal – and thereby short-circuits the forms of judgement embedded in culture and language. Pornography for Marcus, like modernism for Lukács and the eighteenth-century novel for Watts, is both too abstract and too experiential; at once imprisoned in language *and* attempting to by-pass it in favour of an immediate connection with (sexual) experience. As such, it falls short of that form of representation in which the voice of humane consciousness can be heard speaking without doing violence to the tissue of experience recreated in the novel. Pornography, it appears, is a detour or cul-de-sac on the historical path consciousness must travel if it is to rendezvous with the true experience of social life.

But look at the quotations which Marcus uses to make this distinction. The first is taken from the pseudonymous Walter's *My Secret Life*, a vast and detailed journal kept to record and intensify his sexual life. The passage concerns an occasion on which Walter and a friend, dressed as costermongers, go slumming in dockyard pubs in search of sexual excitement.

Thus costumed, we spent the evening at public houses, among sailors, whores, and working men – in an atmosphere thick and foul with tobacco smoke, sweat, and gas. We ordered liquors which we threw under the table or spilt when not observed; we treated some gay women, but in a very modest way, and altogether had a very entertaining evening. It was difficult to act up to our disguise. At one time I had a whore on my knee, and my friend another. We asked the women to bet which of us had the biggest prick, and the girls felt us outside quite openly. There was, however, nothing likely to shock people there. Of lewd talk there was plenty, though no gross indecency was practised. The barmen, or potboys, or the master were always there and checked it. – 'Now you Sally, none of that; or out you go'. – 'Now hook it smart, you bitch', were phrases we heard with others, used by the master or servants when things got too hot. At one house, they turned a woman and a sailor out by force, who were too noisy and rather drunk, 'let's go and fuck, Tom', said the woman who was readier to leave than the man. (Marcus 1964: 106)

Marcus then sets up a comparison with a scene from Dickens's *Our Mutual Friend*, also set in one of nineteenth-century London's dockyard bars. This scene is centred on the character of Miss Abbey Potterson, the publican, with the action provided by a collision on the river outside. Marcus provides no direct quotation, but the following is indicative:

'What is it?' asked Miss Abbey.
'It's summut run down in the fog, ma'am', answered Bob.
'There's ever so many people in the river.'
'Tell 'em to put on all the kettles!' cried Miss Abbey. 'See that the boiler's full. Get a bath out. Hang some blankets to the fire. Heat some stone bottles. Have your senses about you, you girls down-stairs, and use 'em' ...
'If that's Tom Tootle', Miss Abbey made proclamation, in her most commanding tones, 'let him instantly come underneath here.'
The submissive Tom complied, attended by a crowd.
'What is it, Tootle?' demanded Miss Abbey.
'It's a foreign steamer, Miss, run down a wherry.'
'How many in the wherry?'
'One man, Miss Abbey?'
'Found?'
'Yes. He's been under the water a long time, Miss; but they've grappled up the body.'
'Let 'em bring it here. You, Bob Gliddery, shut the house-door and stand by it on the inside, and don't you open it till I tell you. Any police down here?'
'Here, Miss Abbey', was the official rejoinder.

'After they have brought the body in, keep the crowd out, will you?
And help Bob Gliddery to shut 'em out.'
'All right, Miss Abbey.' (Dickens 1910: 458–9)

The action continues with the recovery and resuscitation of the drowned
man, who is restored to the arms of his daughter.

I am not sure if Lukács ever came across *My Secret Life*, and I will
leave the reader to judge which, if either, of these passages is more likely
to strike a chord and 'evoke a response in the broad masses of the people'.
The point at issue is that Marcus uses the first passage to exemplify the
category of pornography while Dickens is wheeled in to represent literary
realism. In other words, the Dickens passage is used to exemplify a form
of representation in which experience can speak to and through a
humane consciousness, while Walter's writing, for all its value as a social
document, supposedly fails to do justice to experience because of its
normatizing and fantasizing detachment and because of its excitatory
function.

I find this account spurious and unconvincing. This is not because of a
mistake made by a particular critic on a particular occasion. Lukács's
denunciation of the modernists as ideologues or Leavis's relegation of
Milton's doctrinal epics in favour of Elizabethan metaphysical lyrics
would serve our purposes equally well. Marcus simply provides a striking
exemplification of what is wrong with all such attempts to evaluate forms
of writing by using pseudo-epistemological terms like 'experience',
'consciousness' or 'representation'. Assume, for the sake of the argument,
that we *are* dealing with a single domain of experience, whose essential
form can only be revealed in the careful staging of events and characters
provided by Dickens's literary language. Then what are we to make of
the absence of some of its characteristic forms of conduct, namely:
getting entertained, getting drunk and getting sex?

Now, in one regard Marcus seems to be quite aware of this problem in
that he says: 'The first thing to learn, then, from such scenes . . . is what
did *not* get into the Victorian novel, what was, by common consent and
convention left out or suppressed' (Marcus 1964: 104; original emphasis).
But, on the other hand, the problem is made to vanish in front of our
eyes. That which is left out, we are told, is really only the residue of a
necessary abstraction from experience. Moreover, this abstraction – like
Lukács's but unlike Walter's – is one which is itself transcended in the
novelistic recreation that leaves the experience intact. Dickens's positive
valuations (which turn the pub into something like a rescue mission for
shipwrecked sailors, presided over by a tough but scrupulously moral
schoolmistress) were already there in Walter's experience of low-life, if
only he had known how to perceive them. 'In Dickens's imaginative
abstraction from and reconstruction of such an establishment, certain
positive values, already inherent in it, are brought into view and focused

upon' (Marcus 1964: 105). This is what sets Dickens apart as 'the supreme novelist, the conscience and consciousness of his age'.

At this point the epistemological concepts used to separate porno-graphic writing from literary realism are spinning idly. 'Positive values' are simply not objects of perception, least of all in mid-nineteenth-century London gin-houses. There may well be reasons for preferring the norms of conduct deployed in the Dickens passage to those governing Walter's writing and action. But these reasons cannot be read off from the allegedly unique representational felicity of literary language.

In the *first* place, the forms of relation to the social domain associated with Walter's journal and the circulation of a Dickens novel are quite specific and quite different. Walter exists at the centre of a dense network of speeches and practices (a network of medical, confessional, familial and pedagogic institutions) which implicates him in a particular type of sexuality. Pubs and brothels of the lowest and most debauched sort figure in this network as elements in the sexualizing apparatus, as sites of particular erotic intensification in the moral geography of London. The dissemination of Dickens, for its part, although it overlaps this network, has its roots elsewhere. His works belong with the social organization of new forms of public morality and decency. Their role lies in the deployment of new behavioural norms and exemplary character types, of which Miss Abbey Potterson is an instance. Each apparatus is capable of equipping individuals with quite different capacities for feeling, judging, acting, and taking pleasure.

Now we can confront the implausibility of Marcus's assertion that the Dickensian norms are already present in Walter's experience of low life, waiting only for an appropriately literary recreation to reveal them. We do so by calling into question the idea that individuals are connected to the social by a single universal capacity or process – experience. In each case what counts as 'experience' must be shown by describing a specific deployment of (for example) techniques of personal discipline (the journal); the spaces of ritual excitation (the public house); moral technologies (the institution of exemplary character types); and so on. In other words, there is no single form of relation to social reality forming a continuous backdrop against which different norms, pleasures, and political judgements can be measured.

Second, now it is possible to see just how unrevealing is the concept of literary representation employed by Watt, Lukács and Marcus. While both of the above passages are presented to us as descriptions, neither of them, to borrow from Wittgenstein, is involved in the *language game* of describing or giving information. To carry on with Wittgenstein for a moment, we can say that the problem with epistemological concepts like 'representation' is that they organize accounts of language around a paradigm or essential case: for example, the description of facts found in the apparatuses of certain sciences, like botany. In fact such descriptions, which *are* implicated in the language game of giving information, may be of recent date and quite marginal, argues Wittgenstein. If this is the case, then there is no need to measure either of the above passages in terms of their distance from this particular language game. The types of relation that exist between the dissemination of forms of writing (on the one hand) and social organizations, individual actions, bodily feelings and sensitivities, historical events etc. (on the other) may simply be too various to be covered by a term like 'representation'.

At the very least the 'descriptions' in Walter's journal constitute a means of disciplining his personal life; a mechanism for regulating certain forms of behaviour (the journal is a point of repetition for medical and family-reform measures which de-sexualize Walter's conjugal relations even while they permit the intensification of his extra-marital pleasures); and a manual of techniques for investing the body with specific capacities for sexual pleasure. In relation to this last, it would be just as fruitless to ask whether these techniques are a good representation of sexual experience as it would to ask the same question about the very different religio-sexual techniques collected in the *Kama-Sutra*. Dickens's 'descriptions', on the other hand, have the primary function of developing new norms of public behaviour and morality, and new forms of character-identification associated with the mass formation of secular conscience. They do not attempt to give information about social life but help to constitute the new 'surfaces' of public morality on which a whole range of formerly tolerated activities (public indecency, drunkenness, profligacy, child labour, dereliction of family duties, etc.) would show up as unacceptable. Miss Abbey Potterson's tavern is an exemplar whose normalizing function is determined by the sustained campaign to clean up London's public houses undertaken during the nineteenth century. This campaign concentrated on severing or policing the relation between ale-houses and criminality, prostitution, and other anti-social activities. Significantly, one of the key measures adopted was to tie the granting of liquor licences to the moral character and social standing of publicans.

It is radically misleading to even attempt a literary-epistemological comparison of the two passages – to ask which is more realistic. The deployment of language is not governed by a general function (representation) in relation to which such a comparison might be made. Nothing about Walter's 'experience' of the world of brothels, gin-houses and licentious pubs could tell him that his relation to this world was 'abstract', or brutally self-enclosed and detached, or that his writing was cut off from the humane tradition of English by the single-minded goal of excitation – nothing except the imposition of new norms of public decency and private conduct. Moreover, these norms are not the creatures of consciousness, or even of language as such. They are deployed within the great correctional apparatuses associated with the regulation of the health and well-being of populations, the reform of family life, the disciplinary investment of children and the policing of the metropolis. If the novels of Dickens provide a different 'description' of the gin-house, the slum, the wastrel father, and the orphaned child, this is not because literary language is more finely tuned to the voice of the humane future speaking through the Victorian experience. It is because novels – disseminated as periodicals or serialized along with other educative 'household words' addressed to the middle-class family – formed part of those social technologies invented by the Victorians (the classroom, the asylum, the nurturing family, the police) which *determined* the future form of individual capacities and collective conducts.

Representational felicity to experience has nothing to do with it. It is a fictitious retrospect to speak of a potentially common human experience here, as if Walter represents a cultural lag, or imprisonment in convention and fantasy, or the failure of the writer to identify with the progress of humane consciousness which is also 'the current of the people's development'. These are simply covers for the fact that during the nineteenth century the forms of government applied to both individuals and populations alter. New social apparatuses emerge deploying new moral norms and requiring new forms of conduct. All that one can say of Walter is that, unlike Dickens, his writing is not connected to the new machinery of social discipline, except perhaps as a perverse relay. Walter is not less humane than Dickens, because the deployment of new moral norms and forms of conduct transform what is to count as 'humane'; which is to say that political morality is not a universal to be derived from experience by an appropriate representation. Instead, it is an artefact of social organization, a positive historical achievement always specified in definite political and moral technologies, such as those associated with the great reform movements of the nineteenth century. Paradoxically, this permits us to agree with Marcus when he says that through the comparison of Walter and Dickens: 'one achieves a renewed sense of how immensely humane a project the Victorian novel was' (Marcus 1964: 105), as long as we understand 'humane project' in the terms provided by the preceding paragraphs.

On the one hand, it is possible to defend the nineteenth-century novel for its role as support for a whole range of disciplinary mechanisms directed at both individuals and populations and responsible for, among other things, the abolition of child prostitution, the improvement of family life, and new levels of public health and security. On the other, these changes cannot be understood as part of the totalizing evolution of culture, or the people, or humane consciousness, anticipated only in the synthetic immediacy of literary language. Dickens is neither more humane nor more far-seeing than Walter in any absolute sense, for example, in the sense that he possesses a language which more fully anticipates the historical emergence of a universal class consciousness. Rather, the forms of conduct and feeling that we associate with the nineteenth-century novel must be treated as artefacts of a different form of social and political organization involving the material installation of new moral technologies.

In other words, it is necessary to abandon the attempts of aesthetico-moral criticism to provide a single general criterion for evaluating writing, based on the allegedly unique appropriateness of literary language to experience. Instead, forms of judgement must be derived from our familiarity with the role that techniques of writing play in different forms of social organisation, for example, the role of techniques of characterization in the institutions of social discipline.[3] In this way, it even becomes possible to offer a limited defence of aesthetico-moral criticism itself, not as the queen of cultural values nor as the custodian of humane consciousness, but as an instrument in the pedagogics of conscience formation. At the same time, we have shown the stagings of experience characteristic of literary realism involve definite, technically secured forms of relation to social organization. It is impossible therefore to dispense with such stagings by treating them as ideological 'experience effects' projected from a mis-recognized linguistic structure.

Structure

Perhaps all that is meant by the formal use of language or its formal analysis is that these make no appeal to the experience of language users. Analysis and use are controlled by explicit rules or procedures. If this is the case, then there are two quite different types of formal analysis. Before beginning our discussion of the formal analysis of literary representation it is worth clarifying this difference.

The *first* type of formal investigation is one which concentrates on the role of specific compositional forms and procedures in the production of public speech and writing. Homeric scholarship is an important source of such analysis, and we can take Albert Lord's reconstruction of the forms of the Homeric oral composition as fairly representative. Lord (1960: ch. 3) describes the stable formulas that permitted the composition and performance of the lengthy epic songs. A given formula will specify 'the names of the actors, the main actions, time and place' and works in conjunction with regular metrical and rhyme patterns which serve a mnemonic function. To learn this ensemble of techniques is to acquire a specific capacity for composition and memory, prodigious by our standards. It is to this capacity that Lord attributes the Homeric epics rather than to the experience of their (collective) author.

Walter Ong also makes use of the concept of compositional formula when discussing writing in the Tudor period. Ong (1971) investigates the Elizabethan pursuit of *copia*, a term that covered both the power of eloquent speech and writing, and the means of achieving it. In doing so he describes the role of commonplace books – literally, books of topics or 'places' in which were lodged proverbs, observations, conceits, adages, turns of phrase, themes, etc., which were common to various discursive purposes. The composition of the materials collected in the technical memory of the places was handled by specific formulas, for example, the formula for the fall of great men or the lives of saints or artists.

> Such organizational formulas provided, among other things, for an ordered progression through a list of topics in praising or blaming a character: for example, Richard Rainolde's *The Foundation of Rhetorike* (1563), an adaptation of the *Progymnasmata* of the fourth-century Greek rhetorician Aphtonius, a favourite textbook in Tudor schools, specifies that for the praise of an individual person one should eulogize in succession his country, ancestors, education, 'actes' (*res gestae* or achievements, that is, his use of gifts of the soul, of the body, of fortune), concluding with some comparison which would show to the advantage of the subject of eulogy. (Ong 1971: 39)

Once again, there is no need to found the eulogy in the writer's experience of the worthiness of its subject. But this does not mean that eulogists were insincere in composing their feelings of admiration. The eulogy was a means by which certain men could be ennobled and acquire a biography and repute, just as it was a means for others to acquire the capacity to feel admiration for such men. In other words, in the commonplace book and the formula, Ong isolates elements of another specific social technology capable of forming *copia*, or the power of speech, without appealing to the speaker's experience. In this sense Lord and Ong exemplify a formal approach to language which, for want of a better word, we might call 'rhetorical'.

The *second* species of formal analysis is quite unlike rhetorical analysis – so different, in fact, that we might say that it belongs in a different historical series or to a time that is distinctly modern, the contemporary publication dates of Lord and Ong notwithstanding. After Saussure the analysis of language is formal in a new sense. Simplifying radically for the purposes of discussion, let us say that nineteenth-century philology provides formal analyses analogous to those we have labelled 'rhetorical'. In Rask's (1811) Icelandic grammar, for example, one finds morphology (word structure) treated in terms of regular patternings of stems, suffixes and prefixes quite analogous to the formulas Lord and Ong identify for higher level patternings – analogous in the sense that they are described without reference to the speaker's consciousness, as a technique to be acquired.[4] Saussure's 'break' with this sort of philological analysis consists, in the first instance, in making the question of the speaker's consciousness central to the description of linguistic formulas and patterns.

In fact Saussure measures his distance from philology by asking two questions which are more or less meaningless given the techniques of analysis employed by the latter: How is language represented to the speaker's consciousness? (I.e., how do we come to recognise linguistic sounds and meanings?) And, how does language represent experience to the speaker? Most importantly, he radically subordinates the second question to the first. In this way, he not only distinguishes his enterprise from philology but also from seventeenth-century philosophical grammar, which had just as radically subordinated the first question to the second.[5]

In fact this new order of questions is the result of a series of shifts which take place in the field of language studies during the nineteenth century:

1 *Language becomes opaque.* In place of the articulated words described by phoneticians and philologists and the evident meanings compiled in the new national dictionaries, Saussure posits enigmatic continua of sound and meaning. The continuum of linguistic experience contains all possible sounds and meanings in an undifferentiated flow. The identity of and relation between discrete bits of sound and meaning is not given in experience; it is the arbitrary result of the abstract organization of language itself.

2 *Formulas become foundations.* If the identity and relation of sound and meaning are not given in experience, then it is fruitless for someone like Rask to describe word structure, for example, directly in the formula or the list. Any given formula or element of a list must have conditions of possibility which are not given in experience. As a result the formulaic lists used in the philological description of word structure receive a striking new deployment. Detached from its practical roles in the transmission and regularization of languages, a list like

	quadru-plex
quadrupes	simplex
quadrifons	triplex
quadraginta	centuplex
etc.	etc.

is used to represent the set of abstract relations that make linguistic experience possible. So, according to Saussure, the identification of *quadruplex* ('four-fold') and its accompanying meaning or experience is purely the result of the 'relations of difference' that link it to the other possible forms.[6] In other words the formulaic list is no longer a rhetorical adjunct to actual speech (*parole*). It is re-deployed as an abstract set of relations (*langue*) and thereby assumes the mantle of general conditions of possibility, or foundations, of linguistic experience.

3 Language becomes systemic. If the recognition and use of any one form of language depends solely on its virtual relations with all the other possible forms, then language (*langue*) clearly constitutes a single system or totality. This allows linguistics to put aside constraints of time and place and to imagine a knowledge of language which approximates the synchronic operation of the entire system – in other words, a knowledge of language that is equivalent to everything that could possibly be said in a language. Hence Benveniste posits a speaker who inherits 'the entire wealth of language' and Chomsky imagines that, in the grammar, the entire calculus of language forms the backdrop to any given utterance. Language and experience become coextensive.

Modern linguistics is sometimes acclaimed as heralding the 'death of the subject'. However, we can treat the above three shifts as marking historical conditions for the *birth* of a distinctively modern conception of the subject. That is what Foucault argues in his archaeology of the human sciences, *The Order of Things*. According to Foucault (1966: chs 8–10), not only linguistics but also psychology, anthropology, and sociology emerge as the result of the introduction of the question of representation or foundations into the 'positive sciences' which make them possible (philology, biology, and economics). As a result, the human sciences enter into a permanently ambiguous partnership with their parent sciences. In the case of linguistics this partnership is typified by the way in which the philological formula (e.g. the morphological list) is at once retained and 'transcended' in its redeployment as foundations. In other words, a space is opened between the practical utilization of the formula as a means of building up local linguistic capacities, and its redeployment as general conditions for the representation of linguistic experience. It is precisely in this space, says Foucault, that the modern version of the subject appears, marked irredeemably by the ambiguous conditions of its emergence. In the human sciences and in linguistics in particular, subjectivity is *both* the mechanical (unconscious) effect of structure *and* the ground where this effect will be represented to a reflexive knowledge. Subjectivity *both* advances beyond structure to the point where it makes contact with, and guarantees, the enigmatic continuum of experience, *and* retreats behind structure, in so far as the latter provides this continuum with its conditions of intelligibility.

These are the circumstances and this the form in which modern linguistics and a new version of the subject of experience emerge inside a field of techniques that had got along quite well without them. To be sure, the ambiguous modern subject is not Descartes' self-knowing fount of ideas, but is a subject of experience nonetheless. Those formal analyses of language based on this recent and distinctive interplay of structure and subjectivity we will call 'structuralist'. It is possible to summarize the distinction between the types of formal analysis that we have been building up in the following way: for structuralist analysis, linguistic relations make up a totality functioning as conditions for the represent-ation of linguistic experience to the subject of this experience, whereas, for the kind of analysis we have been calling 'rhetorical', language is only a general heading for a variable and indeterminate collection of practical techniques involving the use of words. Such uses are not predicated on a general relation to 'experience' (e.g. recognition or, a Saussure would have it, mis-recognition) nor do they presuppose a single underlying systemic structure. Instead, they form part of the piecemeal acquisition of local technical capacities. In what follows I indicate why structuralist approaches to the problem of literary representation miss their mark and why an approach through a 'rhetoric of capacities' is more revealing.

Recent discussions of literary realism have been dominated by the importation of structuralist themes and arguments, and by the accom-modations literary criticism has been forced to make with this intrusion. The transposition has been fairly direct, as critics of realism have based their attack on the same set of moves through which Saussure announced his 'break' with philology. As a result, the structuralist critique has a familiar three-part structure: like philology, literary realism treats experience as given and language as transparent. *Consequently*, it fails to recognize the role of linguistic structure or signifying systems in the formation of experience and the subject of experience. *This means* that the 'experience-effect' of a particular signifying system is enshrined as natural, obscuring both the plurality of other possible meanings in the continuum of experience and reflexive awareness of the linguistic system itself. Catherine Belsey's *Critical Practice* summarizes the net effect of this series.

> Post-Saussurean theory, therefore, starts from an analysis of language, proposing that language is not transparent, not merely the *medium* in which autonomous individuals transmit messages to each other about an independently constituted world of things. On the contrary, it is language which offers the possibility of constructing a world of individuals and things, and of differentiating between them. The transparency of language is an illusion. (Belsey 1980: 4)

We can treat Belsey's book, then, as a convenient and representative example of the structuralist analysis of literary representation.

First, Belsey introduces realism as a discourse lacking sufficient theoretical distance from experience, which it treats as given. Quoting largely from its contemporary critical apologists, she explicates the notion of expressive realism as one presupposing a uniquely privileged use of language; one in which language functions as a transparent medium permitting the co-realization of the author's ideas and values and the immediate experience of reality.[7] For her part, Belsey rejects this privileging of realist discourse by disallowing its pre-theoretical appeal to experience and to the subject of experience. We should note, however, that she does not reject the *category* of experience. Indeed, the assumption of a general stratum of linguistic experience containing all possible sounds and meanings in an undifferentiated continuum or chain plays a central role in Belsey's account.

Second, because of its uncritical acceptance of experience, realism involves a failure to recognize the essentially relational (structural) and linguistic nature of the conditions of experience. Here Belsey paraphrases Saussure to the effect that: 'far from providing a set of labels for entities which exist independently in the world, language precedes the existence of independent entities, making the world intelligible by differentiating between concepts' (Belsey 1980: 38). Meaning does not originate in the individual consciousness of the author but is a value produced by the differential relations of the language system. Literary representation, then, cannot be traced to the experience or thought of an author (even a collective author like Lukács's proletariat) and instead must be revealed in an analysis of the linguistic structure. However, if language is thereby totalized and made coextensive with thought or experience, it is also made to overlap with 'society'. Saussurean linguistics in fact provides two quite different origins for the relations that make up the linguistic mechanisms: on the one hand, they derive from the contingent habits of speech communities, successively sedimented as structure. On the other, linguistic relations are treated as an *a priori* system or calculus (the metaphor of algebra is used) that makes the habits of the speech community possible. It is the oscillation between these poles (modern linguistics cannot do without either) that allows 'language' and 'society' to enter into a relation of circular causality. Linguistic relations, Belsey argues, are thus coextensive with both thought and social relations. The author's location in language is also a position in society.

Third, literary realism can now be defined as a particular type of representation or text, one that conceals its own status as language by producing an illusion or effect of experience. According to Belsey the term 'realism' 'is useful in distinguishing between those forms which tend to efface their own textuality, their existence as discourse, and those which explicitly draw attention to it. Realism offers itself as transparent'

(51). Under these circumstances realism's claim to represent experience can only be a cover for the privileging of *one* of the possible ways in which the continuum or chain of linguistic experience might be cut up. Realist texts thus depend on a double occlusion or mis-recognition: of the structure of the signifying system or discourse underpinning the text; and of the other possible meanings in the chain to which the subject might have access if not locked into a single recognition by the 'experience-effect'.[8]

At this point, Belsey's structuralist account of realism overlaps with the Althusserian conception of ideology. This is no accident. Althusser himself invokes the structuralist account of the relation between subjectivity and language in order to reconstruct this Marxian category. In ideology the subject emerges from the same double misrecognition (of structure and of other possible positions) involved in the recognition of experience, which thus serves as the general mechanism for 'the subject's entry into language'. Belsey's specification of realism thus produces a huge category more or less identical to ideology, which is in turn more or less identical to representation as such. Everything from perfume advertisements and political speeches to the nineteenth-century novel fall under its sway. All involve the occlusion of linguistic conditions of possibility by the staging of experiences through which subjects emerge in language at the price of misrecognizing how they got there.

As a consequence, the way out of the problem posed by realism is equally all-embracing and homogeneous: a new 'critical practice' must set itself the task of revealing the structural conditions of realist representations. If successful, it will reveal the subject's role in the linguistic construction of experience, thereby freeing the subject to explore the 'plurality' of other possible meanings awaiting discovery in the chain.

> It is the recurrent suppression of the role of language which has limited this plurality, and this suppression is in turn ideological. The task of a new critical practice is first to identify the effects of the limitation which confines 'correct' reading to an acceptance of the position from which the text is most 'obviously' intelligible, the position of a transcendent subject addressed by an autonomous and authoritative author. Thereafter it becomes possible to refuse this limitation, to liberate the plurality of the text, to reject the 'obvious' and to produce meaning. (Belsey 1980: 55)

It only remains to identify the plurality of other meanings in the chain with 'desire' and we can start to imagine that this new critical practice will overcome the fixing of the subject in representation and ideology through a liberation of desire.[9]

This, then, is the tripartite scheme in which structuralist themes and arguments have been transposed and adapted to the analysis of literary representation. This schema is clearly quite closely related to the three sets of historical conditions that permitted linguistics to emerge as a human science in the first place; that is, to the conditions which allowed the questions of representation and the speaking subject to be posed in the 'positive science' of philology. It is at least possible, then, that the structuralist critique of literary representation signifies not a complete break with literary criticism but simply a further phase in the forever delayed and uncertain emergence of literary criticism as a human science. If this is the case – and a work like Belsey's does in fact involve introducing problems of foundations and subjectivity into a field of dispersed practical knowledges and techniques – then we should be on the look-out for two tell-tale signs: first, a lack of agreement as to what precisely is to count as 'structure', a characteristic instability resulting from the degree of choice involved in selecting which techniques or formulas should be redeployed as foundations. (Should it be plot structure as in Propp, dictionary entries as in Empson's *The Structure of Complex Words*, semantic relations as in Greimas, signifiers as in Belsey and in Barthes' analysis of myth, etc?) Second, that ambiguous relation, which Foucault treats as representative of the human sciences, whereby practical techniques and knowledges (for example, plot summary, character analysis, scansion, commentary) are not in fact *rejected* but *redeployed* under the sign of 'conditions of experience'.

In order to explore these possibilities we need to clarify the picture of language that emerges from the structuralist critique of literary representation. To this end we can return to Belsey's version and briefly compare it with some of the things that Wittgenstein says about language. One of Belsey's main examples is drawn from the use of colour terms, in fact a privileged example in most structuralist accounts, no doubt because the rainbow or colour spectrum functions as an emblem of experience as a continuum. Different languages produce different organizations or groupings of colours.

> In Welsh the colour *glas* (blue), like the Latin *glaucus*, includes
> elements which English would identify as green or grey. The
> boundaries are placed differently in the two languages and the Welsh
> equivalent of English grey might be *glas* or *llwyd* (brown). (Belsey
> 1980: 39)

This illustrates the point that the difference between colour words or concepts cannot be based on the subject's experience of the difference between colours. According to Belsey, the existence of different systems of colour terms presents us with the following exhaustive alternative:

> We are compelled to argue either that our own language has got its
> concepts 'right' in some absolute way . . ., or that concepts are purely

differential, and that they are determined not by their positive
content but by their relations with the other terms of the system . . .
The world, which without signification would be experienced as a
continuum, is divided up by language into entities which then readily
come to be experiences as essentially distinct. (Belsey 1980: 40)

Most of the main components of the structuralist account are here:
experience, emblematized in the colour spectrum, is an undifferentiated
continuum until divided up by colour terms or concepts. Because experience as such is inscrutable, the identity or meaning of a colour term is
wholly dependent on its relational position in the language system, as is
the capacity to differentiate colours. Hence, if we are not to misrecognize
the action of our own system in the form of a 'natural' experience of
colours, we must analyse it as one *possible* way of dividing up the
continuum or chain of meaning.

It might be argued that Wittgenstein's treatment of colour terms has
the same point of departure in that his remarks are also directed against
the idea that these terms are *names* of experienced properties. Wittgenstein also appeals to the variability of the schema in which colours may be
grouped and organized in order to question the idea that the meaning of
colour terms is determined by certain irreducible or primitive experiences
of colour. But this is as far as the similarity goes. Wittgenstein does *not*
introduce this variability in order to motivate the idea of a continuum of
experience or meaning which can be cut up or 'imagined' in different
ways.

So if someone described the colour of a wall to me by saying: 'It was
somewhat reddish yellow,' I could understand him in such a way that
I could choose approximately the right colour from among a number
of samples. But if someone described the colour in *this* way: 'It was
somewhat bluish yellow,' I could not show him such a sample – Here
we usually say that in the one case we can imagine the colour, and in
the other we can't – but this way of speaking is misleading, for there
is no need whatsoever to think of an image that appears before the
inner eye. (Wittgenstein 1977: 20)

The clue to Wittgenstein's approach lies in his equation of *understanding*
a colour term with the *technique* of 'choosing a colour from a set of
samples'. Our apparatus of samples (the colour wheel, the graduated
palette, the rainbow) places yellow adjacent to red, permitting the choice
of a reddish yellow. Yellow and blue, however, are not adjacent, being
separated by another primary colour, green. Hence the apparatus does
not permit the choice of a bluish yellow.

In Wittgenstein's example, then, the point is not that we cannot
'imagine' or *experience* bluish yellow, not that our *language* occludes

some possible part of a colour continuum. Rather, it is that we happen not to possess a *technique* or *apparatus* that would permit us to engage in a particular set of activities. That we happen not to possess this technique or apparatus does not mean that our (or anyone's) organization of colours is incomplete, or forms only part of 'all the possible organizations contained in the continuum', the reason being that capacities for identifying colours and understanding the meaning of colour terms are local accomplishments resulting from the practical deployment of technologies such as that of the colour sample. Differences in colour concepts must not be traced to different divisions of a continuum of experience of 'chain of meaning', but to the differences in available technologies or 'language-games'.

> Ask this question: Do you know what 'reddish' means? And how do you show that you know it?
>
> Language-games: 'Point to a reddish yellow (white, blue, brown)' – 'Point to an even more reddish one' – 'A less reddish one' etc. Now that you've mastered this game you will be told 'Point to a somewhat reddish green?' Assume there are two cases: Either you do point to a colour (and always the same one), perhaps to an olive green – or you say, 'I don't know what that means,' or 'There's no such thing'.
>
> We might be inclined to say that the other person had a different colour concept from the other; or a different concept of '. . . ish'. (Wittgenstein 1977: 20–1)

When imagining different colour concepts or different capacities for discrimination one does not do so against the backdrop of 'all possible colours' cut up differently by different language systems. The philosopher's licence to think of all that is logically possible is an illusion. It must give way to a more modest investigation of a limited number of techniques, the practical mastery of which tells us what we can mean by colour terms.

> Let us imagine men who express an intermediate colour, between red and yellow, e.g. by means of a binary decimal fraction like this: R, LLRL and like, where, e.g. yellow stands to the right, and red to the left. – Already in their nursery schools these people learn how to choose colours according to such descriptions, and they learn to mix them etc. They would stand to us in the relation of people with absolute pitch to people in whom this is wanting. *They can do* what we can't. (Wittgenstein 1980: 112, original emphasis)

For Wittgenstein, the existence of different colour concepts and capacities cannot be understood in terms of different linguistic positions taken up in relation to a continuum of possible colour experiences. Instead, it must be treated in terms of the different social technologies (the sample, the 'colour calculus') and compulsory practices (choosing between shades, identifying primary colours) that we actually have at our disposal. For this reason, says Wittgenstein, it makes no sense to speak of 'all possible colours', or to picture the formation of capacities as if it consisted in dividing up a field where (as it were) all decisions had yet to be taken. All our investigations began with the existence of differentiated capacities to identify colours. This is not because nature presents itself to us in precisely these hues. But neither is it because different languages each have their own way of dividing up colour experience. Rather, it is because capacities to identify colours are the result of the piecemeal acquisition of competence in a limited number of actual technologies and practices.[10]

Of course, the examples cited from Wittgenstein are only indicative. But they indicate that structuralist accounts of language are quite misleading in so far as they use the difference between sets of colour concepts (for example) to present us with an apparently exhaustive opposition: either we must affirm the absolute correctness of our own set of terms, or we must acknowledge that the meaning of these terms is determined by their place in the system of language. Wittgenstein shows that to imagine the existence of different colour concepts presupposes the mastery of different but definite social technologies. Our 'imagination' is limited to those we have a practical familiarity with and those we can construct by analogy. (Wittgenstein's arithmetical colour notation is just such a construction.) In other words, capacities like those involved in identifying colours and understanding colour concepts do not have general conditions of possibility in the abstract structure of language. They are built up in a positive and piecemeal fashion, depending on the social technology and forms of training embodied (for us) in institutions like the school and the family.

On the one hand, this means that there is no general relation to 'the world' characterized by the (mis)recognition of possibilities in a continuum and signified by the term 'experience':

> The concept of experience: like that of happening, of process, of state, of something, of fact, of description and of report. Here we think we are standing on the hard bedrock, deeper than any special methods and language-games. But these extremely general terms have an extremely blurred meaning. They relate in practice to innumerable special cases, but that does not make them any *solider*; no, rather it makes them more fluid. (Wittgenstein 1980: 119)

On the other hand, it means that there is no need to posit 'the whole calculus of language' as something present in each given use of terms.

Instead, one must look at the role of written and verbal symbols – along with techniques, characteristic ways of acting, etc. – in social technologies which are more or less *regional* in character.

A Rhetoric of Capacities

If the structuralist critique of literary representation is centred on the introduction of the problems of the subject, of representation and of foundations into a field of practical knowledges, then Wittgenstein's later philosophy provides us with a vast collection of examples from which we can deduce the misguided and misleading character of this enterprise. The central plank in the structuralist critique is the 'structuralized' conception of the subject as the ambiguous general site where the enigmatic continuity of experience is resolved by the single foundational agency of the linguistic mechanism. From Wittgenstein's examples, on the other hand, we can form a picture of human beings as bearers of a dispersed array of practical capacities. These are built up through piece-meal mastery of a patchwork of social technologies ('language games'). They possess no general form or conditions of possibility, save those found in actual forms of social organization ('forms of living'). In fact Wittgenstein does not so much provide a new general theory of the 'subject' or 'representation' as a variety of strategies for breaking up and resolving a number of quite different problems grouped under those headings. Nonetheless, these strategies decisively transform our understanding of the field occupied by literary realism and its structuralist theorization.

In the *first* place, if there is no general level of experience and instead only the host of 'special methods' through which particular capacities are maintained, then individuals have no general relation to things (experience, reflection) requiring analysis or explanation. In particular, Wittgenstein's procedural analytics rule out a continuum of all possible experiences whose undifferentiated character motivates the demand for structure and foundations. *How* do we refer to these other possible experiences? asks Wittgenstein. In the case of colours, is it through a practical familiarity with a battery of techniques (the colour sample, the palette, etc.), or with ones we can invent by analogy, or learn from other cultures? Then in this case we are not referring to an undifferentiated continuum of all possible forms of colour experience but to a limited number of differentiated procedures or capacities for identifying colours. Or is it through an appeal to a vision of colour that occurs in advance of any special procedures or techniques or, perhaps, to a vision that embraces a confused amalgam of procedures and techniques? Either way, says Wittgenstein, the appeal is meaningless precisely because it fails to specify any of the particular procedures that tell us that it is colour that is being referred to, rather than shape or size, etc. In this manner Wittgen-stein displaces the notion of 'all possible forms of experience' with a description of 'some actual procedures or capacities'.

There is thus no general problem concerning how forms of repre-sentation are to be justified given the enigmatic continuity of experience. More particularly, the structuralist critique of realism cannot be moti-vated by the alleged failure of literary criticism to pose and solve this problem for literary forms of representation. To be sure, the major defences of realism themselves appeal to the author's capacity to distil experience. But this should not blind us to the fact that here 'experience' refers to highly specific capacities (like the 'Dickensian' sense of appro-priate public conduct or the sense of tact) built up from an ensemble of rhetorical techniques and constrained activities. These capacities for experience are material achievements of social organization possessing their own histories and must be described from case to case. They are not the result of some general philosophical mistaking of structure for experi-ence which allegedly permits some of the 'possible forms of experience' to be arbitrarily privileged over others.

Second, as a result, there is no need to look for a general foundation for experience, or subjectivity, or meaning, in a specifically *linguistic* structure or mechanism. We have already seen that the capacity to identify particular organizations of colour results from acquiring compet-ence in limited and definite techniques and procedures. These techniques and procedures are not essentially linguistic. They may involve, for example, the manipulation of colour samples, the mixing of pigments and the learning of perceptual routines as well as the use of colour words. (We can easily imagine a people, says Wittgenstein, who possess a highly refined sense of colour, built up from the manipulation of samples, but no distinct set of colour words.) Hence, it is futile to attempt to read off the character of capacities or the role of (for example) colour concepts from an analysis of linguistic meaning.

On the one hand, to speak of knowing the meaning of a language is to speak of the specific capacities made available by dictionaries, glossaries, commentaries, the techniques of lexicography and so on. These are the terms in which nineteenth-century philology addresses the question of meaning and they make no reference to the alleged problem of how subjects can identify meanings in the continuum (one simply consults the dictionary), or to the role of concepts in articulating experience. (Accord-ing to Wittgenstein our slogan here must be: 'Meaning is what is explained in explanations of meaning.') On the other hand, one might speak of knowing the meaning of a word in a more general sense where what is involved is a practical familiarity with its role in an ensemble of techniques and regular activities. Here the word behaves exactly like the colour sample in so far as it forms part of a specific capacity resulting from the performance of a set of actions or the mastery of a technique.

Here 'meaning' is not essentially linguistic and only functions as a general heading for a motley array of social technologies with which we have a partial, practical familiarity.

The formation of capacities cannot be read off from the dictionary, yet this is more or less what Saussure and the structuralists attempt to do. Social agency has no general form (subjectivity) whose structure can be read off from a theoretical analysis of meaning or the 'subject positions' made available by a linguistic system. In other words, modern linguistics does not provide us with a foundational science for literature because 'language' as it is conceived in modern linguistics does not provide a general foundation capable of including those forms of agency organized by the apparatus of literature. The description of specifically linguistic artefacts forms only part of the description of literary capacities and forms of agency. And this part is best accomplished by the type of formal analysis which we have earlier described as 'rhetorical'.[11] Needless to say, if literary aptitudes are irreducible to a linguistic foundation, they are even further removed from a foundation in authorial consciousness.

Third, if experience has no general form and if capacities and forms of agency have no general foundation in linguistic meaning, then there is no need to posit a general mechanism in which experienced objects and events are represented in language. In particular, there is no need to posit a general mechanism of knowledge in which the condition of things and events being known is that they appear on a purely linguistic or conceptual surface (for example, the grammar, the paradigm or the problematic).

The forms of social organization in which capacities are built up often include linguistic (colour terms) and non-linguistic (the palette, discriminatory routines) elements. They include 'cultural' (the colour wheel) and 'natural' (the eye) mechanisms. They involve purely symbolic devices (Wittgenstein's arithmetical colour notation) as well as definite forms in which devices are connected to objects, events, and actions. What Wittgenstein rejects is the idea that these elements enter into a single type of relation governed by a general concept of representation or knowledge. For example, it may well be that our colour apparatus involves definite forms for connecting notations to coloured surfaces. Let us say that such a form is to be found in the practice of ostensibly defining colour terms by pointing to coloured surfaces under certain conditions (of observation, light, etc.) deemed normal. Fine, says Wittgenstein. Here one includes 'pointing to coloured surfaces' in the apparatus that forms discriminatory capacities and that tells us what we mean by colour terms. Of course, it is not pointing to coloured surfaces by itself that accounts for such capacities or for our colour concepts. In order to point to coloured surfaces one must already have the mastery of a whole series of special procedures and techniques that discriminate colour from shape, size and so on. But these procedures are, as we have seen, not specifically linguistic or conceptual and they do not constitute a 'deeper' or more abstract level making practical activities like pointing, seeing, etc., possible.

In *this* colour apparatus a notation *is* connected to 'independently existing' surfaces and things, but such connections have no general form, for example, recognition, regardless of how this term is conceived or explained. The relations between colour notations, perceptual routines, and forms for connecting notations to surfaces are not invested in subjectivity, structurally determined or otherwise. Rather, they are set up in definite forms of social organization in which, for example, children are required to learn colour terms, to master special perceptual procedures, and, at a certain time of the day when the light is deemed normal, to connect terms with surfaces.

It is because discriminatory capacities are artefacts of social organization (types of organization which may include biological components like the eye and specific forms for connecting 'notations' and 'things') that they vary. There is clearly nothing inevitable or necessary about the apparatus we have just described. For another people, possessing forms of social organization unlike ours, it might not be stable coloured surfaces that matter, but only colours in transition between other colours. Their paradigm for 'red' might then be the colour of autumn leaves and red in their system would come between green and brown, because they do not privilege rainbows as our system does. (Perhaps, says Wittgenstein, they deal with red as a degenerate green.)[12] The point is that such variations in capacities are not a sign that forms of representation and recognition are purely linguistic or conceptual constructs varying with the ways in which different languages 'position subjects' in relation to a colour continuum. To repeat, the differences are between apparatuses, or organizations of material techniques, special procedures, forms for connecting surfaces with notations (or not) etc. These organizations are always limited and definite. They are not actualizations from an ideal totality of possible forms carved out by a linguistic mechanism. In other words, 'representation' cannot function as a concept in a general theory of the linguistic positioning of subjects in relation to experience. It, too, can only play the role of a general heading for a piecemeal description of a loose collection of apparatuses like the ones we have just looked at.

In different ways both culturalist and structuralist approaches to literature assume that capacities and forms of agency have an essential general foundation in a subject's capacity to represent things. In culturalist Marxism, for example, the development of economic relations is partnered by a development of the forms of representation – a development in which the huge variety of 'special methods' will be synthesized and reflected in a universal class consciousness capable of grasping their functional necessity and, in doing so, escaping it. Great literature, according to Lukács, is the anticipation of this moment. For its part, the structuralist critique assumes that socially organized capacities are called forth by a general linguistic mechanism, in the form of a series of positions which individuals must occupy if they are to become subjects of certain experiences. Literature, like the subject, is both the unconscious effect of this mechanism and the point where it can be known and the ideal totality of positions ('desire') liberated.

What Wittgenstein, and Foucault in a different way, show is that there is no such general foundation for social capacities and forms of agency. Individuals are not divided from or connected to a general social experience either by the functional evolution of forms of consciousness or by the way in which language organizes positions of experience. If this is the case, then it is useless to attempt to base an evaluation of literature on its role in concealing or revealing this general relation or process of representation. In particular, nothing is gained by attempting to reduce the host of social technologies and special procedures of the apparatus of literature to the single point of consciousness, or to linguistic structure. In attempting to do so, both culturalism and its structuralist critique ignore the material organization and social consequences of literary technologies and attempt to derive a politics from a general theory of representation. Both positions in fact remained mortgaged to an enlightenment conception of politics. Political judgement supposedly waits on that mythical moment when a social technique becomes reflexive to its own conditions of possibility (e.g. social or linguistic structure), thereby losing its coercive character and forming the basis for knowing all other forms of social action. When structuralism, for example, invests this moment in the unique character of literary language, then it reduces politics to an enthusiasm for reading 'reflexive' or avant-garde literary works, just as Lukács privileges a different genre of literary techniques as criteria for deciding what counts as authentic class consciousness.

On the contrary, says Wittgenstein, what must be described is not a general process or mechanism, but the fact that the use of such and such a procedure is compulsory: that a particular technique has been installed, that children are required to repeat a particular notation, that individuals master a particular technology for identifying colours or confessing their sins or finding their conscience reflected in literary characters, and so on. These artefacts and the capacities they form are not exhausted by the sorts of knowledge they happen to give rise to. Neither is there any ground for thinking that compulsion and the formation of knowledge are strangers to each other. What is confession, asks Foucault, other than the mandatory acquisition of a set of verbal forms and practical exercises through which individuals acquire the capacity to know their deviation from a norm? Finally, we must resist the temptation to impose a retrospective unity on this indeterminate array of special procedures by imagining that they are 'necessary for' the reflexive subjects of history or language to appear.

There can be no turning back from the position we have reached.

Neither is it a question of looking for a middle ground or compromise between culturalist theories of literary representation and their structuralist critique. That compromise was the condition of appearance of structural literary criticism as a human science. We must leave behind both understandings of literary representation which, as we noted at the outset, have reached a mutually satisfactory division of the field. No general account of representation is possible.

On the one hand, it makes no sense to imagine that the immense variety of techniques, procedures, notations and institutions grouped under this heading have a single point of synthesis in what some individual or class thinks or experiences. Quite the reverse. The sort of things that we are prepared to call 'thinking' or 'experiencing' are wholly dependent on the partial, practical mastery we have of some elements of this variety. On the other hand, it is equally misleading to suppose a single opaque surface of experience (a surface in which all the possible forms of experience exist in some sort of undifferentiated and virtual state) and then to posit an equally general linguistic mechanism through which these forms are made available to subjects as so many instances of recognition. Capacities are not called into being in order to solve philosophical doubts about how experience is possible! All our discussions begin from our actual familiarity with some differentiated and limited capacities, with such and such a procedure, notation or technique. There is no single 'logic' or mechanism, for example, that of (mis)recognition, through which individuals become bearers of capacities.

In place of the empty gesturing to experience, the subject, and to representation Wittgenstein provides a careful and piecemeal description of some of the innumerable 'special methods', the mastery of which determines what we can count as 'experience' or 'representation' under certain circumstances. The important point is that the formation of these procedures into technologies – the deployment of notations, the utilization of biological faculties, the mastery of perceptual routines, the forms of connection to 'things', etc. – is a piecemeal practical achievement of forms of social organization. It makes no sense to posit a single principle for the organization of capacities, the subject (whether conceived as an unfettered consciousness *or* as the surface effect of deep structures) because the forms of social organization are not governed by any single general (epistemological) relation between 'language' and 'the world'.

If we are to understand literary representation then we must be prepared to begin a patient description of an array of procedures and techniques, and of the forms of their organization into specific social technologies or capacities, for example, those of literary reading and writing. Of course, this enterprise will involve the description of linguistic artefacts – of rhetorical schema, of poetic devices, of textual forms and of specific types of notation (character notations, for example). But these will not be treated as instances of a general grammar of experience or subject positions, as they are in structuralist analysis. Literary capacities do not have linguistic foundations. We must be just as ready to describe practical activities or techniques (for example, pedagogical techniques of self-analysis utilizing literary characters) and instrumentalities that connect notations to institutions and political entities (the circulation of periodicals which linked the character notations of the Victorian novel to the family and the family reform movement being a case in point). But these will not be treated as a means by which a society secures its own representation in consciousness by equipping subjects with forms of recognition appropriate to its own (totalizing) development. The formation of literary capacities does not obey a general social logic.

If we describe the organization of a specific literary technology – the deployment of a character notation, of techniques for self-scrutiny, of instrumentalities tying the behaviour of family members to particular norms of conduct, etc. – we must be careful not to allow our description to be subsumed either by an ideal grammar of subject positions or by an historical logic of the forms through which a society secures its own reflection in consciousness. Nothing governs the formation of a capacity except the social organization of 'special methods' which varies from case to case and to which we are tied by practical acquaintanceship. Turning our backs on the grammar of literary representations and the logic of their social causation we can anticipate a different undertaking: a rhetoric of literary capacities whose 'foundations' go no deeper than the available forms of social organization in which such capacities are built up and deployed.

Notes

1. For further discussion see Hunter 1984.
2. For example, those made by Terry Lovell in chapter 4 of Lovell 1980.
3. These are the terms, for example, in which it is possible to develop a policy on pornography. Such an analysis remains within the institutional frameworks that determine the functions and effects of pornographic writing. It sets aside as meaningless the question of whether pornographic writing is appropriate to a common human experience of sexuality or whether it involves an aggressive imposition of fantasies and norms. Instead, it bases its calculations on the current forms in which the law regulates the visibility of erotica in relation to divisions of public space, categories of social agent, and social organization of sexual conduct.
4. Indeed, Rask's researches into the language of the old Icelandic sagas were bound up with the provision of standard techniques of pronunciation, orthography and morphology for the new national languages which were replacing the multitude of Scandinavian dialects. For further discussion see Haugen 1968.
5. A fact overlooked by Chomsky in his attempt to find an origin for modern linguistics in 'Cartesian' philosophical grammar.
6. More precisely, the identification of this (syntagmatic) combination of prefix and stem depends wholly on the fact that each belongs to an (associative) group or class of other such combinations which *might* have occurred at this point. So,

argues Saussure (1983: 126–9), it is only the relational disposition of the parts in the 'linguistic mechanism' that makes identification possible. Compare this with the philological use of morphological lists. Here students are expected to identify prefix and stem directly, for example, through their graphic presentation, often based on Latin exemplars, which must be learned and habitually deployed as a norm.

7. It might be objected to Belsey that realists from Leavis to Lukács in fact give language a much more positive role than is acknowledged in her account of them. After all, Leavis's doctrine of the role of linguistically embodied tradition acknowledges the opacity of language and gives it a positive role in the formation of 'impersonal' structures of feeling and judgement. Lukács for his part does not assume that experience is immediately open to judgement (cf. his attack on naturalism) and traces linguistic forms, in the first instance at least, to social structure rather than to the artist. However, Belsey would not need to set too much store by these objections. She could well respond that Leavis's 'tradition of English', despite his insistence on its role in the formation of the 'individual talent', is finally inseparable from the idea of consciousness because its destiny is to erase language as a particular set of techniques and conventions in favour of an immediate 'embodiment of concrete experience'. Equally, she might reply, as I have in the last section, that Lukács's socially determined linguistic forms are finally reabsorbed by the categories of consciousness and experience because this is precisely what their totalization reveals at the end of history: a universalized class consciousness. Whether Belsey's own linguistic structures escape a similar reabsorption into the subject is of course a different question.

8. This description and criticism of realism – particularly where 'misrecognition' is specified through Althusser's theory of ideology and Lacanian psychoanalysis – was most fully discussed in the journal *Screen* during the mid-1970s.

9. At this point Belsey's account overlaps with deconstructionist and 'reader response' criticism of the sort represented by Hélène Cixous and Stanley Fish. These similarly assume that the production of meaning is a purely linguistic matter and cast their 'politics' in terms of restoring the reader's dubious right to remain in a state of deferred identity in the linguistic continuum.

10. For a more comprehensive outline of the problem of the formation of human capacities, one that avoids competing sociological and biological reductionisms and is compatible with Wittgenstein's treatment of the problem, see Hirst and Woolley 1982: ch. 2.

11. This shows the degree to which the structuralist analysis of literature carried out by Jakobson, Propp, Barthes, Todorov, Greimas, etc. remains useful. To the extent that it can be stripped of its foundational pretentions, to the extent that it can be returned to the role of a practical instrument in the analysis and utilization of verbal artefacts, that is, to the extent that it can be redeployed as a modern rhetoric, it remains important for rethinking the problem of literary representation.

12. It is the contingent variability of perceptual technologies that rules out the realist interpretation of structuralism exemplified in Lovell 1980. In general, realism argues for the language-independent reality of structures by treating them as *necessary* for the explanation of the fact that we experience things in such and such a way. But Wittgenstein shows that the fact that we do experience things in this way rather than that is itself only made available to us by our practical mastery of always definite 'special methods'. In other words, this fact is not something that we contemplate *and then* posit procedures (in the guise of 'causal powers') in order to explain. In 'contemplating' we simply display our mastery of some particular perceptual technology which is neither more or less necessary ('real') than some other.

References

Belsey, C. (1980) *Critical Practice*, London, Methuen.

Dickens, C. (1910) *Our Mutual Friend*, London, The Educational Book Co. (Originally published as a serial in 1864–5).

Foucault, M. (1966) *The Order of Things*, London, Tavistock.

Haugen, E. (1968) 'The Scandinavian languages as cultural artefacts' in Fishman, J. *et al.*, *Language Problems of Developing Nations*, New York, John Wiley.

Hirst, P. and **Woolley, P.** (1982) *Social Relations and Human Attributes*, London, Tavistock.

Hunter, I. (1984) 'Literary discipline', *Southern Review* 17, 2.

Lord, A. (1960) *The Singer of Tales*, Cambridge, MA, Harvard University Press.

Lovell, T. (1980) *Pictures of Reality*, London, British Film Institute.

Lukács, G. (1977) 'Realism in the balance', in Bloch, E. *et al.*, *Aesthetics and Politics*, London, New Left Books.

Marcus, S. (1964) *The Other Victorians*, New York, Basic Books.

Ong, W. (1971) 'Oral residue in Tudor prose style', in his *Rhetoric, Romance and Technology*, Ithaca, NY, Cornell University Press.

Rask, R.K. (1811) *A Grammar of the Icelandic or Old Norse Tongue*. Reprinted by John Benjamins, Amsterdam, 1976.

Saussure, F. (1983) *Course in General Linguistics*, trans. Roy Harris, London, Duckworth.

Watt, I. (1957) *The Rise of the Novel*, London, Chatto & Windus (Page references are to the Penguin edition).

Wittgenstein, L. (1977) *Remarks on Colour*, Oxford, Blackwell.

Wittgenstein, L. (1980) *Remarks on the Philosophy of Psychology*, Oxford, Blackwell.

1984

CHAPTER 8

Discourse and power

John Frow

I

In this paper I seek to outline a semiotic definition of the concept of ideology. Given the force of the arguments against the current usage of the term, it seems to me a gamble as to whether this redefinition is possible.

This is so in the first place because the concept is traditionally defined within a relation between truth and error, as the designation of error. The theorization of error or false consciousness is not possible without establishing a position of authority which would be external to the ideological; but to the extent that this position claims an epistemological and so a political authority, it reveals itself to be complicitous with power, with the will to knowledge which is a form of the will to power. Such a criticism is not in itself conclusive, since it can itself be shown to derive from the same claim to mastery, and because it naively supposes the possibility of an exemption from the field of power. It is a criticism which fails to account for its own conditions of possibility. Nevertheless it has the effect of denying the universality of that standard of rationality that Marxism has ascribed to itself and against which deviation is measured, and of enforcing the paradox that the critique of ideology must itself be relativized to the position of power from which it is enunciated.

In the second place, the concept of ideology is predicated upon a distinction between the symbolic and the real, and hence an exclusion of the symbolic from the real. However much the 'last instance' is, in classical Marxism, mediated and deferred, its eventual finality relegates the symbolic to an epiphenomenal status. The problem that is posed is that of the working through of a further paradox, in which the real would be thought not as substance but as a texture of symbolic systems, and the symbolic would be thought as having a real effectivity. There are additional problems here which have to do with the generality and inclusiveness of the concept of the symbolic, and with the postulation of a single general form of causality.

In the third place, the concept of ideology seems necessarily to pre-suppose a relation between knowledge and a knowing subject. The relation may apply at the level of individuals, but is more generally a relation at the level of social class. In the simplest formulation, class is thought as an expressive unity; more complex formulations for the most part merely qualify this model. In particular, it is not clear that the concepts of hegemony and of the 'relative autonomy' of ideology do not repeat the metaphysical framework that defines the orthodox theoriz-ation of ideology.

These questions cannot properly be answered in abstraction from particular textual constructions of the category of ideology, so I have chosen to examine briefly one particularly lucid account, in one of the great texts of classical Marxism, of the working of ideology. This account is Engels's reading of the city of Manchester – a reading which is doubly instructive, first, in that the semiotic system Engels reads is at once 'superstructural' and directly functional, and second, in that Engels's reading can be understood in terms of quite contradictory methodologies.

II

Manchester in 1844 is built in such a way that 'a person may live in it for years, and go in and out daily, without coming into contact with a working-people's quarter or even with workers,' on condition that he is not seeking to *know* the structure of the city, 'so long as he confines himself to his business or to pleasure walks' (Engels 1975: 347–8). This restriction of knowledge is made possible above all by the fact that 'the working-people's quarters are sharply separated from the sections of the city reserved for the middle class' (348).

This quasi-universal 'person' (part of the text's political ambiguity lies in the status of its inscribed reader) is then specified as 'the members of the money aristocracy,' who

> can take the shortest road through the middle of all the labouring
> districts to their places of business, without ever seeing that they are
> in the midst of the grimy misery that lurks to the right and the left.
> For the thoroughfares leading from the Exchange in all directions out
> of the city are lined, on both sides, with an almost unbroken series of
> shops, and so are kept in the hands of the middle and lower
> bourgeoisie, which, out of self-interest, cares for a decent and cleanly
> external appearance, and *can* care for it. (348)

The effect of this structure is a 'concealment of everything which might affront the eyes and the nerves of the bourgeoisie' (349), and this conceal-ment is at the same time *motivated*, there is a relation of distorted representation, of concealment/manifestation, between the façade and the districts behind it:

> True, these shops have some affinity [*Verwandtschaft* – Marcus (1974: 170) translates this well as 'concordant relation'] with the districts which lie behind them, and are more elegant in the commercial and residential quarters than when they hide grimy working-men's dwellings; but they suffice to conceal from the eyes of the wealthy men and women of strong stomachs and weak nerves the misery and grime which form the complement of their wealth. (348–9)

Engels seems to be using the model of a truth which is hidden beneath an 'external appearance' and which is nevertheless revealed on the surface *in an alienated form*. One can *infer [schliessen]* what lies beneath appearances ('Anyone who knows Manchester can infer the adjoining districts, from the appearance of the thoroughfare') but it is nevertheless *invisible*: 'but one is seldom in a position to catch from the street a glimpse of the real labouring districts' (349). The 'separation' between working-class and middle-class districts would therefore be the bar between a signifier (the thoroughfares) and its repressed signified (the working-class districts); the 'concordant relation' would be a relation of signification, or rather of (mis)representation.

But it is not only the middle-class thoroughfares that Engels reads; elsewhere the text reads, with great thoroughness, the working-class districts themselves. The *whole* city is a semiotic system. The 'separation', then, is not that between a signifier and a signified but that between two sets of signifiers, one of which (the thoroughfares) stands synecdochally for the whole and one of which is repressed. The working-class districts are not the *truth* of the city, nor are they the deep structure which generates an illusory surface structure. They are that part of a semiotic system which is significantly invisible to 'the eyes and the nerves of the bourgeoisie' (349).

What is produced by this asymmetrical relation between two sets of architectural signifiers is not so much a single and necessary structure of 'illusion' (since 'anyone' can read the city, by using their feet) as a structure of *positions of reading* through which individuals will inscribe themselves within the semiotic system. There are two main positions (two types of reader): (1) the bourgeois reader, who is affirmed by the city as a universal subject (and the text confirms this universality: the bourgeois reader is 'anyone'); and (2) the proletarian reader, who is a non-subject (the text confirms this, at least at this point, by excluding this position). A third, synthetic, position is that of the theoretical reader who, in speaking the repressed discourse of the working-class districts and relating it to the discourse of the middle-class enclaves, produces a total, structural reading of the relation between the parts of the signifying system, and relates this total system to the system of class relationships within which it is overdetermined.[1] These positions are not *imposed* on agents, they are merely *potential* positions. The position of a theoretical reading, in particular, is not a fixed *class* position (Engels is a middle-class business-man), and although it has the potential to be translated into revolution-ary practice, it can also be used – this is suggested by the fact that the text is addressed to an implied *bourgeois* reader, who is *warned* of the consequences of capitalist oppression – to defuse revolutionary action (e.g. 581).

This is one sense in which we can speak of the 'relative autonomy' of ideology; another sense is discussed in terms of the *origin* of this 'peculiar' structure. Here the text grapples with the problem, which it cannot adequately theorize, of a causality which is both structural and yet corresponds to the objective *intentions* of the bourgeoisie. The construc-tion of the city is 'hypocritical' (*heuch-lerisch*), although it is based on straightforward economic considerations:

> I know . . . that the retail dealers are forced by the nature of their business to take possession of the great highways; I know that there are more good buildings than bad ones upon such streets everywhere, and that the value of land is greater near them than in remoter districts. (349)

Nevertheless the exclusion (*Absperrung*) of the working class is 'syste-matic'. But immediately Engels concedes that 'Manchester is less built according to plan, after official regulations, is more an outgrowth of accident, than any other city' (349). However, even if its construction is not *controlled* by the bourgeoisie, the *effect* of this random construction is that it can be translated directly into a propagandistic meta-discourse:

> When I consider in this connection the eager assurances of the middle-class, that the working-class is doing famously, I cannot help feeling that the liberal manufacturers, the 'Big Wigs' of Manchester, are not so innocent after all, in the matter of this shameful method of construction. (349)

One sentence crystallizes these contradictions and suggests a possible resolution: the sharp separation between working-class and middle-class quarters comes about 'by unconscious tacit agreement, as well as with outspoken conscious determination' (*durch unbewusste, stillschweigende Übereinkunft wie durch bewusste ausgesprochene Absicht*, 348). 'Determ-ination' may refer only to the control exercised by one class; but 'agreement' indicates the unconscious concurrence of both classes in the exclusion operated on the proletariat. As Marcus notes, this astonishing and outrageous arrangement cannot be fully understood as the result of a plot, or even a deliberate design, although those in whose interests it works also control it. It is indeed too huge and too complex a state of organized affairs ever to have been *thought up* in advance, to have pre-existed as an idea. (1975:172)

III

Engels's analysis mobilizes the classical tropes of an empiricist reading: the relation between the surface and the hidden, between seeing and not seeing, between will and accident. At the same time it can be read as putting into play a possible contradiction between two distinct strategies of reading: the one he deploys, which we could call 'interpretation' and which is partly blind to Engels's own inscription as a reader in the text of Manchester; and a second strategy which reads the determinants of reading, the system that makes possible both those interpretations based directly in class interest and those directed against it. The concept of ideology produced by this second strategy would concern, not the translation of an originary class position, but the effects of an objective and conventional system of signification – that is, the allocation of a differential structure of interpretation. Any semiotic system will generate specific possibilities of reception: it will construct both a semantic structure and a limited set of formal positions from which this structure can be interpreted.

At one level the contradiction between these two strategies can be referred simply to conflicting epistemological presuppositions. If structure is located in the real, then ideology will be seen to be generated directly by this real structure. The theory of commodity fetishism in *Capital* is close to this position: the structure of commodity production involves as a necessary effect the production of surface forms which are illusory and opaque. Misrecognition of the structure is a consequence of the distinction *within* the real between deep structure and surface structure. In a similar manner, capitalist production directly produces the illusions of the contractual equality of socioeconomic agents, or of the givenness and ahistoricality of the social order. Ideology is *imposed* by reality in the sense that limits are set to the immediacy of 'experience': a worker, for example, will draw a finite set of possible deductions from the hierarchical and serial organization of the work process according to the position that he or she occupies within that process. 'Reality (the object) determines the place of the subject within it and, therefore, the conditions of its experience of it. Reality determines the *content* of ideology; it generates false recognitions of itself by subjecting subjects to circumstances in which their experience is distorted' (Hirst 1979: 41). What is assumed in the thesis of ideology as a representation of an alienated reality is, first of all, preconstituted subjects who represent to themselves an objectivity which presents meaning directly to them; and second, that there is a necessary congruence between the subject's position in the production process and their ideological position. Ideology is a simple effect of an auto-effective process. Thus 'it is not that the subject is mistaken [*se trompe*] but that *reality deceives him* [*le trompe*], and the appearances in which the structure of the production process are concealed are the starting point for the way individuals conceive of reality' (Godelier 1966: 832).

Althusser's critique of this empiricist position, and indeed his general critique of economism and historicism, seem to me to remain more powerful than any countervailing response, and I won't argue the case for them here. Their consequence is that, if structure is located, conversely, in the systems of signification through which the real is constituted as an object of knowledge, then ideology will be seen as an unmotivated system which is a product of social determinations but is discontinuous with the structure of production. It will not be the expression or the transformation of a concealed deep structure (the structure of production which would be its secret truth). Rather, it will represent the intrication of relatively self-contained semiotic systems in the field of antagonistic class relations rooted in relations of production.

The counterpart of this rejection of an expressive conception of ideology is a critique of the epistemological problematic of the possibility of a correspondence between representation and the real, and the consequent move towards a non-epistemological conceptualization of knowledge and its objects. This shift is perhaps most dramatically exemplified in Hindess and Hirst's argument that theoretical objects are constituted 'within definite ideologies and discourses' (1975: 318), whereas the 'distinction and the correlation characteristic of epistemology depend on objects which exist independently of knowledge, and yet in forms appropriate to knowledge itself' (1977: 20). Epistemology works by presenting an appropriate form of order to theoretical discourse which will guarantee the fit between the theoretical grid and the order of the real. The bases for this closure of discourse are: (i) the construction of privileged and tautological criteria of validity; (ii) normative requirements concerning the mode of operation of discourse; and (iii) an aprioristic conception of the process of production of knowledge (1977: 11–17). But discourse in fact remains stubbornly *unlimited*, because 'the forms of closure of discourse promised in epistemological criteria do not work. They are silent before the continued discourse of theories which they can never correspond to or appropriate' (1977: 8).

The occasion of this critique is a rejection of the definition of ideology as 'false consciousness' (and of the scientism that accompanies it). If ideology is defined – as Althusser, for example, defines it, in Lacanian terms – as the 'imaginary', then the forms of the 'imaginary' cannot arise spontaneously from the subject (that would convert recognition into *imagination* and restore the constitutive subject), equally, they cannot be given by 'reality' (that would restore a simple reflection theory). The forms of the imaginary should, if these positions were to be avoided, have the status of *significations*, representations which are reducible neither to a represented which is beyond them, nor to an origin in a subject, but which are effects of the action of means of representation. (Hirst 1979: 63)

The signifieds of discourse (including the 'referential' discourses of science or history) are generated not from an extra-discursive real to which we may appeal as a final authority, but within specific processes and practices of signification. The decisive criterion of analysis could thus no longer be the relation between discourse and a reality which would be external to it, since discourses would be 'interpretable and intelligible only in terms of their own and other discourses' constructions and the categories of adequacy which they apply to them' (Hirst 1979: 19). Instead, the relevant criterion would be that of the relations between discourse and *power*, the intrication of power *in* discourse. We would be specifically concerned with the institutions, the forms of transmission and diffusion, and the pedagogical forms which impose and maintain discourses and which contain dissenting or marginal positions within certain limits. It would still be possible to apply specific *local* criteria of adequacy and appropriateness (although not of validity), but there could be no appeal to the epistemological unity of a knowledge process in general.

The danger here is that of simply reversing the empiricist argument by postulating the auto-effectivity of discursive systems and reducing all signification to the single model of highly autonomous symbolic systems which produce a uniform mode of being of the subject. But ideological systems work in very disparate ways and through very different forms of constitution of their subjects. There can be no single model of ideological structure because there is no hard and fast line between the 'real' and 'symbolic'. The distinction between the 'real' and 'symbolic' realms is not ontologically given but is a social and historical result. The discursive is a socially constructed reality which constructs both the real and the symbolic *and this distinction between them*. It assigns structure to the real at the same time as it is a product and a moment of real structures. It therefore covers a spectrum of semiotic systems from both 'realms'. Thus 'material' structures – for example, specific work processes – are also immediately symbolic structures (structures of power, that is, the meaningful position of individuals within these processes). Conversely, symbolic systems cannot be conceived only on the model of intellectual formations transmitted through special institutions to empty subjects.

They involve varying degrees of motivation, explicitness, and systematization; they are directly or indirectly linked to the process of material
production; and they are appropriated by agents (and by different classes
of agents) in different ways.

IV

The political implications of the abandonment of Marxism's epistemological certainties are of course bitterly disputed, and much recent work
seeks to reclaim the Real and the Material as sources of epistemological
(and hence political) authority for Marxism. Perry Anderson, who played
so important a role in opening up English Marxism to European philosophy, has attacked structuralist theory in a rhetoric reminiscent of
nothing so much as a religious denunciation of atheism. Structuralism's
'speculative aggrandizement of language' and 'free-wheeling nescience'
have brought about an 'attenuation of truth' and a dismissal of the
'referential axis' (1983: 45–7). In the 'abyss of Parisian relativism' (65)
the imperialism of the linguistic model has destroyed the possibility of
causal explanation and so of 'history proper' (50), and brought about the
disappearance both of the historical theme of 'man' and of the subject or
agent of knowledge (52). Derrida is said to have 'liquidated' the 'last
vestige' of the 'autonomy' of structures: the subject; to have 'freed'
structures from subjects; and so to have brought about the reign of
'absolute chance', 'a subjectivism without a subject', indeed 'a finally
unbridled subjectivity' (54). In short, the linguistic model 'strafed meaning, over-ran truth, outflanked ethics and politics, and wiped out
history' (64). In similar vein Terry Lovell argues that in a 'relativist' and
'conventionalist' problematic theoretical terminology is defined systemi-
cally rather than referentially; but this model 'is not open to Marxist
materialism. Signs cannot be permitted [sic] to swallow up their referents
in a never-ending chain of signification, in which one sign always points
on to another, and the circle is never broken by the intrusion of that to
which the sign refers' (1980: 16): somewhere there must be an end to
signification, an ultimate non-signifying ground. At one point Lovell
finds it in the Holocaust, which she mobilizes as a sign of the ultimately
Real: but that of course is precisely the ideological function of the
Holocaust, to act as a *sign* of the real, as an argument. Elsewhere she
devastates the heretics with splendid metaphors: whilst Althusser 'sails
dangerously close to the wind,' the post-Althusserians 'abandon caution
and openly embrace conventionalism' (1980: 17). For Lovell everything
turns on the category of the 'material', as the object of 'experience' and
as the solid ground against which to measure the symbolic. But in this
kind of context (where it is set against the 'ideal' or 'spiritual') the
concept is a metaphysical one and is only contingently related to Marx-

ism. More importantly, it ensures that the distinctive criterion of Marxist analysis becomes the materiality of the commodity rather than the inscription within it of the process and the relations of production which determine its value and which are not, strictly speaking, material.

Against any such dichotomous conception of a 'material' economic base and an 'immaterial' superstructure it seems important to argue that *all* social systems are *semiotic* systems producing significations realized in material sign-vehicles. The system of natural and physical objects is necessarily always also a system of social values; and the materiality of the body is a support of the complex gender systems through which sexual difference is constituted. The economic system is concerned precisely with the transformation of quantities of matter-energy into information: at one level into use-values, at a second level into the complex signification of exchange-value which endows qualitatively different commodities with a symbolic equivalence and so permits their circulation as signs within a generalized equation (cf. Wilden 1972: 204). The political-juridical system articulates and consolidates class positions on a secondary and self-contained plane of power relations and categories of subject which is constrained by, but not necessarily fully congruent with, the structure of relations of production, and which in turn is functionalized in the struggle to secure the appropriation of surplus value. And the ideological system, which mediates the categories of the other systems and allows individuals (as 'subjects') to construct their relation to these constraining structures, works as a system of signification only through its embedding in material forms.

There can therefore be no absolute ontological distinction (of the order 'material/immaterial' or 'real/symbolic') between the systems whose complex intrication constitutes the social structure. Rather, social structure can be thought in terms of a play of constraints, determinations and restrictions exercised upon each other by a range of semiotic practices and institutions. This play will result in particular states of balanced tension which will shift as the complex convergence of forces at any one point shifts: there are no necessary outcomes or 'stages' of struggle, and there can be no *general* model of the relation between components of social structure. To substitute in this manner an overdetermined series of semiotic formations for an ontological dichotomy is not to argue that each formation is equally determinant of each other formation, or that any one formation is the expression of others, or that a social structure is no more than a system of symbolic systems. Any of these arguments would ignore the fact that value systems have the particular function of realizing relations of *power*. Power is equally a 'symbolic' value but it has direct material effects. It involves 'need, work, and exploitation, that is . . . factors which brutally beset the human body of man in its psycho-physical materiality and not just the sign systems practised by him' (Rossi-Landi 1975: 16).[2] Power is realized in all formations (possession of economic, political and ideological values, and optimally also of the means of producing them), but this realization is *asymmetrical.* In class societies control at the level of relations of production *tends* to be realized in terms of hegemony in other formations; but these relations of control and determination are fought out within each formation in terms and within formal constraints which are peculiar to each formation.

One of the effects of this asymmetry of social systems is a *displacement* between semiotic formations, such that one formation cannot be seen as the direct translation of the production of values in another. This 'relative autonomy' of practices – the historical result of the uneven realization of power at different levels by the hegemonic class in complex and dynamic social systems – renders invalid an expressive model which reduces social systems to a central deep structure of which each level would be the isomorphic transformation. Further, economic practice is not a 'last instance', a final and therefore absolute determinant of social structure imposing a necessary teleology on the development of this structure. Rather, the specific structure and temporality of each formation produce a limited range of *possible* developments; the actual course of development is realized in the play of the class struggle, where the limited teleology of class goals is worked out.

V

I take the following to be the general requirements of a working theory of ideology. First, that it not assert a relationship of truth to falsity (and so its own mastery over error) but concern rather the production and the conditions of production of categories and entities within the field of discourse. Second, that it not deduce the ideological from the structure of economic forces or, directly, from the class positions of real subjects of utterance; that it theorize the category of subject not as the origin of utterance but as its effect. Third, that it not be an ontology of discourse, deriving effects of meaning from formal structure, but rather theorize the multiple and variable limits within which relations of power and knowledge are produced.

These requirements are largely negative, and there is perhaps a strong argument to be made against the normativeness of any conception of ideology – an argument that one should more properly attempt a description of the determinations according to which discourses have historically been distributed between the true and the false (cf. Foucault 1980: 118). But that would still leave unproblematized the position from which this description would be made. Marxist theory is inescapably involved in making political judgements about discourse, on the basis of categories which are necessarily provisional and themselves positionally constituted. This political force of the concept of ideology must be retained. But if the ideological is not to be ontologized, it should be regarded as a *state* of discourse or of semiotic systems in relation to the class struggle. Rather than being thought through an opposition to 'theory' (a space external to the determinations of ideological production) it would be thought as a differential relation to power. Given that all discourse is informed by power, is constituted *as discourse* in relation to unequal patterns of power, then political judgements can be made in terms of particular, historically specific appropriations of discourse by dominant social forces.[3] Note that this involves two distinct theses: first, that of the productivity of power; second, that of the inequality of powers. This means that power isn't simply on one 'side', and hence that the 'sides' in any situation may be mobile and tactically constituted; they are not necessarily pre-given (except in the limited case of *simple* social contradiction) and can't necessarily be specified in advance, since ideology is both constituted by and is involved in the constitution of social contradictions. But it also means that power is never monolithic, stable, or uniform in its effects. Every use of discourse is at once a judgement about its relation to dominant forms of power and either an assent or a resistance to this relation.

In so far as power invests all discourse, the category of ideology is a description of systems of value in which all speakers are enclosed and which is the productive basis of all speech. In so far as power is always asymmetrically split, the category describes a particular political functionalization of speech. It is both a 'universal' category and a category that refers to the tactical appropriation of particular positions by a dominant social class (in Engels's text, the 'universalizing' capture of the thoroughfares on behalf of the bourgeoisie). But it does not refer to specifically 'class ideologies' or class cultures. Here I follow Poulantzas' argument against a 'number-plate' theory of ideology according to which each class would possess its own distinct and characteristic view of the world, and his contention that 'the dominant ideology does not simply reflect the conditions of existence of the dominant class, the pure and simple subject, but rather the concrete political relation between the dominant and the dominated classes in a social formation' (1973: 203). The hegemonic practice of the ruling class attempts to ensure that subordinate classes operate within limits defined by the dominant ideology. 'Subaltern groups are always subject to the activity of ruling groups, even when they rebel and rise up; only 'permanent' victory breaks their subordination, and that not immediately' (Gramsci 1971: 55).

This is not an argument that subordinate classes accept the tenets of a distinctly defined and externally imposed 'dominant ideology', nor is it an argument for the necessary effectivity of such an ideology in integrating a social formation and securing the reproduction of the relations of production. Abercrombie, Hill, and Turner have mounted what I think is a correct critique of functionalist conceptions of ideology (including a large part of recent Marxist theory) which assume that there *is* social coherence, and that ideology is instrumental in securing it. My argument concerns not 'an' ideology which would be separately specifiable, but rather the differential, and differentially effective, investment of discourse by power, and in particular by ruling class power. What is at stake in this process is the consolidation of class power (through the integration, in the first instance, of the disparate factions of the ruling class, and then, in so far as possible, of other classes) and the reproduction of the conditions for the extraction of surplus value (conditions which are always a combination of economic structures, the juridical and political relations buttressing them, judicial and military force or its potential, and the 'consent' of the working classes). But to describe what is at stake is not to describe an actual and necessary effectivity. Hegemonic strategies establish a shifting and tense balance between contradictory powers and concede greater or lesser degrees of autonomy to discursive positions occupied by subordinate classes (although even in yielding ground, such hegemonic strategies tend to define the terrain of struggle: to set the agenda of the thinkable and to close off alternative discursive possibilities). Hegemony is a fragile and difficult process of containment. Further, there are historically quite distinct degrees of coherence of the 'dominant ideology'. It may either be the case that one discursive domain (for example, religion in the feudal period) is so heavily invested as to constitute in itself the 'dominant ideology', or the investment of power may range across a number of domains, no single one of which is dominant. It may be the total structure of a discursive domain which is appropriated because of its high correlation with a social function, or it may be one particular set of categories within a domain or across several discursive domains (the concepts of 'nation' or 'individual', for example, which draw upon and pull together quite different discourses and practices); and it may be the case that the resulting stresses are neither coherent nor non-contradictory. It is quite true to say, then, that 'the functional relation of ideology and economy is ... a contingent one, specifiable only at the level of concrete societies. There cannot be a general theory of ideology' (1984: 185). Here, however, I attempt no *a priori* specification of which discursive domains were most heavily invested or appropriated in particular periods, since this is precisely a matter for reconstruction from textual analysis.

In the function of ideological investment (in Freud's sense of *Besetzung*) is to bring about an acceptance or a tolerance of the hegemonic position of a dominant class, resistance is nevertheless written into the structure of all discourse. If power is no longer thought simply as a negative and repressive force but as the condition of production of all speech, and if power is conceived as polar rather than monolithic, as an asymmetrical dispersion, then all utterances will be potentially splintered, formally open to contradictory uses. Utterance is in principle dialogic.

Both 'ideology' and 'resistance' are *uses* of discourse, and both are 'within' power. Ideological utterance is marked by redundancy, by an automatization which appears as a kind of semantic crust proclaiming its authority and its status as second nature (cf. Lukács 1971: 86). Resistance is the possibility of fracturing the ideological from within or of turning it against itself (as in children's language games) or of reappropriating it for counter-hegemonic purposes. This turning is an application of force. In both cases the conditions of possibility are given in the structure of discourse (although they are not necessarily grammatically marked), but they are not intrinsic qualities of the language; they take the form of enunciative acts, and of judgements about the status of those acts.

VI

The concept of ideology has generally been reserved to systematic and immediately political or propositional conceptualization – to 'opinion' or 'world view'. But by ascribing political value only to what openly claims the status of political or philosophical discourse, this restriction of the ideological sphere impoverishes our understanding of the area in which class conflicts are fought out. In class societies, where the production and circulation of meaning function as a determined and determinant level within antagonistic social relations of production, all meaning is, in the fullest sense of the word, political. The concept of ideological system therefore needs to comprise not only explicitly conceptual systems, but the totality of codes and values through which speakers make investments in the construction of realities. A theory of ideology is a theory of semiotic value, because within the symbolic order the position and intensity of values are the index of a mediated tactical assertion, the site of a struggle for symbolic power and charged with the traces of that struggle. The ideological structure is co-extensive with the *semiotic field* – with the totality of signifying systems. Bakhtin/Voloshinov makes this point when he writes that 'the domain of ideology coincides with the domain of signs. They equate with one another. Wherever a sign is present, ideology is present too. *Everything ideological possesses semiotic value*', and 'without signs there is no ideology' (1973: 10). This is not to claim the falsity of all signifying systems but to stress the arbitrariness of the sign – the fact that it signifies only by virtue of a social consensus, and that where this consensus is founded on social relations which are contradictory, the symbolic order is necessarily involved in this contradiction.

However, Bahktin/Voloshinov's conception of the sign as an entity which 'reflects and refracts another reality outside itself, i.e. possesses meaning, represents something other than itself' (1973: 9) ignores the extent to which meaning is produced by structural interrelationships within the signifying system, and instead locates the process of semiosis in the isolated act of representation, the relation between the sign and its referent. But ideological value does not reside in the falseness of a particular act of representation. It is only at the level of the articulation of the sign in a particular structure of signification that we can speak of a production of meaning, and here 'meaning' must be conceived strictly as a function of the diacritical coherence of the structure. Signification depends not on the correlation of signs with bits of reality, but on the order of signs amongst themselves. A meaning is not the sign of something irreducible to which it points as its essence but a sign of its own position in a differential system.

Within the semiotic order language holds a privileged position in so far as the values generated in all other signifying systems can be translated into linguistic form: 'The field of linguistic value corresponds entirely to the field of meaning' (Rossi-Landi 1975: 139). At the lowest level of semantic structure the semiotic order could thus be defined as a collection of abstract positional units formed within a number of distinct systems of differential relations but corresponding to the signifieds of the language system.

At this level of definition the axioms of structural linguistics are crucial. Saussure's conception of the purely relational character both of the signifier and of the signified destroys the traditional empiricist notion of signification as a relation between a material signifier, an abstract concept, and a 'thing' for which the word 'stands'. Language is no longer a secondary formation, an accretion superimposed on a naturally articulated reality, but rather it actively articulates our representations of reality. The assumption that the sign simply associates a word with the thing it names presupposes 'that ready-made ideas exist before words' (Saussure 1966: 65); whereas Saussure's conception of the closedness of the sign stresses the gap which founds the *systematic* structure of language and the dependent independence of thought. It establishes that relative arbitrariness which enables us to grasp systems of representation as particular kinds of game rather than as a reflection of the real; and it demolishes the privileged position that *substantives* enjoy in any empiricist typology, making it possible to think of relations, processes and qualities, as well as entities, as objects of signification.

Language thus, in Eco's words, establishes a 'cultural' world which is neither actual nor possible in the ontological sense; its existence is limited to a cultural order, which is the way in which a society thinks, speaks and, while speaking, explains the 'purport' of its thought through other thoughts' (1976: 61). The referent cannot therefore be understood as a transcendental signified external to the order of language, since

> the so-called 'thing itself' is always already a *representamen* shielded
> from the simplicity of intuitive evidence. The *representamen* functions

only by giving rise to an *interpretant* that itself becomes a sign and so on to infinity. The self-identity of the signified conceals itself unceasingly and is always on the move. (Derrida 1976: 49)

Meaning is an endless chain of semiosis, a movement between units which are virtual, positional, and therefore irreducible.

However, the articulation of the semantic realm into pure differential values depends on an implicit hypostatization of the signified (or more correctly of the empty content-form) as a position defined outside of particular systems of signification. It deals in atomized units and rests on something like the lexicographer's convenient fiction of the existence of stable lexemes. In fact, the *double* relationality of the levels of form and content means that the correlation of signifier to signified, and so the production of meaning, takes place only *within specific relations of signification.* The system of these relations I shall refer to as discourse (I include in this term non-verbal semiotic systems). If we follow Foucault's terminology we will say that the mode of existence of language in discourse is the statement (*énoncé*), whereas the sentence is the relevant unit of analysis at the level of grammar or language-system (*langue*). What distinguishes the statement from the sentence, the speech act, or the proposition is not an *addition* of meaning (since isolated sentences and propositions can be meaningful) but the mobilization of the complex of rules and conventions of the language games that constitute meaning in use. The statement is not a *unit* of discourse but rather a function cutting across the other domains of structure such as grammar, and acting as the condition of possibility of linguistic manifestation in these domains (Foucault 1972: 87–8). Statements are by definition contextual, but they are not the direct projection of an actual situation. Rather, the statement is always a component of 'an enunciative field in which it has a place and a status.' It belongs to textual and intertextual systems, so that 'if one can speak of a statement, it is because a sentence (a proposition) figures at a definite point, with a specific position, in an enunciative network that extends beyond it' (Foucault 1972: 99).

On this definition, discourse cannot be equivalent to 'speech' in the linguistic sense of *parole* (it is closer to the extended sense that Derrida gives to *écriture*). Here again it is Bakhtin who has done the pioneering theoretical work. Holquist summarizes it this way:

Utterance, as Bakhtin uses it, is *not* . . . unfettered speech, the individual ability to combine *langue* elements with freely chosen combinations. As he says, 'Saussure ignores the fact that besides the forms of language there exist as well forms of combination of these forms.' If we take into account the determining role of the other in actual speech communication, it becomes clear that there is not only system in language independent of any particular articulation of it, but there is as well a determining system that governs any actual utterance. We might say the world of *parole*, like the sphere of *langue*, is controlled by laws; but to say so would be to change completely the definition of *parole* as used by Saussure. (1983: 311)

Recent linguistic analysis, however, has largely failed to move beyond the *langue/parole* opposition. It has been dominated on the one hand by a formalism which treats the text as an extension of the syntactic and logical structuring of the sentence, on the other hand by an embarrassed empiricism which, in attempting to take into account the role of context and enunciation in the shaping of text, finds itself unable to formalize the infinity of possible speech situations (for the second position cf. van Dijk 1977: 91). In both cases the result is a renewal of the traditional dichotomy between text and context or between *énoncé* and *énonciation*, in which only the former is seen as properly linguistic, and the situation of utterance is conceived as contingent, circumstantial, 'subjective', non-systematic.

VII

Here I can do no more than briefly sketch in some of the requirements of a more adequate theory of discourse. Let me propose in the first instance that utterances are produced within the framework of a number of distinct *universes of discourse* (or discursive formations) – the religious, scientific, pragmatic, technical, everyday, literary, legal, philosophical, magical, and so on; and that it is not possible to assign a cognitive privilege to any one of these universes (even, paradoxically, to that within which this statement is made): each must be regarded as having equal epistemological validity, but as performing different (and variable) *functions*; that is, each will have a different mode of authority within the discursive economy as a whole and in relation to the distribution of social power. These formations govern the production of relatively autonomous semantic realms; forms of referentiality and figurality which are specific to each realm; and the production and reproduction of the subject as subject-of-signification through its positional inscription within these overlapping and often contradictory semiotic horizons.

At a more specific level – the level of the situation of utterance – I want to argue that the production of meaning is a function of the *genres of discourse* which Bakhtin/Voloshinov defined as normatively structured clusters of formal, contextual and thematic features, 'ways of speaking' in a particular situation (1973: 20). Each genre is stratified as a social practice through the importance of 'language-etiquette, speech-tact, and other forms of adjusting an utterance to the hierarchical organization of society' (21). The production of meaning is thus always highly specified by the rules of the discourse structure in which it occurs, and the structure of the genres of discourse is directly correlated with the semiotic constraints of the speech situation. These concepts have been given more precise theorization in Halliday's elaboration of the concept of register, which I take to be roughly equivalent to that of genre. By understanding the speech situation, not spatio-temporally but semiotically as a situation-*type*, Halliday is able to establish correlations between normative contextual constraints and the three interacting dimensions of discursive structure which make up the complex unity of register and which he calls field, tenor, and mode (Halliday 1978). These dimensions specify organized fields of semantic material, layered in depth and in complex relation to other fields; positions of enunciation, of authority, and credibility, and patterns of strategic interaction; and linguistic and rhetorical options.

Registers, or discourse genres, are thus systems of metalinguistic rules governing the production, transmission and reception of 'appropriate' meanings by 'appropriate' users in 'appropriate' forms in particular social contexts. That is, they are normative systems (whose rules can be broken or changed or parodied) specifying what can and cannot properly be said at a given time and place. The concept refers to the relation between discursive practices and the *systematic* structuring of discourse. Todorov remarks that 'any verbal property whatsoever which is optional at the level of the language system can be made obligatory in discourse; the choice that a society makes between all the possible codifications of discourse determines its *system of genres*' (1978: 23). Discourse is therefore not the random product of a free subject operating 'outside' or 'above' the language system, and it is not 'an aggregate of conventional forms of expression superposed on some underlying content by "social factors" of one kind or another (Halliday 1978: 11). It is the production of a unified cluster of semantic, structural, and contextual meanings in accordance with generic norms. Discourse is not *parole*, and a theory of the systematic structure of discourse renders invalid the Saussurean dualism on which modern linguistics is founded. Pêcheux has proposed that the opposition of *langue/parole* be replaced by the couple *langue/ processus discursifs*, intending by this an opposition not of the abstract to the concrete, the necessary to the contingent, the objective to the subjective, but of two types of system (1975: 81). In this model discourse is the crucial level at which meaning is produced, and the lexical and morphosyntactic levels are subordinated to their functionalization within discourse; they represent category options whose uses and effects are indeterminate until they are subsumed within a higher level of codification.

If meaning is produced in accordance with generic discursive norms, it is therefore not an *abstract* potential but is closely tied to the structure of the context of utterance. Foucault argues that relations of signification can only be assigned within 'a specific, well-stabilized enunciative relation' (1972: 90), because language is based on a principle of thrift which gives rise to homonymy and synonymy, and therefore to an unsteady sliding between signifier and signified which is only eliminated in a higher order of contextual codification, where the fixing of signifiers to signifieds and the selection from complex networks of implied predicates attached to a cultural unit takes place. Pêcheux similarly claims that words receive their meaning from the discursive formation in which they are produced: 'The meaning [*le sens*] of a word, an expression, a proposition, etc., doesn't exist "in itself" (that is to say in its transparent relation to the literalness of the signifier), but is determined by the ideological positions brought into play in the socio-historical process in which words, expressions and propositions are produced' (1975: 144). Polyvalence is a function of the semantic shift that occurs in the passage from one discursive formation to another. The particular enunciative frame taken as applying in any particular situation determines the probability and the conditions of appearance of discursive objects, their possible functions, and whether and to what extent they are to be assigned the status of referentiality and truth.

Questions of semiosis and epistemology are thus not separable from questions of modality – that is, of the truth-status, the degree of seriousness, and the degree of authority carried by an utterance. Speakers enter discourse by way of subject positions inscribed in the structure of genre. These positions are modes of relation to *authority*, but, as Foucault argues, 'the subject of the statement should not be regarded as identical with the *author* of the formulation – either in substance or in function . . . To describe a formulation *qua* statement does not consist in analyzing the relations between the author and what he says (or wanted to say, or said without wanting to); but in determining what position can and must be occupied by an individual if he is to be the subject of it' (1972: 95–6). The formalization of registers over time means that there will not necessarily be a direct correspondence between the social position of speakers and the position they will occupy in discourse. Rather, there will tend to be a simple binary structuration of most genres, specifying a dominant (unmarked) position as that of a ruling class adult male and a repressed position as that appropriate to members of dominated classes, females, and children. In the case of those registers reserved to dominated groups this coding will be reversed. In practice this binary codification into appropriate and inappropriate users means the *excodification* of certain classes of user whose status as non-subjects is then concealed by the pseudo-universality of dominant registers.

In my reading of Engels's analysis of Manchester I argued that the ideological status of this discursive system (the city) derived not directly from the socioeconomic positions of the agents occupying it but rather from its construction of a set of formal positions which structured the distribution of semiotic authority (the distribution of power *within* this system). The most important factor here is the discontinuity between discursive positions and the actual social position of a speaker. The positions of utterance and reception which are specified as appropriate are empty and normative positions which may be filled, or rejected, or ironized, or parodied, or replaced with alternative positions; the speaker may fill them consciously or unconsciously, or may fuse them with other positions, or may simply be unaware of them or incompetent to fill them. There is thus a complex network of subject positions available to the speaker of a language (enabling the transformation of existing registers and the generation of new ones), and this means, in Foucault's words, that

> the subject of the statement is a particular function, but is not necessarily the same from one statement to another; in so far as it is an empty function that can be filled by virtually any individual when he formulates the statement; and in so far as one and the same individual may occupy in turn, in the same series of statements, different positions, and assume the role of different subjects. (93–4)

The crucial question for a theory of ideology must be that of the possibility of disruption of discursive authority, and of the integration of this disruption into general political struggle. This possibility can be thought in terms which don't rely upon the postulation of a realm of freedom external to discourse: that is, it can be thought in terms of a non-correspondence between socioeconomic *locus* and discursive position and in terms of the uneven articulation of subject positions inscribed in different domains. The overlap and contradiction of genres of discourse produces at once an effect of semantic stability (an effect of the unity of Being as guarantor of the variant repetition of meaning) and an effect of semantic contradiction (realms of Being fail to correspond). Silverman and Torode write that, against the assertion 'that "members" in consensual fashion work to sustain a single social fact world, it appears to us that speakers articulate conflicting relations between voices. This occurs both within the repertoire of a single individual, and between individuals' (1980: 185). These voices, and the realities they sustain and are sustained by, are not neutral, and the relations between them do not constitute a dialogue. The clash of voices is a clash of power, and the analysis of discourse is an analysis of and an intervention in this politics.

Notes

1. One could perhaps define a further position, that of the petit bourgeoisie, the very ambivalence of whose class position would play a major role in the production of ideological effects. Engels's text is interesting in terms of the 'buffer' role of

this class, but there is no suggestion that it has an autonomous ideological position; the model I am using is not that of a direct correspondence between class position and ideological position; it is that of a contradictory coding, within which the non-categorical classes will fit themselves.

2. The ultimate material irreducibility of the body is the basis of the social and of power, the limit to meaning, the final source and measure of value: but the body then in turn *becomes* meaning in the social order; it is the canvas for elaborate semiotic differentiations, in particular for the construction of gender, and it is the measure of other signifying systems: it feels pain and joy, but it also talks.

3. Anthony Giddens (1983: 18) argues that the concept of ideology 'is *empty of content* because what makes belief systems ideological is their incorporation within systems of domination,' and that 'to understand this incorporation we must analyze the mode in which patterns of signification are incorporated within the medium of *day to day practices.*'

References

Abercrombie, N., Hill, S., and **Turner, B.** (1984) *The Dominant Ideology Thesis*, London, Allen & Unwin.

Anderson, P. (1983) *In the Tracks of Historical Materialism*, London, Verso.

Bakhtin, M., Voloshinov, V. (1973) *Marxism and the Philosophy of Language*, New York, Seminar Press.

Derrida, J. (1976) *Of Grammatology*, Baltimore, The Johns Hopkins University Press.

Eco, U. (1976) *A Theory of Semiotics*, London, Macmillan.

Engels, F. (1975) *The Condition of the Working Class in England, Marx/Engels Collected Works*, Vol. 4, London, Lawrence & Wishart.

Foucault, M. (1972) *The Archaeology of Knowledge*, London, Tavistock.

Foucault, M. (1980) *Power/Knowledge*, New York, Pantheon Press.

Giddens, A. (1983) 'Four theses on ideology,' *Canadian Journal of Political and Social Theory* 7: 1 and 2.

Godelier, M. (1966) 'Système, structure et contradiction dans *Le Capital*,' *Les temps modernes*, November.

Gramsci, A. (1971) *Selections from the Prison Notebooks*, London, Lawrence & Wishart.

Halliday, M. (1978) *Language as Social Semiotic*, London, Edward Arnold.

Hindess, B., and **Hirst, P.** (1975) *Pre-Capitalist Modes of Production*, London, Routledge & Kegan Paul.

Hindess, B., and **Hirst, P.** (1977) *Mode of Production and Social Formation*, London, Macmillan.

Hirst, P. (1979) *On Law and Ideology*, London, Macmillan.

Holquist, M. (1983) 'Answering as authoring: Mikhail Bakhtin's trans-linguistics', *Critical Inquiry* 10: 2.

Lovell, T. (1980) *Pictures of Reality: Aesthetics, Politics and Pleasure*, London, British Film Institute.

Lukács, G. (1971) *History and Class Consciousness*, London, Merlin Press.

Marcus, S. (1974) *Engels, Manchester and the Working Class*, New York, Random House.

Pêcheux, M. (1975) *Les Vérités de la Palice*, Paris, Maspero.

Poulantzas, N. (1973) *Political Power and Social Classes*, London, New Left Books.

Rossi-Landi, F. (1975) *Linguistics and Economics*, The Hague, Mouton.

Saussure, F. de (1966) *Course in General Linguistics*, London, McGraw-Hill.

Silverman, D., and **Torode, B.** (1980) *The Material Word*, London, Routledge & Kegan Paul.

Todorov, T. (1978) *Les Genres du Discours*, Paris, Seuil.

van Dijk, T. (1977) *Text and Context: Explorations in the Semantics and Pragmatics of Discourse*, London, Longman.

Wilden, A. (1972) *System and Structure*, London, Tavistock.

Name Index

Character and story index

Subject and non-fiction book title index